THE INWARD ODYSSEY

THE INWARD
ODYSSEY

The Concept of *The Way* in the
Great Religions of the World

EDITH B. SCHNAPPER

London
GEORGE ALLEN & UNWIN
Boston   Sydney

First published in 1965
Second edition 1980

GEORGE ALLEN & UNWIN LTD
40 Museum Street, London WC1A 1LU

© George Allen & Unwin (Publishers) Ltd. 1965, 1980

British Library Cataloguing in Publication Data

Schnapper, Edith Betty
  The inward Odyssey.
  1. Mysticism
  I. Title
  149'.3   BL625

  ISBN 0-04-291015-3

Typeset in 11 point Plantin by Computacomp (UK) Ltd, Fort William, Scotland
and printed in Great Britain
by Biddles Ltd, Guildford, Surrey

PREFACE TO THE FIRST EDITION

In a Japanese text it is said 'Oh the joy of those who take as their guide the teaching of the Way of the Gods'. This I found to be true, for a sense of joy and adventure prevailed throughout the years I was working on the present book. Time and again I delighted in, what were to me, new and exciting discoveries in spheres, visible and invisible, and I found precious friendships with fellow-seekers both of the East and the West.

It would be difficult to mention by name all those who, by their written or spoken word, or frequently by their mere presence, have helped me in my researches and to thank individually the many friends who have so generously given of their knowledge and experience. However, I wish to express my gratitude, here, to Mrs Nora Briggs for her encouragement and counsel, particularly in the early stages of the book, to Mr P. W. Martin for reading the typescript and offering constructive criticism, to Dr Carmen Blacker for her stimulating comments and helpful advice at all times, and to Miss Morwenna Donnelly for her inspiration and for sharing with me the many problems and delights of the 'Inward Odyssey'.

Finally I should like to record my indebtedness to Miss Lorna Billinghurst for her suggestions regarding the choice of illustrations and to the authors, translators and publishers for their permission to use copyright material from the following works: M. Smith, *The Sufi Path of Love* (Luzac & Co.); Sir J. Singh, *The Persian Mystics, Ansari* (John Murray); L. Barnett, *The Heart of India* (John Murray); W. de la Mare, *The Traveller* (Faber & Faber) by permission of The Literary Trustees and the Society of Authors as their representatives; T. S. Eliot, *Four Quartets* (Faber & Faber); L. Menzies, *The Revelations of Mechthild of Magdeburg* (Longman, Green & Co.) by permission of The Iona Community, Edinburgh; A. Carmichael, *The Sun Dances* (The Christian Community Press, 34 Glenilla Road, N.W.3).

Cambridge
October 1964

E.B.S.

PREFACE TO THE SECOND EDITION

Years have passed and not only has the central message of the Inward Odyssey remained as relevant as ever but its immediate urgency to our time has palpably increased.

The dominance of the materialistic outlook on life has taken on frightening proportions and has led, on the one hand, to a growing neglect and even rejection of spiritual values and, on the other, to an intensified longing and search for abiding norms to give guidance and meaning to life. In this pursuit, the fields of symbolism, of comparative religion, of yoga as well as of studies into states of consciousness and religious experience have been explored widely, both on the academic and the popular levels, resulting in a considerable number of publications dealing with these subjects in a variety of ways. Where applicable these have been taken into account so as to bring the new edition in line with recent researches.

In view of this wider climate of interest and the greater urgency now prevailing, it is hoped that the present study, in bringing to light the timeless character of the religious quest, will foster between the various traditions a deeper understanding of their mutuality and a growing realisation of their common roots in the universally valid truths of spiritual experience.

I should like to express my renewed gratitude to Dr Carmen Blacker for her sustained encouragement and her many discerning suggestions, to thank Dr Michael Loewe for his wise counsel regarding the new edition, and Mrs J. C. Calvert for her practical help and her cheerful companionship as a fellow pilgrim on the Way.

Hempstead   E.B.S.
March 1979

CONTENTS

ILLUSTRATIONS

This book it chalketh out before thine eyes
The man that seeks the everlasting prize;
It shows you whence he comes, wither he goes;
What he leaves undone, also what he does;
It also shows you how he runs and runs,
Till he unto the gate of glory comes.

It shows, too, who set out for life amain,
As if the lasting crown they would obtain;
Here also you may see the reason why
They lose their labour, and like fools do die.

This book will make a traveller of thee,
If by its counsel thou wilt ruled be,
It will direct thee to the Holy Land,
If thou wilt its directions understand:
Yea, it will make the slothful active be;
The blind also delightful things to see.

John Bunyan: *The Pilgrim's Progress*

Ah! Lord! What shall this book be called to Thy Glory? It
shall be called *The Flowing Light of My Godhead* into all
hearts which dwell therein without falseness.

Mechthild of Magdeburg

INTRODUCTION

The unity of mankind and the creation of one world – these are the great ideals of modern man. He strives passionately for their realization and, indeed, the last hundred years have witnessed the widening of horizons, the crumbling of dividing frontiers, and the drawing together of lands once far apart. By his scientific discoveries man has gained the tools that make possible rapid communication on a hitherto unprecedented scale. The pooling of knowledge and resources is an everyday occurrence and carries in it new possibilities of co-operation and friendship. It seems, indeed, that this vast drive towards world unity includes in its range not only mankind but the whole of nature and is even reaching out into the space beyond our planet.

There is a contrasting picture equally typical of modern man. It is a picture of unities of whatever size, families, groups, nations, splitting apart, of new and deep gulfs appearing, of the erection of fresh barriers, of separation and strife. The inventions of science are employed to divide nation from nation, and the means of communication are used in the service of destruction that threatens to invade not only the earth but the skies.

Both pictures must be taken together for they are two sides of the whole, the psyche of modern man. They reflect the profound fissure in the human mind which makes itself felt in all departments of life. Religion is no exception. On the one hand, there is deeper mutual understanding and tolerance, on the other, there is a sharp division into individual faiths, denominations and sects, all stressing their exclusiveness and superiority. Inter-religious fellowship is as characteristic of our time as is religious faction and intolerance.

These conflicting trends are thrown into high relief by the far-reaching change that is occurring in the field of religion today, a change that equally affects East and West. As far as the West is concerned, a silent but effective influx of eastern religiosity has taken place and it is no longer the question whether we want this to happen, or, indeed, whether we wish our lives to be influenced by it or not, for our world has already been revolutionized, whether we approve or disapprove of the trend as a whole. Here is a vital challenge, do we accept it and allow it to enrich our religious outlook, or do we try to pretend that nothing has happened and even erect defences against it? The answers we give depend on another question. Can we open ourselves to the timeless treasures the East has to offer without being disloyal to our own precious heritage, our own commitments and beliefs?

Many who have pondered this have become aware of the fact, so often forgotten, that the man who is religiously committed solely on the level of literal interpretation and understanding has not enough freedom of movement, not enough give and take to partake usefully in what has lately been termed the dialogue of religions. Conversely, the man committed on the deeper level of immediate experience finds, as devoted men and women of all races and times have found, that there in the depth common ground is touched and that mutual fructification becomes not only possible but natural. There, too, dogma and belief, individual creeds and symbols, instead of being regarded as mutually exclusive, are seen to balance and compensate one another and, in their various historical contexts, to become once more charged with vital energy, forming one great organic whole.

The religious commitment of the individual must always be unique and the particular path he chooses is inviolably his own, and the only one to which he can give himself wholeheartedly; but, if contact is maintained with the unity found in the depth of experience, he will be able to drink deeply of the truth and wisdom offered by other approaches. The knowledge that such a point of unity exists in a world divided as it is, seems so comforting and full of hope that in this study the attempt is made to outline 'The Way' leading to it and to show that only through acceptance of the paradox residing at the heart of religion, where uniqueness and universality fuse, can religion become one with life.

I

THE INHERENT PATTERN

I

The Way – a Paradox

> Just as if, brethren, a man travelling in a forest, along
> a mountain height, should come upon an ancient
> track, traversed by men of former days, and should
> proceed along it: ... Even so, brethren, have I seen
> an ancient Path, an ancient track traversed by the
> Perfectly Enlightened ones of former times.
>
> SAMYUTTA NIKAYA

> The Path has not been long! *Is* there a Pathway
> there?
> Or is it I who dreamed of a Sun
> Whose Rays pierced through Itself and made Space
> And *were* for a million of years—or a moment,
> And were not again?
>
> DAR-U-SALAAM

'The Way' is known to all religions. Always it stands for the truth and
the dynamic manifestation of the truth in the holy life, the life divine; a
fact superbly epitomized by Christ in his words 'I am the Way, the
Truth and the Life'. Indeed it may be said, that the Way is not just one
religious concept amongst many others, or even the central concept in
any one religion, but religion and the Way are synonyms. One of the
oldest religions in existence today, Shinto, denotes 'the Divine Way' or
'the Way of the Gods'; Buddhism regards itself as a vehicle progressing
along the nirvanic path, and Judaism is called 'the Way of the Lord',
and a highway for wayfaring men, of which Isaiah says 'It shall be
called the way of holiness'. A Christian follows the Way of Christ, and it
is now a generally accepted fact that Christianity was originally known
as the religion of the Way or the Way of God, in the same manner as
the Islamic term for religion in general is *mazhab*, the Way.

Just as there is religion and there are many religions so there is the
Way and there are many ways. The first, the outpouring at the source,
the second, the network of waterways issuing from it. One cannot be
separated from the other. The Way divorced from its ways is a dead
abstraction; the ways without being nourished by the Way cannot live.

A study of the Way must, therefore, necessarily be concerned with
both; with the hidden source and its endlessly varied manifestations;

with the dynamic unity residing in the depth of religious experience and the individual pursuits which derive their meaning and purpose from it. The subtle relationship between these two strata is shown in a most simple but beautiful way by the Lord Krishna in the Bhagavadgita when he says 'However men approach me even so do I welcome them for the path men take from everyside is mine'.[1] The same is expressed in an often-used simile; it is said that whatever our religion we are all fellow pilgrims travelling by various routes towards the same goal, from different sides we are all converging to meet at the summit of the mountain of religion.[2]

What is the peculiar structure of this mountain? It appears that an answer can be found not so much in the hard and fast rules of official doctrines and creeds but in the records left by those who have attempted the climb. One of the most striking features of these records, of whatever origin, is that they are strangely paradoxical; in fact, it seems, that a description of what happens on the Way cannot be given without the use of paradoxical utterances. E. Underhill's characterization applies universally: 'At once a journey, yet a development; a stripping off, yet a completing; a victory, yet a self-loss; only in a paradox can its supernal nature be made clear.'[3]

To attempt an explanation at this point, why this should be so, would be premature; what is vitally important, however, is, neither to ignore the prevalence of paradoxical statements in the relevant texts nor to explain it away but to realize it and accept it fully.

Wherever man has trod the Way there he has met with certain landmarks which, taken in their entirety, reveal the underlying pattern of dynamic growth. One of the basic characteristics of this pattern is mentioned in a Buddhist scripture:

> Just as, brethren, the mighty ocean deepens and slopes gradually down, hollow after hollow, not plunging by a sudden precipice,—even so, brethren, in this Norm-Discipline the training is gradual, progress is gradual, it goes step by step, there is no sudden penetration to insight.
>
> *Udana* V, 5

The Way, then, is gradual, both in the sense that 'The method of heaven and earth proceeds gently and gradually',[4] and in the sense that it is graded, that is, displaying the characteristics of a ladder or scale. In fact, the symbol of the ladder is almost as universal as that of the Way itself. At the beginning of religious history it appears as the 'Scale of Osiris' in the *Egyptian Book of the Dead* and is addressed thus:

Homage to thee, O ladder of the god, homage to thee O ladder of Set. Set thyself up, O ladder of the god, set thyself up O ladder of Set, set thyself up O ladder of Horus whereby Osiris appeared in heaven when he wrought the protection for Rā.

(p. LXXIII–IV Introduction)

The 'ladder of the god' has been set up wherever man has aspired to reach out beyond the plane of material existence, and it has become the 'scale of perfection' as Walter Hilton has called it, or the 'ladder of divine ascent' as a Christian mystic of the Orthodox tradition has named it who himself was known as St John Climacus, St John of the Ladder.

A scale or ladder is composed of steps or rungs and so is the Way for it is said to consist of certain stations or degrees which are inter-connected, yet individually distinct and different from each other. They represent rallying points in which the previous phase finds its consummation but where, at the same time, lies embedded the seed for further growth. Thus each step stands for a new level of development and a new departure; one conditioning and, in a transmuted form, being contained in the other.

These steps are vital and the various religions exhort their followers with one voice that 'One must not wish to leave out the steps between and penetrate directly'[5] for this would spell danger. Whether the way is pictured primarily as a track gradually leading up a mountain side or as a ladder to be climbed rung by rung, this warning applies; the continuity of the process, as well as the sequence of the steps, whatever this may be in each individual case, must not be interfered with.

Running counter to this picture are a host of images used in this context which seem to express the exact opposite. They indicate not gradualness and slowness but instantaneity and suddenness; not continuity but discontinuity. The fact transpires that the words in Revelation 'Behold I come quickly'[6] are as much the keynote of the Way as their counterpart, the slow ascent of the soul to God. It is for this reason that the symbolism of entering a door or gate, and of undoing a lock or seal is used, for what all these images point to is a sudden entrance into, and opening of, a realm of experience which is closed, and therefore unknown, until the flash of realization occurs and the threshold is passed. It is at that moment that two different worlds touch and that the clash of values takes place; for this realization is instantaneous like a thunderbolt out of the blue sky, resulting in an unprecedented experience of all things made new. It happens 'in the twinkling of an eye' that 'we shall all be changed'[7] or, in the words of the Old Testament it is 'the quick understanding in the fear of the

Lord'.[8] Other religions speak of the tearing aside of the veils hiding the face of truth, or of a sudden awakening of the soul from sleep. The immediacy and abruptness of the experience overwhelms and often bewilders. Many pilgrims have felt this; to them the gift of vision appears to be too sudden and seemingly undeserved and they exclaim: 'The thought of enlightenment has arisen within me I know not how even as a gem might be gotten by a blind man from a dunghill.'[9]

The long preparation, the arduous climb, the gradual progress, seem nothing compared to the sudden insight and splendour of the new vision. And yet one is as characteristic of the Way as the other, and this applies not only to the higher stations of enlightenment or union with God but, in equal measure, to every single rung of the ladder of perfection. Only by sustained and untiring effort, slowly and gradually working within man the necessary change, can the individual steps be gained. This is the preparation; the actual attainment, however, is as instantaneous and new as it is seemingly without connection or relationship to what has gone before.

In this sense every attainment on the Way is 'both our own, yet not our own', as mystics of all times have observed. It is our own, for we have become pilgrims following the Way by our own toil, yet the fruit of our action is not ours, for attainment comes we know not how. The change will be wrought in a moment of no duration which does not touch the sequence of passing time. 'Betwixt that one and the other shall be no time, and then shall all be brought to joy.'[10]

This 'ecstasy of an awakening which opens the door of life eternal',[11] we cannot claim for ourselves; it comes to us from another world, as something we can neither understand nor control and which the Buddhist scriptures liken to the rising of the morning sun, 'O wonderful! the sun rises and all the world is lighted, so awakens the mind to Truth, and men benighted in error see its brightness, and adore the pure form of the Blessed One'.[12] What is experienced here the Bible calls grace, of which St Paul says clearly that it does not belong to us but is a gift of God.[13]

Many a time throughout history the question has been asked which of the two is the true Way, the slow ascent or the sudden leap. This is a question typical of the dualistic view of life which sees all opposites as mutually exclusive. The perfect answer was long ago given by Eckhart who said: 'Thy opening and His entering are but one moment.'[14]

The transformatory power of that 'moment' reveals itself in yet another paradox, or so it seems to the outsider who, lacking the immediate experience, has to judge by the testimony of those who have lived through it. Both continuity and discontinuity, both gradualness and suddenness are not pertinent any more, the new description of what happens stands over and against all these. The metaphors employed point to an attainment which does not happen once for all times, as climbing and eventually reaching the topmost rungs of a ladder, or, as the sudden break-through into a new world would suggest, on the contrary, what is attained is something which happens all the time, something which forms part of nature's cycle of becoming and growth, something, furthermore, which engenders the most intimate feeling of familiarity, proximity and even identity. The Way leads through territory one seems to remember, and past well-known landmarks which yet give rise to the question where and when?

In the overwhelming strength of the experience, some forget what has gone before or are convinced that up to now all has been illusion; they know, so they assure us, that there is no such thing as a ladder of becoming or a sudden lifting of a veil, revealing an unknown life different from that lived from day to day. They laugh at their former foolishness and say that they stand where they have always stood and have not moved an inch. Others remember the toil of the ascent but insist that they have now returned whence they started and that the Way, therefore, cannot be straight, neither can its steps lead altogether away from its beginning, for they know that they have come home and that, in fact, they have moved in a circle. They would agree with Plotinus' words:

Self-knowledge reveals the fact that the soul's natural movement is not in a straight line, unless indeed it has undergone some deviation. On the contrary, it circles around something interior, around a centre. Now this centre is that from which proceeds the circle, that is the soul. The soul will, therefore, move around the centre, that is around the principle from which she proceeds; and trending towards it, she will attach herself to it, as indeed all souls should do.

Enneads VI, 9, 8

What Plotinus here calls self-knowledge is, in far eastern terms, 'satori', the sudden insight into one's own self-nature which, again, reveals the circular movement.

Satori is 'an existential leap' which means also an existential leaping-back. In our spiritual life there is no 'one way' passage; the movement is always circular, the going-out is the going-in, and *vice-versa*.[15]

To say that the going out is the going in and the end is the beginning is to say that not only the Way itself but also its destination, the goal of all endeavours, can only be approached by means of the paradox. And such indeed is the case as all who know assure us. What is the goal of the Way? Many and varied answers have been given but it appears that they divide into two main categories of which one is found more frequently in the East, the other in the West. There are those who teach, and ardently believe, that the seeking soul at the summit of her search becomes reabsorbed in the infinity of the divine being, thus losing its separate identity and becoming one with the All. This is their aim and towards the fulfilment of this they strive and live. Others say an emphatic no to this, maintaining that at the peak of the ascent there is bestowed the gift of the transformed life, a life which fulfils itself in loving and constant communion with its transcendent source. The first goal is annihilation in the absolute or Godhead and of those who feel drawn towards it, it has been said:

Canst thou wonder, that they who walk in the true path, are drowned in the sea of adoration? They disregard life through affection for its Giver; they abandon the world through remembrance of its Maker; they remember their Beloved, and resign to Him both this life and the next. Through remembrance of God, they shun all mankind: they are so enamoured of the Cup-bearer, that they spilt the wine from the cup.[16]

The second goal is not to become annihilated but to become a perfect instrument of God's purpose, not to flee from life but embrace it in the 'good life', the 'holy life'.

He hath shown thee, O man, what is good; and what doth the Lord require of thee, but to do justly, and to love mercy, and to walk humbly with thy God?

Micah. 6, 8

Once more we are faced with a seemingly irreconcilable contradiction appearing at the most vital point of the Way, its goal, and we must remind ourselves of the truth that 'only in a paradox can its supernal nature be made clear'. This contradiction should, therefore, not be regarded as standing for two mutually exclusive approaches to the Way, as this has so often been the case, but it should be left intact and accepted in its entirety for only thus can it act as a pointer to an altogether different level of meaning where the conflict is resolved and the true nature of the path's goal becomes apparent.

NOTES FOR CHAPTER 1

1. IV, 11.
2. For an interesting survey of the symbology currently attached to 'The Way' and 'The Mountain', see chapter 1 of Marco Pallis' book *The Way and the Mountain*.
3. *The Spiral Way*, pp. 17–18.
4. *Yin Fu Ching* III, 6.
5. R. Wilhelm, *The Secret of the Golden Flower*, p. 23.
6. 22, 20.
7. I Cor. 15, 51–2.
8. Isaiah 11, 3.
9. Santideva, *Path of Light*, III, 14, p. 46.
10. Julian of Norwich.
11. *Kena Upanishad*, II, 4.
12. *Avatamsaka Sutra*, XXIV. See also Psalm 84, 11.
13. Eph. 2, 7.
14. Predigten, 3.
15. D. T. Suzuki, *Living by Zen*, p. 125.
16. Dārā Shakūh. In: M. Smith *The Sufi Path of Love*, p. 144.

2

The Labyrinth

And the quaint mazes in the wanton green
For lack of tread are undistinguishable.
W. SHAKESPEARE: *A Midsummer-Night's
Dream*

I give you the end of a golden string
Only wind it into a ball,
It will lead you in at Heaven's gate
Built in Jerusalem's wall.
W. BLAKE: *Jerusalem*

I saw a great Cathedral, which at the hour of united
meditation became flooded with golden light ...

The music ceased to sound, and the people gathered
in a great circle round the walls, forming a wheel.
Once again the great organ pealed, and they moved
inwards. And there on the floor of gold and alabaster
and mosaic they danced the eternal rite, of the spiral,
of the star and the stair, of the spear and the cup, of
the rose and the cross.
C. CAMERON: *The Cathedral*

The picture which emerges from our investigations so far is not only
complex but perplexing and we may well ask with Evelyn Underhill
what is that 'curve that marks our progress—that "Way", as the
mystics call it, which is a journey and a transmutation in one?'[1] In
agreement with her and other seekers of all times, our reply is that, if we
want to portray this inner development in terms of time and space we
should liken it to a spiral motion. For here in the image of the spiral we
have that universal and dynamic pattern, ordering and governing the
almost breathtaking diversity which marks the Pilgrim's Path.

This pattern is triune in structure. It consists of a first phase, the
departure from things familiar, and the venturing forth into new
territory, leading to a turning point and with it to the beginning of the
second phase which reveals itself to be not only of an openly contrasting
nature, as compared with the first, but which involves a total reversal of

direction. The third phase, again heralded by a new departure stands, at the same time, for a return and for the passing of the last thresholds separating the traveller from the more abundant life of truth and union.

Such is the triple movement which constitutes the inner dynamics of the Way, whether the metaphors speak of climbing a ladder, of undertaking a pilgrimage or crossing a river. It is always the spiral curve the seeker has to follow, a curve which both the East and West have recognized as expressing a universal law of growth. We meet it in nature in microcosmic phenomena like the chromosomes or the nuclear spin, as well as in macrocosmic structures, such as the spiral nebulae, and we find the recognition of its universal validity from the earliest human cultures down to our present age. It appears as an ornament in many different forms, with round or square scrolls, single or double, and a similar pattern is used symbolically in religious art and practice where it is depicted either two or three-dimensionally or enacted ritually. Its interpretation has varied through the ages and to trace all the ramifications of its use, spread far and wide, calls for a study in itself.[2] Here we have to limit ourselves to pointing to one strand of meaning which emerges in different cultures and countries and which has an important bearing on our present investigations.

Life's inherent motion follows the line of the coiled serpent, for in death it turns upon itself only to lead to a new departure in a new birth. Many cultures have depicted the twofold journey from birth to death and from death to a new life by the double spiral, the centre as the turning point, standing for both death and rebirth. As such it symbolizes the Way of all life and is one of those universal images which in their seeming simplicity are taken for granted and regarded as self-explanatory but which, in reality, are immensely rich in meaning and only yield their secret messages to him who is able to make them come to life and experience them as a dynamic force.

The symbol of the spiral as a basic pattern, together with its almost endless and often highly elaborate variants, is like a many-storied building; it is not only many-sided but many-levelled, each level of meaning, complete in itself, standing for one particular aspect of the cyclic sequence of birth, death and new birth. All these levels interpenetrate and in so doing they tend to obscure one another; furthermore, emphasis on one strand of meaning often brings about a change in the symbolic pattern used, a new variant appears, and the old is frequently lost sight of.

Among the many aspects of the spiral symbolism three are of outstanding importance in this context. They are all expressive of the life—death—life cycle, each representing a different angle. First, there is the spiral pattern found in connection with the enactment of ritual death, the gateway to regeneration and the return of the life-giving power. On another level the spiral appears as a symbol of the 'journey of the dead' leading to a new life beyond the grave; and on yet another, it is expressive of the inner death as experienced by the religious aspirant; it is the death of the old Adam and the birth of the new man.

It is likely that, wherever in religious practices the symbol of the spiral way appears, all three levels of meaning are present although one or the other may take first place and surpass the others in immediate importance. Thus in its fullness, the phenomenon of death, seen from the point of view of religion, always comprises within itself these three main strata: ritual death as encountered in fertility and regeneration rites as well as in the sacraments of the highly developed religions; physical death, the lot of all mankind and equally suffered, often sacrificially or vicariously, by the founder or central figure of a religion; and lastly the death of the lower nature in man, the unregenerate self which has to die in order to be transmuted. The same threefold pattern applies to the idea of birth where the cyclic repetition of ritual rebirth stands against both rebirth in another life as well as 'the second birth', the invisible birth of the new creature here and now. First and foremost, it is the third strand of meaning which will be traced here but, as will be seen, it is often impossible, and indeed would be wrong to attempt, to treat it in isolation for the various aspects condition each other and they can only be understood if their intimate relationship is taken into consideration.

The pilgrim of the Way, setting out as a seeker, finds the path not only baffling in its twists and turns but fraught with dangers. There are many who lose their way, who falter and are led astray for the spiral road reveals itself to be both a testing ground and a perilous venture that easily turns into a nightmare; the pilgrim finds himself caught in a maze and a labyrinth. This indeed men of all ages and traditions must have experienced for the spiral elaborated into a labyrinthine pattern[3] proves to be a universal symbol spontaneously produced and spontaneously responded to by the human psyche.[4]

The symbolism inherent in the labyrinth is complex and as difficult to unravel as the intricate design itself. Many interesting facets will have to be ignored here and only such aspects mentioned which have a direct bearing on the spiral way as an image of death and rebirth.

It is in connection with the temple of Amenemhet III that the name *labyrinth*[5] appears first in classical texts. This temple, erected near the king's pyramid, belongs to the middle kingdom, but researchers have shown that from the end of the old kingdom onwards we must consider the temple as the labyrinth, and we must remember that it was the centre of the secular administration of the country as well as the place of religious ritual.[6]

It seems that in the earliest times the royal tomb was constructed as a labyrinth and it was here, too, that certain rituals were performed to ensure life after death. When later the royal temple and the royal palace, where the king resided, became identified, another rite is known to have been practised also expressive of death and rebirth. Its purpose was not life after death but new life for the king, both in the sense of annual regeneration and royal procreation. The question arises why these temples, tombs and pyramids all follow a similar pattern as indeed did the holiest of holies, the funerary temple of Osiris.[7]

W. F. J. Knight has answered this question convincingly. He points out that a building, constructed on the spiral pattern of a labyrinth, has two main objects. One is the defence of, and exclusion from, the centre, the other is conditional admission and penetration to this very centre. There is no doubt that wherever a labyrinth is found, in any of its many different forms and functions, these two ideas are present. However, what has been said regarding the different levels of meaning applies equally here. Defence and exclusion may refer to the material safe-keeping of a tomb, a palace, a temple or a whole city. Where this aspect is predominant we have the 'tactical labyrinth'[8] which may be found not only at the very beginning of Egyptian history, but also in other cultures and periods.

To force the intruder to follow a long and circuitous route gives untold advantage to the defender. It seems highly probable that the city of Troy was built in such a manner, its outer and inner walls forming a maze of defences so that even those who succeeded in penetrating the outer ring were not likely to reach the heart of the city.[9] The ground-plan of the Castle of the St Angelo in Rome, formerly a mausoleum, follow the same idea, and so do many other such defensive structures as, for instance, Maiden Castle in England.[10]

The world knows many different types of intruders who are out to violate a sanctuary, of whatever kind this may be. Apart from the human intruder there are the evil spirits, and adverse influences in general, which have to be warded off and in this task, judging by its widespread use, the spiral pattern in its labyrinthine form has obviously proved highly effective.

According to Chinese belief, evil spirits can only proceed in a straight line; if this is made impossible by obstructions that force the unwanted visitor to twist and turn, an effective defence is the result. The Chinese spirit-walls which halt the straight flight of the evil spirits immediately behind the entrance to an inhabited place, be this a town or a house, are built to this purpose.[11] The same symbolism is present almost everywhere maze-like patterns are found.[12] As will be shown later, this is also one of the ideas underlying the many and varied threshold designs reported from various parts of the world. It appears than an intricate maze pattern, traced on a strategic spot like a threshold, proves as effective in warding off undesirable elements as does the labyrinth-structure itself.

On still another level the unwelcome intruder to be kept out is not the man who is out to attack and destroy, neither is it an evil spirit but it is everyman, every seeker who is unworthy of entry, unworthy of the great boon awaiting the steadfast at the centre. For here the labyrinth or maze represents the way of man, and in particular the way of the pilgrim, and as such constitutes an ordeal and a trial and admits to its innermost recesses only those who pass the test and prove themselves. To the unworthy the sacred centre is unreachable for they either become weary of the intricacies of the pathway or succumb to its perils. This, surely, is one of the ideas behind the complicated lay-out of some of the great temples, for instance Barabudur in Java, where the whole edifice is one great spiral whose volutes lead the faithful gradually to the sanctuary where the divinity resides.

From all this the interesting fact emerges that the 'good way' is not short and straight but long and winding and this fits in admirably with all descriptions of the Pilgrim's Progress. It is intricate and tortuous and weeds out those who are unable to unravel its mystery; they are swallowed up and are lost to the world.

For the labyrinth represents the world and the path to the nucleus is everyday existence, either lived foolishly, when man becomes ensnared by it, or lived wisely, when it reveals itself as a gradual journey to the promised land, the point of transformation, lying at the very heart of life itself.[13]

This is expressed clearly on the labyrinth in Piacenza Cathedral where the following verse appears:

> This labyrinth shows the picture of the world,
> Free to him who enters
> But very narrow to him who returns,
> But he who is ensnared by this world and is weighed
>   down by the delights of vice,
> Will find it difficult to solve the riddles of life.[14]

When Daedalus constructed his famous labyrinth at Knossos in the island of Crete he did so by using the Egyptian pattern, so Pliny assures us. Whether this is true or not, indeed, whether there ever existed such a structure as it is described in Greek myth, the fact is that the whole imagery contained in the tale of Theseus and the Minotaur spread far and wide and can be traced, often in a form adapted to local tradition, in many parts of the world.

Judging by classical texts it seems that the Cretan labyrinth was constructed as a double spiral. At its centre lived the *Minotaurus*, the man-bull, to whom the tribute of seven maidens and seven youths had to be sent every year only to be devoured by him. It was Theseus who undertook to enter the labyrinth, from which no mortal being had ever returned, and slay the monster. He did so with the help of Ariadne who furnished him not only with a magic sword, but, even more vital, with a skein of thread and a crown or wreath of light so as to enable him and his companions to find their way back to the world.

This well-known tale[15] contains all the main features of the labyrinth symbolism. At the nucleus resides death in the form of a creature which is both animal and man.[16] This dual nature, standing for darkness and light as well as death and life, is revealed in the two names by which the guardian of the centre was known; Minotaur, the man-bull, spelling death, and Arterious, the star, giving light and dispelling darkness. Both names occur side by side in Greek mythology.[17]

The centre, then, clearly stands for both death and life, death to all those ignorant of the Way, life to the hero who 'threads' his way back to the world. He does so by means of his light-crown which expels the darkness of the labyrinthine underworld and the clew of thread[18] which, according to some versions of the myth, the architect of the labyrinth himself, Daedalus, and not Ariadne, had given to him. A clew is wound spiralwise[19] and this is not just a curious coincidence. On the contrary, here we have the spiral Way in material form as a double journey to and from the central turning point where light and darkness coalesce. This interpretation is borne out by two northern myths in which a clew of thread figures prominently.

A Finnish myth relates how sun, moon and fire disappear from the world and are lying hidden in a rock. Ukko, the sky god, resolves to create another sun out of a single spark of fire. This precious spark, concealed in a golden bag in a silver chest, is lost and finally discovered in the stomach of a pike in which there is a salmon trout who has previously eaten a smaller salmon, and it is here inside the small salmon that two clews are found, one blue the other red; it is in the centre of the red one that the spark is discovered. The obvious connection implied in this myth between the clew and the spiral course of the sun will have to be taken up later, at this stage, the point to be noted is the light which resides at the inner-most volute of the spiral; it is here that the hidden treasure is found, at the point of no-return which reveals itself to be, at the same time, the turning point from which new light rises to illumine the whole world.

The second myth which comes from the Faroes is mainly concerned with another equally characteristic feature of the spiral ball. Here a young boy has to flee from a giant who demands him as a tribute after winning a game of dice with the father of the boy. The boy is his unless the father can hide him effectively. After various attempts Loke is asked for help and he advises to prepare a clew of thread with a wide pathway into it which is to contain an iron bar. In pursuit, both the boy and the giant approach the clew. What happens next is succinctly told in the following verse:

> Ran the boy in a great flurry,
> Ran through his father's clew in a hurry,
> Ran through his father's clew with a skill,
> Pursued by the giant suspecting no ill;
> Caught was the giant in his track,
> Burst did the iron bar in his head.[20]

The broad way leads to death, the narrow and winding way to life, and he who can unravel the ball and make the double journey will, like Theseus, deliver the world from the dominance of the forces of darkness.[21]

Christianity absorbed the labyrinth symbolism in all its richness and, throughout its history, made ample use of it. Since earliest times it was accepted as one of the symbols of the Christian way of salvation, and it is interesting that the Church by no means deemed it always necessary, as many examples testify, to change the iconography as it had been handed down from antiquity. Theseus fighting the Minotaur appears in Christian churches at the centre of the labyrinth, for instance in the church of St Michele Maggiore at Pavia (eleventh century); in the cathedral of Lucca (twelfth century) all three main actors of the Cretan story, Daedalus, Theseus and Ariadne are mentioned in the inscription accompanying the labyrinth, and in the greatest of all church mazes, that of Chartres (twelfth century), it is said that the blank space at the centre was once filled by a representation of the famous hero-fight. The biblical equivalent of this fight is shown in St Michele Maggiore, Pavia, it is the fight of David and Goliath or, in New Testament interpretation, the fight of Christ against Satan. For Theseus, in Christian symbolism, represents Christ, the Minotaur the forces of evil, and the labyrinth itself the path of redemption, leading the pilgrim through a world of temptations and snares to the point where sin is wiped out and death and resurrection accomplished.

Christianity has shown a preference for one particular version of the labyrinth which the French call 'labyrinthe de pavé'. In most instances the maze-like design is let into the floor of the church, usually near the entrance, sometimes in the nave or choir (Auxerre), but always in a strategic position where it cannot be missed. Many of these floor mazes survive today but their meaning is all but lost. There is a vague notion that it is 'supposed to have originated as a symbolic allusion to the Holy City' (*Catholic Encyclopaedia*) or again, that it represents the world and man's passage through it. If there were no more than that to it why should Christian churches from the earliest period (Orléansville, fourth century) down to modern times (Ely, nineteenth century) have persisted in its construction? It seems established that practically all the great French cathedrals had it at some time in their history, medieval churches of Italy contain it and it can be found in both Germany and England.[22]

There is no doubt that, especially in medieval times, the Christian Church was intensely alive to the deeper aspects of the labyrinth symbolism. They can all be traced, all in a Christian garb. The idea of the 'labyrinthe de pavé' itself is pre-Christian for such a labyrinth is not only mentioned in the Daedalus myth, as having been constructed by him for the amusement of Ariadne in the form of a dance floor, but it also appears as a floor mosaic in a theatre in Athens, as well as near the Cestius Pyramid on Egyptian soil. The question arises why it was this version of the labyrinth above all others which was preferred by the Christian Church. The labyrinth which at one time figured prominently in the cathedral of Reims points to the answer. It was called 'Chemin de Jerusalem' (just as the one in Chartres was known as 'lieue': mile) and it is known that there existed a guide book entitled '*Stations au Chemin de Jerusalem, qui se voit en l'église de Nôtre Dame de Reims*'.

Included in the rituals of the Church is another way equally consisting of a number of stations, the Way to Golgotha. The imagery of the 'stations of the cross' was used freely in all places of Christian worship in the Middle Ages and is still being used in Roman Catholic churches today. As in olden times it is customary 'to do' the stations, that is to walk from image to image, offering certain set meditations and prayers and contemplating their meaning. This 'pilgrimage' is mostly performed inside the church where the events which took place on the road to Calvary appear in the nave, pictorially or sculptured, usually adorning the main pillars or columns leading to the altar. In a place of pilgrimage, however, the stations of the cross are often placed outside the church, winding up a hill, following each other in an ascending sequence or again, they are laid out in an open space in the vicinity of the church. It is said that the custom of walking the Stations of the Cross first made its appearance after pilgrimages to the Holy Land became impossible because of its conquest by the 'infidels'.

The history of the 'Chemin de Jerusalem' in Christian churches affords a curious parallel to that of the Road to Calvary. Both were used in an almost identical manner and all the main features mentioned in connection with the stations of the cross are found again, adapted to suit the special characteristics of the labyrinth. Here, too, the image appears mostly in the nave, sometimes in or near the west entrance (Bourne, Ely, Chartres, etc.) or in front of the altar (S Michele, Pavia). It is along this line, the vertical arm of the cross, that the faithful walk to the sanctuary. Occasionally the labyrinth is found immediately outside the church or in its vicinity, as is the case in a number of English villages where the maze, mostly cut in turf, adorns the village green (Saffron Walden, Hilton, etc.).[23] It seems highly probable that the church labyrinths were used in very much the same way as the Stations of the Cross. This surmise is confirmed in many and various ways.

Three possibilities in which they could have been used are usually mentioned. If the maze was large enough it could be walked, as this is still, or better again, being done near the Church of Wyck Rissington in the Cotswolds;[24] as a means of penitence they could be done on one's knees or, again, where its size did not allow this, its winding path could be followed with one's finger (Lucca). Whatever the manner, the booklet of Reims shows that, whilst 'doing' it, certain meditations, and undoubtedly prayers, had to accompany the tracing of the labyrinth and, what is more, a number of indulgences seem to have been attached to it.[25]

To find more substantial proof of such practices is difficult; according to both Pliny and Shakespeare[26] mazes were 'trod' and it is known for certain that the former labyrinth in the cathedral of Auxerre, as will be mentioned in more detail later, was danced, probably in a very similar way as this is reported to have been the case, at different periods, in many parts of the world.[27]

According to traditional belief, equally difficult to track down to its source, the church labyrinths came into use for precisely the same reason as did the Stations of the Cross, namely the conquest of the Holy Land by the Turks, and the consequent cessation of pilgrimages.[28] All the available evidence clearly points to the fact that the church labyrinths were undoubtedly used and this is by far the simplest explanation of their presence in so many churches all over Europe, for it is difficult to see why they should have been constructed if they had no place in Christian worship and practice.

Furthermore, if the reason for the permission of the Church to walk or do the labyrinth is based on the idea of providing a substitute for the pilgrimage to Jerusalem, in the same way as this is the case with the Stations of the Cross, it is more than likely that it was at the main places of pilgrimage where labyrinths would be constructed for the use of pilgrims. This is certainly confirmed as regards the great French cathedrals, as well as Ely[29] and the Italian churches mentioned above. All these contained shrines sought by the pilgrims and it seems that other places of pilgrimage made use of an outside maze for the same purpose. In so doing they took over and continued a pre-Christian tradition and, what is more, in all probability used and often maintained 'pagan' structures more often than not situated in or near a village or other settlements.[30]

In this context another puzzling question presents itself. Why should these church mazes or labyrinths be found, almost exclusively in France, England, Germany and Italy? Their date affords a clue. The majority belong to the eleventh to the thirteenth centuries. Although there are both earlier and later ones, this is the period when it appears to have been the fashion to build labyrinths in or near churches. It is also the period of the Crusades when the idea of pilgrimage was rife certainly all over Europe, but especially in the countries mentioned, for they in turn provided the leaders for the campaign.

Pilgrimages have, of course, existed at all times and in all countries, but for the Christian world the Crusades spread this religious practice widely and made it into a potent ferment which, from that period onwards down to the Reformation, made every true Christian heart long to prove itself and join the many thousands who were seeking the blessings of one or the other of the many holy centres dotted over the map of Europe.

Thus it seems highly probable that the presence of a ground labyrinth in or near a church points to the fact that at one time this church contained a shrine which attracted pilgrims. Here the faithful from all parts of the world foregathered and, by passing over or walking the labyrinth, they symbolically undertook the greatest pilgrimage of all, that to the Holy City itself, which stood for both the death of the old and the birth of the new Jerusalem. They were reminded that their pilgrimage in itself was a labyrinthine way in search of the sacred centre, the cross, which traditionally was regarded as standing at the hub of the world. Having reached the centre the pilgrim stands face to face with the last great barrier, death; Theseus and the Minotaur are engaged in battle. The cross, the great symbol of both darkness and light, of both death and new life, confronts man.[31]

The point where in the Christian story the darkness of the grave and the radiant light of the new life meet is at Easter, the festival of death and resurrection. That the Middle-Ages were acutely aware of the fact that in the labyrinth symbolism was contained the story of Easter finds confirmation from many different sources.

In the Museum of Lyons there is preserved a stone inscription in Latin which obviously once belonged to a labyrinth. It says:

Look upon this mirror and behold in it thine own mortality!
Thy body shall become dust and food for the worms.
But though thyself shall live eternally; this life is hard to live.
Beg and pray to Christ that thy life may be lived in Christ
That by the Easter Festival thou mayest be awakened and come out of the labyrinth.
By these five lines of verse I instruct thee in the secret of death.[32]

The great Easter hymn *Victimae paschali* contains these words:

'Death with life contending; combat strangely ended!
Life's own Champion slain, yet lives to reign.
Tell us, Mary: say what thou didst see upon the way.
The tomb the living did enclose; I saw Christ's glory as he rose.'

Slain yet reigning, buried yet alive. It was this hymn which for many centuries was intoned in Auxerre Cathedral when, on Easter day, the bishop and his clerks 'danced' the labyrinth, inlaid in the floor at the west end of the nave. According to a decree dated 1396, the dean held a ball given to him by one of the canons and a chain[33] was formed of all the priests present with the dean at its head. Whilst intoning the Easter sequence the chain of priests danced the 'tripudio', the three-step dance, following the volutes of the labyrinth, and throwing the ball in a prescribed way. The joy of the resurrection in which all take part can hardly be better and more clearly expressed. The labyrinth, the words of the Easter hymn, the chain of dedicated men, dancing their way through the central point and back to the beginning, and the ball linking them all with the head, the dean, all these are expressive of the great message of Easter, the renewal of life through the darkness of death.[34]

The presence of a ball in connection with the labyrinth symbolism is not a new feature. In the Cretan story the ball of thread figures prominently and, as has been mentioned, in folklore such a ball is known to represent the labyrinth itself. The other suggestion made by several scholars is that the ball represents the sun, the newly born light, itself following a spiral path. These interpretations do in no way contradict each other. As the Finnish myth tells us, the spark of the new sun was found hidden in a clew of thread; out of it, as Theseus out of the labyrinth, rises the new sun. This in Christian language is Christ, the new Theseus, who is the sun of righteousness, and the light of the world. By walking, dancing, singing and throwing the ball, man not only contemplates the hidden meaning of the labyrinth, but he makes it come alive, he partakes of it and lives it with body, soul and spirit. This ritual dance was performed for many centuries, probably until its significance was forgotten and it became an empty shell, repulsive to those who only saw misplaced gaiety in it and eventually banned it.[35]

The motion inherent in a two-dimensional spiral pattern is directed inwards, towards a nucleus where the direction is reversed. This expresses the inner journey of a seeking soul *par excellence*. Where, however, the journey is mainly concerned not with the pilgrimage through life but with the passing from life to death and the realm beyond, the inherent dynamic pattern changes. The goal of the 'journey of the dead' is not a point within but a point outside, it is the attainment not of a transmuted life here and now, but of a future life beyond. The pilgrim's aim is the way *through* the labyrinth and not its centre, and instead of the return journey back to the world of the living, he presses on towards the abode of the dead, where he hopes to find renewal in another plane of existence.

To isolate this aspect of the spiral from the other aspects referring to life on earth is hardly possible; this is true especially where early phases of development are concerned when rebirth always meant both rebirth after death as well as rebirth in this life after ritual death. As Layard has shown for Malekula, however, the knowledge of the manifold layers of meaning is easily lost. In Egypt, for instance, the 'journey of the dead' tended to become divorced from any great significance for the living and developed into a mortuary rite. At this stage funerary temple and labyrinth part company; on Egyptian seals the human figures are shown outside the labyrinth whereas on earlier seals they occupy its centre.

There cannot be any doubt that the motive power behind this change is the new orientation of the labyrinth traveller which is directed predominantly neither towards physical nor spiritual regeneration but towards renewal in another life. When this happens, the symbolic design itself, the spiral or labyrinth, is affected and two main changes appear to take place; first, the centre tends to be left blank, for it is no longer the point of return but a place of transit. One is here reminded of some of the Church mazes where exactly this is the case.[36] The second change is more drastic. The labyrinthine design based on the idea of a coiled spiral is stretched, as it were, and becomes a structure which, in reality or symbolically, is entered at one end and, after many twists and turns, left at the other, the exit opening to the beyond.

The labyrinth pattern here represents not so much the winding path, leading to a great treasure within, but a threshold or gate over or through which man must pass if he wants to gain the renewal of life, awaiting him the other side. Unless he can perform this feat the boon of the future life is barred to him which means that, in this form also, the labyrinth acts as a testing ground permitting entry to the worthy and refusing it to the unworthy. This function is disclosed in a most colourful way in Malekula, an island belonging to the New Hebrides. The belief is that the guardian ghost is encountered at the threshold from this to the next life. The dead man is said to have lost his way and without the knowledge of the way he cannot pass beyond, for there is traced on the threshold one half of a maze-like design whose complicated pattern he has to complete.

A strangely similar myth comes from West Ceram, one of the Indonesian islands, where it is related that the maiden Hainuwele was killed by the people on the ninth night of the Maro festival whilst standing at the central point of the spiral dance, distributing gifts to the people. One of the virgin goddesses of the island, Satene, decided to punish the people for their evil deed.

So she built on one of the dance grounds a great gate, consisting of a ninefold spiral[37] like the one formed by the men in the dance; and she stood on a great log inside this gate, holding in her two hands the two arms of Hainuwele. Then, summoning the people, she said to them, 'Because you have killed, I refuse to live here any more: today I shall leave. And so now you must all try to come to me through this gate. Those who succeed will remain people, but to those who fail something else will happen.' They tried to come through the spiral gate, but not all succeeded, and everyone who failed was turned into either an animal or a spirit.[38]

Both these myths belong to a primitive cultural level but the idea they contain of the spiral or labyrinth as a gate or threshold design is by no means confined to that level. On the contrary, such designs are known to have been used and indeed are still being used in many different traditions. In popular belief they address themselves not to the dead, as is the case in Malekula, but to the living. Where the church mazes are situated in the extreme west end of the building, these, too, can be regarded as threshold designs, acting in the same way as Satene's spiral gate, separating the wheat from the chaff.

It is mainly in South India that many of these designs are found; they are mostly traced in sand or rice-flour and appear in both temples and on the threshold of houses. They are called 'Forts', stressing their defensive character but, at the same time, they are drawn so as to attract the attention of Lakshmi, Goddess of Prosperity. Others are dedicated to the God of Obstacles, Ganesh, whose help is thus secured to keep out destructive elements, whereas it is reported from another locality (near Madras) that these designs are known as 'Gates of Heaven'.[39] But here, too, there is a deeper level of meaning. It transpires when the time of the year in which these designs are mostly drawn is taken into consideration. It is in the month of Margali, which is generally considered as unlucky, that every morning women trace maze patterns afresh on the doorsteps of their houses. Margali is the month of the winter solstice when the sun dies only to be reborn anew giving new life and new light.[40]

To the two levels of meaning mentioned, there can be added yet another; for in Indian, mainly Tibetan (both Hindu and Buddhist) initiations to the path of discipleship, threshold designs have been used for centuries and the knowledge of their hidden meaning and power handed down from generation to generation. In the complicated ritual attending such an initiation all the symbolic aspects of the spiral or labyrinthine way as a threshold design are present; the pattern is drawn with coloured rice powder or by means of threaded cords,[41] or again is engraved on some suitable material. The most popular of these designs is the *Yantra* consisting of a complicated arrangement of triangles, guarding the central point, surrounded by a series of concentric circles. The fact that they are threshold designs is emphasized by the presence of gates at the cardinal points of the outermost rim which, for instance, in Tibet are protected by fear inspiring monsters called 'guardians of the doors'. The disciple, on his spiritual quest, must find his way past the protecting outer rings and past the guardians to the sacred centre which is beyond time and space and signifies the land of bliss and peace.

India is not the only country where such threshold designs are known. We need not go far afield for they are found in Scotland, in the Isle of Man, the Wye Valley, Newmarket and the Isle of Lewis. They are known as tangled thread and are more often than not traced in sand. A charming couplet is traditionally said to explain the meaning of these names. It runs:

Tangled thread and rowan seed
Gar the witches lose their speed.[42]

What is perhaps one of the most interesting survivals of this old custom is practised at Knutsford in Cheshire. Here the art of sand drawings has apparently never completely died out and at the May Day Festival, at the ceremony of crowning the Queen of May, such a 'tangled thread' drawing plays a prominent part. Its meaning is made abundantly clear by a closely related custom also practised at Knutsford. Traditionally an intricate sand tracing is executed outside the bride's door at a wedding feast. An old song explains this:

> Then the lads and lasses, their tundishes handing,
> Before all the doors for a wedding were sanding,
> I asked Nan to wed, and she answered with ease,
> 'You may sand for my wedding whenever you please'.[43]

The hero must conquer the intricacies of a labyrinth in order to receive his princess who, by the same token, is safely guarded and secure from the intrusion of the unwanted. Symbolically the marriage takes place when the way has been found to the centre, and out of it issues regeneration and new life.

It is curious to see the way the symbolism of the spiral pattern persisted through the ages, always expressing on different grades of meaning, the idea of a circuitous pathway leading to a highly prized goal; coupled with it is the emphasis on two main aspects of the Way, the aspects of light and darkness, death and life, hell and heaven and the aspect of probation, of initiation and with it of selection and exclusion.

Sometimes all that is left of the rich meaning is the idea of creating an intricate pattern for purely ornamental or playful purposes. Such is the case in many hedge mazes figuring in gardens and parks (e.g. Hatfield and Hampton Court) and such is also the case in that outdoor game which children, certainly all over Europe,[44] love to play. The name given to this game is a reminder of its true significance, it is called Heaven and Hell.[45] It consists of a spiral line, resembling a snail's shell, traced in sand or drawn on the pavement. The space between the spine is divided into a number of compartments and the difficult feat to be performed is to push a stone from number to number with the foot whilst hopping on one leg, until the centre, called Hell, is reached. From there the return journey has to be undertaken in the same way, and the winner is he who has successfully accomplished the double journey; this apparently is Heaven. The symbolism of the spiral way could not be expressed more clearly. Here, as in other spiral representations, the emphasis which is put on either the positive or the negative aspect of the centre varies. In the latter case there is the need for the return journey, for finding one's way back,[46] in the former case the final goal is the centre which then becomes 'Heaven' or 'Home'. This indeed is found in a variation of the above mentioned game. In England, at the beginning of this century, this particular version was called 'Klondyke'. Once again the spiral had become the symbol of the way to the great treasure, the 'mine of gold'.[47]

Some scholars have maintained that the image of the spiral in its many different forms, as well as the labyrinth myths such as that of Theseus and the Minotaur or Heracles' quest for the Golden Apples, represent the annual descent of the sun into the deathlike region of winter from whence, resuming its spiral course,[48] it, like the hero, is reborn to give new light and life to the world.

The sun's setting and rising, ever new and yet the same, has indeed, from time immemorial, been regarded as the visible manifestation of the hidden mystery of the recurrence and renewal of life, symbolized through the ages by the image of the spiral. A striking example is found in the stone relief adorning the four great gates of the Buddhist Stupa at Sanchi. Here are depicted peacocks whose tails enclose a huge spiral ornament. It is generally agreed that the sun spiral is referred to but the presence of peacocks adds a new element. The peacock is believed to symbolize immortality for its tail contains all colours and thus stands for all-inclusiveness and attainment;[49] furthermore, every winter the peacock sheds its tailfeathers only to recover them again in all their beauty when spring comes. They die and are reborn like the sun and like the pilgrim who passes through the temple gates in search of truth. The same belief in Christian language is found in a passage by Saint Antonio of Padua (thirteenth century).

> The reflection of temporal glory is symbolized by peacocks. For it is known that the peacock casts off his feathers when the tree casts off its first leaves, and afterwards down grows on it when trees begin first to grow green and bushy. The first tree was Christ ... but at the general resurrection in which all trees (that is, the saints) begin to grow green, that peacock who has thrown the feathers of mortality will receive the feathers of immortality ...[50]

So far no mention has been made of the spiral in its three-dimensional form, i.e. the corkscrew. Instead of the coils winding round a central point in an approaching or receding motion, they curl, mostly taking the form of a snake, around the length of an upright staff. In its symbolic meaning this variant shows a close relationship to the two dimensional form. This is immediately apparent in its classical representation, the Caduceus, the double serpent of the rod of Hermes, a motive which seems to be as universal in character as it is varied in appearance.

Hermes' (or Mercury's) main function was that of guide and friend (Psychopomp)[51] to the souls of the departed on their journey to the realm of darkness; but this same journey is also one which leads to the regions of light. This Prudentius makes clear when he says 'For Mercury knows well the Thessalonian magic and the rumour goes that his staff guides the souls of the dead to the heights of light'.[52] What is here referred to is most likely that aspect of Hermes' activities which Praxitiles depicts when he shows the God as playing with the Dionysos child or when he is seen receiving a newborn babe out of the hands of a goddess who is rising out of the earth.[53] Hermes' staff here guides those souls who are ready to be born on earth, leading them from the darkness of Hades to the light of the world.

Hermes, or Mercury, thus reveals himself as the God of the Way and the wayfaring men both in its literal and symbolic meaning. He carries as emblem of office the spiral staff, in the same way as it is the sign of office of both the Tibetan and Christian initiates. The Lama carries the single or double *dorje* or sceptre which, when represented pictorially, is seen to consist of a central spiral, opening out into the crowned lotus flower. The Bishop and other high Church dignitaries carry the crozier which, traditionally, terminates in a spiral scroll or crook, whose innermost point is often adorned by some allegorical figure, denoting the goal, the journey's end. One reason given for this curved end is that 'the head is bent or crooked in order to draw in and attract souls to the ways of God'.[54] There cannot be any doubt that whenever they appear, these symbolic designs, whose real meaning like that of the cathedral maze, is all but lost, represent the unfolding along an intricate spiral path of the human mind and spirit.[55] The guide, like Hermes, is the consecrated bishop, guru, or lama, the man who has travelled successfully along the labyrinthine way of total transformation.[56,57]

NOTES FOR CHAPTER 2

1. *The Spiral Way*, p. 12. See also J. Mitchell, *The City of Revelation*, p. 13.
2. One of the most comprehensive surveys is found in J. Purce, *The Mystic Spiral*. See also D. A. Mackenzie's *The Migration of Symbols*.
3. The main difference between a spiral and a labyrinthine design, apart from the

latter's more intricate pattern, is twofold. First, the reversal of direction, occurring in both, is of a different type, the relative position of the traveller to the centre being maintained throughout in the case of the spiral but not in a labyrinth. Second, the basic pattern of a labyrinth is usually threefold; an approach to the centre, a turning away from it and a renewed approach; this can be repeated several times. In the (two dimensional) spiral the initial approach is maintained until the centre is reached. (E. Wedepohl, 'Versuch über Labyrinthe', *Der Architekt* VII, Vulkan Verlag, 1960.)

4. For its great antiquity and wide dissemination, see A. Gibson, *Rockcarvings which link Tintagel with Knossos. Illustrated London News*, Jan. 9. 1954.

5. According to recent researches, 'labyrinth' derives etymologically from the Greek λαύϛα meaning rockpath, way of stone, paved path, defile, gutter, and thence house or place of stone, quarry, mine with many shafts, grotto, stone caves or stone passages. In the middle ages a walled-in monastery, a cell, or hermitage made of stone was called λαύϛα or λαβϛα (see H. Güntert, 'Labyrinth', *Sitzungsberichte der Heidelberger Akademie der Wissenschaften*, Phil.-Hist. Klasse, 1932, p. 14 ff.)

   Another derivation is from the word 'labrys', double-axe; the sign of the double-axe was found in several places in the palace of Minos, Crete, and it is thought that the Greeks, noticing the emblem, called the palace 'the house of the labrys', or the labyrinth.

6. C. N. Deeds, *The Labyrinth*, p. 16.

7. Deeds, *op. cit.* p. 21. Spiral designs of labyrinthine character also figure prominently in the Irish Royal Tomb of New Grange, which, in all probability, belongs to the second millennium B.C., and on the Holywood Stone said to date back to the Middle Bronze Age.

8. W. F. J. Knight, *Cumaean Gates*, p. 62ff.

9. The name Troy derives in part from a common derivation meaning to turn and twist.

10. A dramatic description of such a 'fort' occurs in the Indian epic *The Mahābhārata* and, what is more, its labyrinthine design is shown in a frieze at Halebid in Mysore. (S. C. Brooke, *The Labyrinth Pattern in India*.)

11. Also reported from Germany.

12. Another typical example is found in the so-called 'Tombeau de la Chrétienne' in Tipasa in Algiers. This subterranean grave, which is likely to be pre-Christian, is reached by a long and winding path, following a spiral pattern. Three transverse walls act as additional obstacles. (See A. Rosenberg: *Die Christiliche Bild-Meditation*, Note 2, p. 295.)

13. It is this aspect of the labyrinth which the seventeenth-century writer and historian Jan Amos Komensky (Comenius) elaborates in his famous poem: *The Labyrinth of the World and the Paradise of the Heart*. New editions, both in German and English, have appeared recently.

14. E. L. Backman, *Religious Dances*, p. 70.

15. Its most recent interpretation is that the youths and maidens were toreros and toreras who practised the feat of bull-jumping, and that the term 'minotaur' refers to a participant in a religious ritual or dance who wore a bull-mask. Pictures or statuettes illustrating these practices are extant. Theseus, it is thought, conquered Knossos by penetrating to the innermost chamber of the labyrinthine palace, the Throne-room, where he slew the Minoan king whilst the latter, wearing a bull mask, was engaged in some ritual to save his people. (C. Seltman, *The Listener*, March 19, 1953.)

16. A curious parallel is found in Egyptian mythology. The animal sacred to the Egyptian god Min was the white bull, and the god's symbol was that of the spiral, furthermore, he was mainly worshipped as protector of travellers and those journeying through the desert. (Larousse, *Mythology*, pp. 37–8.)

17. K. Kerényi, *Labyrinth Studien*, p. 56. Coins from Knossos, which incidentally use both the round and the angular version of the labyrinth, show as its centre either the Minotaur, or, in some cases, a star.

18. In this connection it is interesting to note the way idioms in common usage, sometimes point to an otherwise forgotten strand of meaning. 'Thread' is the spiral part of a screw and to lose the thread is to get lost in argumentation. Likewise, the clew, or ball of thread, used to guide through the labyrinth has now become 'clue', i.e. abstract, a line of thought, the thread of a story or a guiding principle.

19. It is depicted as a spiral on an Etruscan bowl. See K. Kerényi, *Labyrinth Studien*, p. 47. See also J. Schwabe, *Archetyp und Tierkreis*, B. Schwabe. For an Indian version of the Daedalus-Thesaur myth, see S. C. Brooke, *op. cit.*, also note 10.

20. Free translation. See J. Schwabe, *Archetyp und Tierkreis*, p. 534f.

21. There exists a curious parallel to this whole imagery in certain myths, fairytales and traditions. The symbol they all have in common is the ear and, keeping in mind that the volutes of the ear carry the name of labyrinth, the connection becomes clear. In fact, the ear, as a symbol of transformation, occurs in many traditions and its relationship with the sun is often stressed. Thus Karna, the son of Surya, the Hindu sun deity, was born from his mother's ear just as, in the middle ages, the belief was prevalent that the Holy Ghost entered through the Virgin's ear and thus was conceived the new sun of the world. In mainly Russian, Irish and Celtic fairytales we find the following: A boy, often dull-witted or awkward, enters the ear of a horse, giant, or other creature and comes out of the other ear transformed into a hero. In the Celtic myth of Conn-Eda, the young prince on his journey to the fairy realm, in search of three great treasures, rides a magic horse; one of its ears contains 'the sacrificial knife for the ritual immolation' and the other the elixir 'all-heal', the symbol of new life. It is significant, to say the least, that the volutes of the ear carry the name of the labyrinth. Furthermore, as H. Kayser has shown, the shape of the ear follows, or better represents in material form, the vibrational pattern of sound. The tone-figures transposed three-dimensionally, become the tone-spiral. One is here reminded of the 'Eargate' in John Bunyan's *Pilgrim's Progress* and of the 'Path of the Ear' mentioned in *The Tibetan Book of the Dead*. (See H. Von Beit, *Symbolik des Märchens*, I, 154, 422; II, 425–7; H. R. Zimmer, *Integrating the Evil*, Guild of Pastoral Psychology, Lecture 39, 1943; H. Kayser, *Vom Klang der Welt*; D. A. MacKenzie, *The Migration of Symbols*, p. 143.)

22. The best known church mazes are as follows:

> FRANCE: Chartres, Sens, Auxerre, St Quentin, Arras, Reims, Amiens, Toussaint, Chalons sur Marne, Poitiers, St Omer, Bayeux.
>
> ITALY: Ravenna: St Vitale, Piacenza: St Savino, Pavia: St Michele Maggiore, Lucca: Cathedral, Cremona: Cathedral, Rome: St Maria Travestere and St Maria in Aquiro.
>
> GERMANY: Cologne: St Severin, St Gereon.
>
> ENGLAND: Ely, Bourne.

For full list, see W. H. Matthews, *Mazes and Labyrinths*. Also J. Bord, *Mazes and Labyrinths of the World*.

23. For further examples see N. Pennick, *Caerdroia. Ancient turf, stone and pavement mazes*.

24. In an explanatory leaflet we read: 'The Wyck Rissington Maze embraces symbols of life, death, paradise and heaven. A recent visitor described his experience on the paths as "better than all the sermons I have ever heard". It will appeal more to the "pilgrim" than the sightseer, it preaches the gospel in a unique way. The maze, like some other ancient ones, is designed for "processions". If the correct paths are chosen 600 people can walk on them without the head of the procession ever running into the tail. On St Laurence Day, August 10th, the Rector leads a procession of this kind, and the parishioners follow behind: it is their annual pledge that they will tread the Christian path of life.' Is it a coincidence that St Laurence is traditionally shown as leading a soul from purgatory, an activity in which he is reputed to be engaged every Friday?

25. L. Ch. Cerf, in his *Historie et discription de Nôtre Dame de Reims* (Dubois, 1861), says that the 'Chemin de Jerusalem at Reims was also known as "Lieue" ' and adds this footnote, 'On l'appelait ainsi, dit M. I. Paris, parce que l'on mettait une heure la parcourir à genoux', p. 77. He goes on to say 'Ces allées inestricables étaient, pour le fidèle, une image du pelerinage de cette vie, ou un souvenir douloureux de la passion du Sauveur, comme l'indique le nom de Chemin de Jerusalem ... Des indulgences étaient attachées à cette pratique de devotion.' (p. 78.)

26. Pliny: *Nat. Hist. XXXVI*, 19, 91; Shakespeare: see supra p. 10 and, for instance, *The Tempest*, III, 3.

27. It appears that labyrinth dances constitute one of those universal rites which must have been practised since the dawn of religious history. It is said that Theseus and the Athenian youths performed such a dance after their escape from the labyrinth (Plutarch, *Aenead* V, 545–603 and similar dances still form part of Greek life today. W. O. E. Oesterly (*The Sacred Dance*, p. 70ff) mentions a pictorial representation on an Etruscan vase and quotes a description of this dance found in Homer (XVIII, 590–606). Furthermore, there exist, mainly in northern Europe, curious structures known as 'Walls of Troy' which are, in fact, mazes in spiral form built of stones, hedges or turf, and which date back to the Bronze Age. What these structures were used for is still somewhat obscure but the general idea was undoubtedly to perform the double journey from the circumference to the centre and back. This could have been done either as a game or as a religious rite. Both possibilities find confirmation in various ways. We know, for instance, that in early times a game of armed horsemen was a custom in Italy which went under the name of Troia, Truia, or Trojan Game. Such a game is described in Virgil's *Aeneid* V, 545ff, in connection with Julian, a son of Aeneas. It has been suggested that the name of 'Julian's Bower' for a maze may be derived from this. It is portrayed on the often-mentioned vase of Tagliatella whose whereabouts are, however, uncertain. Here the emphasis is clearly on protection and defence as this was also the case in the Salien Dance, known to have been performed round the city walls of Rome. Other labyrinth dances stress the idea of conditional penetration, for instance the initiation dances in Malekula (New Hebrides) and the Maro Dance (Ceram, Indonesia). The latter proceeds around a central figure, the maiden Hainuwele. Here, as in many myths and fairytales, the maiden, in a place difficult of access, stands for fertility and, generally, for the renewal of life. The traditional names given to some of these labyrinthine or mountainous places bear this out, i.e. Nun's Fence, Maiden Bower, Maiden Castle.

In this connection it is interesting to see that the centre of the earliest known church labyrinth bears the word 'Ecclesia', standing for mother church, offering a new birth and a new life to her children.

For literature on maze dances, etc., see W. F. J. Knight, *Maze Symbolism, and the Trojan Game*, in *Antiquity*, IV, 1932, pp. 445 ff; K. Kerényi, *Labyrinth Studien*, and H. Güntert, 'Das Labyrinth' in *Sitzungsberichte der Heidelberger Akademie der Wissenschaften*, Phil.-Hist. Klasse, 1932, p. 14. Also A. Rosenberg, *Die Christliche Bildmeditation*, p. 277.

28. E. L. Backman, *Religious Dances ...*, p. 71.
29. The Labyrinth in Ely Cathedral is late nineteenth century, but is undoubtedly going back to, and reviving, a much older tradition.
30. A comprehensive survey of these outdoor mazes is to be found in W. H. Matthews, *Mazes and Labyrinths*. See also J. Bord, *Mazes and Labyrinths of the World*. One such maze, it is claimed, once existed on Glastonbury Tor. See G. R. Siekmann, *The Mystery of Glastonbury Tor*.
31. There exists a Scottish stone cross whose four arms are filled with maze-like ornaments and in whose centre appears a double spiral, constructed, however, in such a way that entrance and exit do not coincide. The centre of the cross usually symbolizes the place where the mystery occurs, it stands for the *coincidentia oppositorum*, the death and resurrection of Christ. (See D. A. Mackenzie, *The Migration of Symbols*, pl. VII.)
32. E. L. Backman, *Religious Dances*, p. 71.
33. Clearly, the labyrinth dance mentioned by Lucian and Plutarch (*Pollux IV*, 101) was performed in the same way by a double line of dancers each holding on to the back of the dancer in front, thus forming a human chain. An illustration of this dance is apparently found on the so-called François vase, mentioned by W. Meyer. (See 'Ein Labyrinth mit Versen', *Sitzungsberichte der Philos. Philol.- Hist. Classe der K. Bayr. Akademie der Wissenschaften*, München, 1882.)
34. E. L. Backman, *Religious Dances ...* p. 67ff. There is a saying attributed to Erasmus, 'Mia est pila', I got the ball, meaning I have obtained the victory. See C. Hardwick: *Traditions ...*, p. 72.
35. Similar ceremonies must have existed at other places of Christian worship, but, without a written record, it is difficult to trace them at a time when practically all knowledge of the original meaning of the labyrinth symbolism has long vanished. Thus tradition tells that the maze dance of the youths near Brandenburg was closely associated with Easter and the Ascension and Backman (p. 71) reports from a place in north Holland that it was the custom there to walk the nearby labyrinth on Easter day.
36. S. Vitale: Ravenna, Chartres, St Quentin, Toussaint.
37. K. Kerényi gives an illustration of such a spiral gate from New Zealand, consisting of a female figure prominently ornamented with spiral designs. Illus. 6 in: *Labyrinth Studien*.
38. Quoted in J. Campbell, *The Masks of God*, p. 175.
39. Virgil in his sixth *Aeneid* describes a similar 'gate', a Cumaean Gate – on which the Cretan Labyrinth is depicted and which stands at the threshold to the underworld.
40. See J. Layard, 'Labyrinth Ritual in South India.' *Folklore*, 48, 1937, pp. 115ff, and S. C. Brooke, *The Labyrinth Pattern in India*.
41. Closely related in symbolic meaning to these threaded cords or tangled threads (see p. 23) are the intricate line designs as well as the complicated knots which fascinated such men as Dürer, Leonardo da Vinci and El Greco. Knots which only the hero can unravel, figure in myths, fairytales and legends and both knots and 'tangled' thread designs appear in profusion in medieval, mainly Irish, illuminated manuscripts. Their symbolism comes close to that of the Labyrinth. (See G. R. Hocke, *Die Welt als Labyrinth*.)

42. M. M. Banks, *Folklore*, 46, 1935, p. 170.
43. G. Long, *Folklore Calendar*, p. 120.
44. Also reported from India.
45. Significantly children only play it in the spring when the sun is reborn. In other parts of Europe it is called 'Walls of Jericho' and it is also played by Icelandic, Norwegian and Roman youths. See W. Meyer, *Ein Labyrinth in Versen*, p. 277.
46. At Hilton the return journey is the difficult part of 'Walking the Maze', not the way to the centre.
47. One is here reminded of the so-called Monk's Game, a form of solitaire which consists of an intricate circular pattern surrounding a nucleus; a small ball has to be negotiated past the many obstacles guarding the centre. Similar games are known in various parts of the world and they seem to date back to remote antiquity. The Fitzwilliam Museum, Cambridge, possesses such a game from Egypt and G. R. Hocke mentions a social game popular in the sixteenth century called the labyrinth of Ariost. (See G. R. Hocke, *Die Welt als Labyrinth*, p. 88.)
48. The sun's spiral path symbolizes not only the bestowal of new life but also the constant renewal of time. Leisegang and others have shown that the well-known relief of Mithras, encircled four times spiralwise by a serpent and surrounded by the signs of the Zodiac, is of Orphic origin and represents the Orphic God Phanes. The serpent stands for the sun's course and, according to the texts, it bears the double name of Heracles, meaning the coiled serpent, and Chronos, the God of Time and the creator of the Aeon. (Leisegang, 'The Mystery of the Serpent', 'Eranos', *Mysteries*, p. 210ff.) Proclus clearly knew of this imagery for he refers to people 'who celebrate time as a God, eternally, boundless, young and old, and of spiral form'. (Timaeus.)
49. Sri Aurobindo calls the peacock the bird of victory, and there is a Sufi saying that when the divine light first saw itself reflected in a mirror it saw a peacock with tail outspread.

    To this day, peacock's feathers are used for initiations and other religious rites in both Hinduism and Buddhism. Furthermore, the peacock's outspread tail, round like a wheel, has, since olden times, been regarded as an image of the starry sky. The Sanskrit term for peacock is Sahasraksha, 'the thousand eyed', or 'thousand starred'. This is also a name for Indra. (See J. Schwabe, *Symbolon*, p. 155.)
50. E. R. Goodenough, *Jewish Symbols* VIII, 2, p. 53.
51. The same applies to the Egyptian god Min. See note 16.
52. H. Rahner, *Griechische Mythen in Christlicher Deutung*, p. 244.
53. Scene on the Vase of Kertsch.
54. *Catholic Encyclopaedia.*
55. This is charmingly illustrated by the medieval painter Butinone. In his picture 'Christ disputing with the Doctors' (see plate 1) he shows the Christchild in the temple, with sceptred orb in hand, sitting on a spiral structure, strongly reminiscent of the Babylonian ziggurats. Similar structures, mostly carrying a divine image or temple on the top, are found all over the religious world.
56. In our time, total transformation is the goal symbolically expressed in the ground plan of Auroville, the international 'City of Dawn', inspired by the teaching of the modern sage and Yogi, Sri Aurobindo, which is in the process of being built in India. The plan shows a spiral whirl, standing for both a centrifugal and centripetal motion. The design is open-ended, indicating its oneness with, and openness to, the world at large.
57. According to tantric teaching, this 'Royal Road' is also the path of the *Susumma*,

the central life channel in man around which is wound the double spiral of the
female or dark, and the male or light energy. The path of enlightenment, as taught
in certain schools of Hinduism and Buddhism, is intimately bound up with this
inner process. According to traditional illustrations it is depicted either in a form
essentially identical with the staff of Hermes, or it takes the form of the Kundalini
Serpent coiling round the creative point in the centre. In both cases emphasis is on
the spiral nature of the process, a fact which C. G. Jung confirmed in modern
times when he says 'We can hardly help feeling that the unconscious process
moves spiralwise round a centre, gradually getting closer, while the characteristics
of the centre grow more and more distinct.' (*Psychology and Alchemy*, p. 207.)

3

The Cyclic View

There is a thing inherent and natural,
Which existed before heaven and earth ...
I do not know its name,
If I am forced to give it a name,
I call it Tao, and I name it as supreme.
Supreme means going on;
Going on means going far;
Going far means returning.

Tao Te Ching XXV

The flowing out of God always demands
a flowing back.

JAN VAN RUYSBROECK

We shall not cease from exploration
And the end of all our exploring
Will be to arrive where we started
And know the place for the first time.

T. S. ELIOT

Progress along a spiral path necessarily involves three basic motional patterns, a cyclic, a graded and a linear. Taken either in its two- or in its three-dimensional variant, the spiral path is always a synthesis of all three, but approached from different angles, any one of these patterns may appear to overshadow the others, giving rise to seemingly contrasting symbols and metaphors employed in the portrayal of the Pilgrim's Way.

Thus some traditions stress the cyclic aspect, the repetitious motion which returns to its starting point; others emphasize the aspect of scale, seeing the Way primarily as an ascent composed of distinct steps or stations leading ever higher towards perfection. To the first, the most vital feature is the turning point reached after the initial setting out, the inversion of direction which follows and the coincidence of the journey's end with its beginning. To the second it is the attainment of ever new grades of being which fascinates the pilgrim and obscures all else. Others, again, see the Way as a continuous rectilinear progression which holds its initial course throughout and leads slowly from a less to a more advanced evolutionary stage. There is nothing here of the broken rhythm of the scale nor of the curvature of the circle.

Whichever aspect predominates in any one culture or period imposes its own laws and leaves its unmistakable imprint; if held exclusively it may even result in a pattern of life which stands in striking contrast to those created by a different vision of the Way.[1]

It has long been recognized that the Far East feels itself drawn towards the cyclic aspect of the spiral way, towards its intrinsic repetitions, its closed nature, where beginning and end are one, and its element of recoil, and change of direction. Everything that lives seems to be expressive of a rhythmic motion comparable to the swing of a pendulum. Birth and growth revert into decline and death, spring and summer into autumn and winter. This succession, like in- and out-breathing, is ever the same in eternal repetition. It is the visible outflow of an invisible divine order, which embraces man and nature alike. To live in accordance with its laws and conform to its ordinances should be man's aspiration and hope, for to go against it, or even to deviate from it, inevitably leads to misery and disaster. In the *Tao Te Ching*, the Taoist classic, it is written 'Where Tao is, equilibrium is. When Tao is lost, out come all the differences of things'. 'The great virtue as manifested is but following Tao.' What the following of Tao involves is stated unequivocally 'Returning is the motion of Tao'.[2]

The idea of a rhythmic alternation between a going forth and a return pervades all Chinese thought. Both are not only seen as mutually dependent but as phases of a greater circular motion which blends all things together into one harmonious whole and without which things would fall apart and lose their meaning. 'In order to contract a thing, one should surely expand it first.'[3] The same idea, taken a step further, is found in chapter XXV where Tao is named supreme. 'Supreme means going on; going on means going far; going far means returning.' In those words 'going far means returning' is contained the intrinsic law of all circular motion; the departure, the reaching of a turning point and the return to the beginning. In such a return is seen the goal of all life, as it is said:

> All things come into existence,
> And thence we see them return.
> Look at the things that have been flourishing;
> Each goes back to its origin.
> Going back to the origin is called peace;
> It means reversion to destiny.
> Reversion to destiny is called eternity.
> He who knows eternity is called enlightened.
> *Tao Te Ching* XVI

What is perhaps the most elaborate treatment this cyclic view has ever been accorded is found in that curious text which has influenced Chinese thought for century after century, the *I Ching*, or 'Book of Changes'. Here the eternal cycle of becoming and passing away is regarded as synonymous with life in all its manifestations. Being cyclic in character, this dual motion is not to be identified with cause and effect much less with two mutually exclusive opposites. 'That which makes this cycle possible is the overlapping of the polar forces. The force of the Yin principle, representing form and concentration, does not become effective only when the force of the Yang principle, representing content and expansion, has spent itself, but is already secretly active when the other force has reached its summit.'[4] Each principle contains the seed of the other and, what is more, for the circle to be closed, both are needed. The cyclic motion is the higher entity which is made possible through the interplay of the opposites.

Furthermore, the *I Ching* teaches that this interplay, contained in the cyclic nature of the immutable whole, gives birth to two types of change or movement. Continuous change and cyclic change. The question presents itself whether, what is here called continuous change, covers the same phenomena as does the concept of evolution or continuous development in one overall direction. Wilhelm denies this emphatically. He maintains that, although China knows the principles of progress and development, here they do not represent ultimate values. They are seen as embedded in, and part of, a much more comprehensive dynamic pattern. 'There does not exist a forward movement beyond a certain limit, for at the extreme point the counter-movement sets in, which makes life's pendulum swing back to the beginning.'[5] Thus, however far evolutionary change proceeds, its inner law is that of the cycle and 'the idea of continuous change is really a ring-shaped thought, even if we have to think of this circle as being sufficiently big to include the whole history of mankind and of the cosmos.'[6]

What is true of nature, of history, of the outer world, is also true of man's inner world. Here, too, the circular movement is seen as the great goal for it alone conforms to the eternal motion of Tao. As is shown in the *Secret of the Golden Flower*, 'A Chinese Book of Life', the hope of man lies in the circulation of the inner light. This, however, cannot be accomplished until the outward flowing movement of energy, demanded in everyday life, is counteracted by the backward-flowing movement. The return has to be effected, the circle to be closed. It is only then that the 'Golden Lotus' within can come into blossom. 'Therefore the meaning of the Golden Flower depends wholly on the backward-flowing method ... when the light is allowed to move in a circle, all the powers of heaven and earth, of the light and the dark, are crystalized.'[7] In the words of the *I Ching* 'In returning we see the mind of heaven and earth'.

Throughout the ages wherever man has sought for the meaning of life and its hidden laws he was confronted with the same obstacle. What he was seeking lay beyond the reach of conceptual thought and its language. What other tools could he use? Older than the language of concepts is the language of symbols and it is this language which alone can express the hidden, intangible and ever changing dynamics of life. Symbols are the outflow of, and address themselves to, the whole of man, and it is that whole which, in turn, is activated and responds; here lies their efficacy but also the reason why they crumble and lose all power the moment they are imprisoned in the realm of intellectual reasoning. They are then literally explained out of existence.

The wheel of life[8] is such a symbol, standing for the cycle of becoming and passing away; it is expressive of one aspect of life's ultimate meaning and as such it carries in it great potentials of energy as indeed it is clear from the powerful influence it has yielded upon whole cultures over long stretches of time. This influence can be felt and traced in all human activities. Life is seen as the stage on which, in rhythmic repetition of in- and outflow, Tao, itself changeless, manifests in constant change. Contraries for ever follow one another but, at the same time, they complete and engender each other, and in so doing, they follow the returning motion of Tao.[9]

What of the irreversible progression of passing time? To a mind which has its gaze fixed on the cyclic aspect of life's motion such a view is incomplete. It mistakes the part for the whole. Passing time is only one beat in the vast rhythm pulsating through the universe. The next beat contains the turning point and the seemingly straight line of time's progression is seen to be curved. The return follows as surely as night follows day. The non-recurrent character of passing time is therewith nullified. The forbidding irreversibility of time, its now or never, becomes a mere illusion. What matters are not the separate phases but the circular movement as a whole. In its entirety it is timeless and absolute, and it is against this timelessness that its relative aspects, the different phases of passing time must be seen. Any sequence of events, including history, is looked upon as a pattern taking shape within a larger ever recurring pattern and not as irrevocably fixed in time. Its significance lies in its relationship to the whole not in its exact position in a chronologically ordered succession.

L. Abegg gives interesting examples of this view of reality:

Unlike us, they (the East Asians) have never thought in terms of a chain of connected dates, but often used very short periods as the basis of their chronology ... The East Asians have, therefore, no fixed point in their chronology such as we have in the year of Christ's birth; chronologically they remain somehow suspended in mid-air, exactly as in their attitude to life, they conceive neither of a beginning nor an end, but only of eternal flux.[10]

This eternal flux, however, they do not regard as ultimate. As their religious attitude shows, they look beyond to that which knows no flux, to the changeless source of all change, the perfect all-embracing circle or wheel, the grand unity, T'ien.

Just as time is seen to conform to the circular pattern so heaven and earth. The image as used in the *I Ching* is that of an eight-spoked wheel, showing not only the four quarters with their subdivisions but nature's changing seasons together with the main elements, sky, wind, water, mountain, earth, thunder, fire and sea. These are seen to correspond to eight human qualities, the creative, the gentle, the precipitous, quietude, the receiving, the exciting, the clinging, the cheerful. In fact, there does not seem to be a sphere anywhere, from the most exalted to the most trivial which is not secretly or openly guided by cyclic motion. There are wheels within wheels.

Even the arguments expounding this view are circular in nature; the underlying thought-process does not advance in a straight line, the inherent motion of logical thought, but 'consists of enveloping or encircling moves'.[11] The approach to the core of the argument is by ever narrowing circles; once arrived, the movement is put into reverse and returns, by way of widening circles, to the all-enveloping round which can now be put into relationship to the central point.

This method is, for instance, applied in a well-known passage from the *Ta Hsüe*,[12] which is introduced with the revealing words 'to know what is first and what is last will lead near to what is taught in the Great Learning'. A circular course of action is described which begins with the desire of the ancients 'to illustrate illustrious virtue throughout their kingdom', and ends with the realization of that desire. This is the large enveloping round, it is filled with a number of concentric circles, standing for smaller and smaller units, the family to be regulated, the person to be cultivated, the heart to be rectified, the thoughts to be made sincere, things to be investigated. With the latter the inner limit is reached which carries in it the reversal of direction, for the investigation of things means extension of knowledge. We are now led back, touching the same successive landmarks on our way out until the

original encircling round is reached again, standing for the happiness of
the whole kingdom.

The cyclic view, wherever it is taken as the guiding principle,
engenders in its followers an attitude towards life which is unmistakable.
For man to pit himself against the rhythmic motion inherent in all
creation would be folly for he would be crushed in the ever turning
wheels of the world. To ignore or neglect it would be equally foolish for
it would mean being tossed about helplessly between the opposites
constantly replacing each other. What is asked of man is a different
attitude, one which is rooted in acceptance and non-interference but
which, at the same time, strives, through spontaneous co-operation, to
become identified with the rhythmic swing of life's pendulum and
therewith reach out towards that still-point where the pendulum is
suspended, and from whence all movement proceeds.

Non-interference and acceptance, coupled with spontaneous co-
operation and inspired action, is this possible? Religion says it is and
the Chinese see in it the all important means of attaining to Tao; they
call it *wu wei*. In trying to portray an attitude for which the West,
although it is known to it, has yet no concept, scholars have proposed
many different translations. Literally the term means 'not-doing', 'do-
nothing' or 'non-action' but this expresses its negative aspect only and
ignores its undercurrent of active participation of which, although it is
hidden, the Chinese mind is acutely aware. It has, therefore, been
rendered, more elaborately as 'be effective without exertion', 'be
effective through your being', 'absence of self', 'to practise virtue
naturally', 'striving through the power of the inner life', 'non-
interference', or 'refraining from activity, contrary to nature'. In the
Tao Te Ching, wu wei ranks next to *Tao* and *Te*[13] in importance.
'There is no other doctrine that is grander than the doctrine of Tao, and
no other teaching that is more universally potent than the teaching of
wu wei.'[14,15] If only man were able to embrace this principle then all
things would develop spontaneously according to their own nature.
Chapter 48 of the *Tao Te Ching* reveals the process involved:

> He who pursues learning will increase everyday;
> He who pursues Tao will decrease everyday.
> He will decrease and continue to decrease,
> Till he comes at non-action;
> By non-action (wu wei) everything can be done!

This verse brings out in full relief the most essential feature of *wu wei*.
It is neither just non-action nor action but, by making use of the

language of paradoxes, it points to that hidden stratum of existence which includes the world of opposites, yet goes beyond it. 'Act non-action' is the maxim repeated in different ways throughout the *Tao Te Ching*. In other words, if man would surrender to the law of the eternal Tao which is non-action, spontaneous and harmonious action on the temporal plane would naturally flow out of it; for the great Tao is the perfect round, the closed circle which, as the eternal One, knows no change and no action. Yet it is at the same time the Mother of the Universe and as such embraces and produces all things out of the primal opposition of Light and Shade.

Seemingly, there are two worlds, the world of Tao and the world of the 'ten thousand things' but in reality there is only one, for in its interaction and entirety the world of ceaseless change is that perfect round, the complete circle, which, being ever the same, must be regarded as non-changing and non-acting. This is the world of the return where such opposites as existence and non-existence, the visible and the invisible, action and non-action interpenetrate.

> The non-existent can enter into the impenetrable.
> By this I know that non-action (wu wei) is useful.
>
> XLIII

or, in terms of the Zen sect of Buddhism which was deeply influenced by Taoist ideas:

> If you are desirable for the truly immovable, the immovable is in the moving itself.[16]

The goal of *wu wei*, then, is to embrace, in and through the diversity of phenomena, that hidden unity which binds all things together. What is demanded is a conscious act of surrender to its spontaneous manifestations which include both the ceaseless play of opposites and the perfect round enclosing them. Laotse answers the question what it is which has to be surrendered in no uncertain terms. 'The perfect sage ... works without grasping and therefore succeeds in whatever he undertakes.'[17] The sage 'desires the desireless' and 'has no self to call his own'. What is taught here is the universal principle of non-attachment, and selflessness, the absolute pre-condition for Tao and Te to become active in man. For to be guided by selfish desires leads to constant interference in the natural interplay of forces, to man pitting himself against nature, giving him a sense of action which, however, is as fruitless as it is deluding. The pursuit of selfish desires, therefore, results in wrong activity whereas selflessness makes possible non-interference (*wu wei*) in, and therefore living in harmony with, the dictates of heaven and earth.

NOTES FOR CHAPTER 3

1. In spite of this, the other aspects are never altogether absent in any one religious culture. Compensatory trends are always at work and, in any case, the teaching of the Way, in its wholeness always presupposes recognition, and the active interplay of all three of these basic patterns.
2. XVIII; XXI and XL.
3. *Tao Te Ching*, XXXVI.
4. R. Wilhelm, *Chinesische Lebensweisheit*, p. 85.
5. ibid., p. 106.
6. L. Abegg, *The Mind of East Asia*, p. 74.
7. R. Wilhelm, *The Secret of the Golden Flower*, p. 34.
8. See p. 180ff.
9. As J. Needham has shown, the Taoists were especially impressed by cyclical change, not only of the seasons and of birth and death, but as visible in all kinds of observable cosmic and biological phenomena. This is what Hou Wei-Lu calls the doctrine of cyclically recurring differences, '*hsun huan i pien lun*'. (Needham, vol. 2, p. 75.)
10. *The Mind of East Asia*, pp. 308–9.
11. L. Abegg: *The Mind of East Asia*, p. 31.
12. *Ta Hsüe* I.
13. *Te*: Intrinsic Virtue.
14. XLIII.
15. Or, in the words of Chuang Tzu, who regards *wu wei* as the highest virtue, 'Perfect happiness and preservation of life are to be sought for only in inaction. Let us consider, Heaven does nothing; yet it is clear. Earth does nothing; yet it enjoys repose. From the inaction of these two proceed all the modifications of things. How vast, how infinite is inaction, yet without source! How infinite, how vast, yet without form. The endless varieties of things around us all spring from inaction. Therefore it has been said: "Heaven and earth do nothing, yet there is nothing which they do not accomplish". But among men who can attain to inaction?' (Needham, vol. 2, p. 69.)
16. Hui-neng. See D. T. Suzuki, *Manual of Zen Buddhism*, p. 88.
17. XLVII.

4

The Ladder of Perfection

A man who has renounced the world and everything
in it with unfailing faith, believes that the merciful
and generous God will accept those who come to
Him repentant; and he knows that from dishonour
God leads His slaves to honour, from extreme
poverty to riches, glorifies them through abuses and
degradation, through death makes them heirs and
participators of eternal life. Such a man strives to go
forward by these means ... like a thirsty stag,
towards the immortal spring; and by them to ascend
on high, as by a ladder. On this ladder angels ascend
and descend to help the climbers, while God stands
above it awaiting such labours and efforts as are
within our powers ...

God does not allow those who strive towards Him
with all their zeal to fall completely off this ladder, but
seeing them exhausted, helps and supports them,
stretching out the hand of His power and leading
them to Himself.

ST SIMEON *the New Theologian*

Count Keyserling once said that the Indian mind proceeds from state to
state, and that in doing so it puts itself in opposition both to the Far East
and the West. In India the religious quest is seen as consisting primarily
of a series of distinct phases of transformation, affecting the inner as
well as the outer life. The aspect of scale here comes to the fore,
expressing perfectly the Indian view that man's true goal is the
attainment of more and more exalted planes of being. The ascent
envisaged leads, step by step, towards heights unimaginable to those
who are still bound to the round of existence, ever repeating itself.
Cyclic recurrence, symbolized by the circle or wheel, is experienced as
a burden unto death.

A world-without-end, is this round of birth and death. No beginning
can be seen of those beings hindered by ignorance, bound by
craving, running through the round of births and death. Thus for a

long time, brethren, have ye experienced ill, experienced grievous pain, experienced misery, and swollen are the charnel fields. So that ye may well be disgusted with, well turn away from, well be released from all the activities of existence.

Samyutta Nikāya II, 178ff

The keynote here is not return but liberation, not rhythmic repetition but escape from it and, as seen from both the Hindu and Buddhist point of view, the Way has only one savour, the savour of release, gained by gradually climbing ever higher on the scale of perfection. Although India retains the cyclic view on the cosmic plane, she utterly rejects it on the human plane; indeed, here the scale or ladder becomes the great symbol of freedom, standing over against the image of the cosmic wheel of time, revolving *ad infinitum*, ever the same, yet ever new.

From earliest times it was acutely felt that here, in the gradual aspect of the spiral way, lay man's fairest hope. The main concern of every type of religious teaching in India is, therefore, the detailed mapping out of this ascent with its well-defined sequence of evolutionary states or steps, the description of their foremost characteristics, and the necessary instructions for their attainment.

The sixfold division envisaged in the *Katha Upanishad* is symptomatic of this type of thinking.

Beyond the senses are their objects, and beyond the objects is the mind; beyond the mind is pure reason, and beyond reason the great Self. Beyond the great Self is the Unmanifest; and beyond the Unmanifest, the Spirit. Nothing is the beyond the Spirit: He is the Path supreme and the end of the Path.

Katha Upanishad I, 3, 10/11

Also in the Upanishads is found the Vedantic teaching of the four states of consciousness, basic to much of Hindu thought. It tells of the great ascending scale, leading from the senses and their objects to the high goal, the spirit supreme, from the 'waking life of outward moving consciousness' through the life of dream and deep sleep to the 'awakened life of supreme consciousness'. This last is the awareness and experience of absolute unity and is synonymous with the fully enlightened mind.[1]

Fourfold, too, is the scale underlying the way the Buddha taught. Discipline and purification, themselves manifold, are followed by meditation and concentration with their different grades of intensity, giving rise to intuitive knowledge and enlightenment, and eventually leading to release, the gateway to Nirvana. Out of this scale, which forms the backbone of Buddhist teaching, issue other processes of transformation, of which the most important is the graded sequence known as conditioned genesis. It traces a long chain of causations, including in its wide scope such vital activities as feeling, desiring, craving and becoming, and, by stopping them all one by one, connects the first link in the chain, the disappearance of ignorance, with the last, complete freedom from fear and suffering.[2]

If it is asked how this process can be put into effect, the answer is by the acceptance of the four holy truths, themselves forming a fourfold rise from the realization of suffering, the cause of suffering, the extinction of suffering, to the way to bring about the end of suffering. This is the middle way, the Buddhist Eightfold Path. It, like the Hindu way of liberation, is the great bridge, spanning the river of ceaseless recurrence and leading to the further shore. He who has crossed over is a 'stream-winner' for he has conquered the first stage on the long journey from bondage to freedom. Mastery of the second lap transforms him into a 'once-returner' from which station he proceeds further to the third phase of the never-returner. The fourth and highest part of the journey, at the summit of achievement, is trodden by the *Arahat*, the enlightened human being, who has accomplished his fourfold pilgrimage and is ready to enter Nirvana.[3]

That the teaching of the gradual ascent is still foremost in the Indian mind today, as it has been since ancient times, is born out by such masters of the spiritual life as Sri Ramakrishna, Sri Ramana Maharshi and, above all, Sri Aurobindo. In his essay on the *Synthesis of Yoga* and even more so in his monumental work, *The Life Divine*, Sri Aurobindo traces in detail the peculiar features of the 'stair of ascent', as he frequently names it, and he insists that it would be wrong to regard its individual rungs as entirely clear-cut and separate. There is interpenetration and, what is more, progress is not so much an uninterrupted climb but rather takes the form of an oscillation between higher and lower states. Of this line of transition the following picture is given:

This line is, as all must be, governed by the natural configuration of the stair of ascent: there are in it many steps, for it is an incessant gradation and there is no gap anywhere; but, from the point of view of the ascent of consciousness from our mind upwards through a rising series of dynamic powers by which it can sublimate itself, the gradation can be resolved into a stairway of four main ascents, each with its high level of fulfilment. These gradations may be summarily described as a series of sublimations of the consciousness through Higher Mind, Illumined Mind and Intuition into Overmind and beyond it; there is a succession of self-transmutations at the summit of which lies the Supermind or Divine Gnosis.[4,5]

According to Indian teaching, the inner law governing the 'stair of ascent' is that of transformation through absorption; the lower plane is absorbed into the higher in a transmuted form and individual and seemingly isolated phenomena become integrated as the ascending movement continues. The watchword, here, is not completion, as is the case where the cyclic view of life predominates, but transformation. What matters alone is the grade to which the seeker has attained, for it is this which determines the interpretation of, and attitude to, the world. Both these necessarily change as man progresses and they must, at no stage, be regarded as final. The manner we appraise both the world within and without is seen as the direct result of where we stand on the ladder of transformation.

Although it is true to say that each step is self-contained, as it were, and follows its own dynamic pattern, it yet does not disclose its real meaning unless seen in relation to the hierarchy as a whole. Taken in isolation it can only convey a limited and therefore easily misleading picture of life. Thus each level has its own peculiarities and colours our outlook accordingly. Objective truth is only approached at the very end of the journey, only then is gained the ability to see things as they are. Only the highest principle can be said to be ever real and ever existent, all else is only relatively so. As Lord Krishna teaches:

The unreal has no existence, the real is never non-existent; the conclusion about both these has been perceived by the seers of the truth.

Bhagavadgita II, 16

The different states of awareness pertaining to the lower reaches are mainly characterized by the degrees of illusion which still prevail. The dualistic view of life, for instance, belongs to a certain stratum of awareness; the man who is wholly immersed in it will regard it as ultimate. Yet even a small shift away from it gives access to an entirely new vista and doubt as to the validity of the former judgment appears. What was regarded as true and satisfying to the understanding turns out to be only partially true and thus unsatisfying. In this way, the need for re-interpretation and reorientation constantly arises.

What is offered here as a solution to the riddle of the opposites which make up the world, is not that they are complementary and as such necessary for the understanding of the all-comprehending whole, but that their concreteness and their very existence is in truth not only relative but ephemeral. Only the man who stands on the lowest rungs of the ladder of becoming will accord absolute reality to the pairs of opposites; once a more advanced stage has been reached, these false imaginings are left behind, and the whole world of phenomena becomes 'a mere appearance of existence ... like a mirage in the air'.[6]

Realizing this, the seeker engaged on this ascent is ever intent to climb higher, and in doing so to shed previously cherished notions and beliefs, and what is more, to guard against the danger of being caught by the illusion of permanency which every step, taken in isolation, presents. This is the snare of *Maya* and he who is ensnared by it, is faced with stagnation and the arrest of all progress. The often repeated call which reaches the pilgrim from the various holy scriptures is, therefore, to awake, to arise and to strive towards the heights. Scale upon scale stretches in front of him and wherever he turns there is a new evolutionary grade which, in some mysterious way, is 'wholly other', yet forms part of himself.

As within, so without. Corresponding to the inner transformation as outlined, Hindu teaching also grades man's sojourn in the world into four stages, the four states of the Brahminical life. The first is that of instruction, study, and initiation (*Brahmachari*), at the beginning of which the young Brahmin is invested with the triple cord, symbolizing the need of control over the three constituents, the body, speech and mind. The second state is that of the householder. The Brahmin who has married and become a father is called a *Grahastha*; every action of his daily life is regulated along certain lines of conduct and repeatedly during the day he has to utter a number of set prayers and invocations, perform ablutions and attend to various ritual actions. Having reached the third state, that of dweller in the jungle (*Vanaprastha*), he retires with his wife from the active life of town or village, and lives forthwith in retreat in some secluded spot. Here his life is regulated by strict rules of continence and asceticism and all his leisure time is to be devoted to the various degrees of concentration and meditation, leading to union with Brahman. The last and highest state belongs to the holy man, the *Sannyasi*, who has entirely renounced the world, has left his wife and children and treads the earth, a man who has severed all ties, lives on alms and calls nothing his own. He has only one object in life; it is to prepare himself for the final stage of identification with the supreme deity.

Just as the human life, rightly lived, represents a graded ascent, so does the society man lives in. The Indian caste division is one of the oldest social systems known to mankind. From and by birth it grades every Hindu and assigns to him the station in life where his duties lie and to which he unalterably belongs. Tradition has it that it was Brahma himself who established this fourfold hierarchy on earth in which each group is again subdivided in varying degrees, often depending on the locality or province in which it occurs.

All are clearly defined with their attendant duties and sometimes distinguishing marks are worn or painted on some part of the body. Whatever the prevailing hierarchy, it is, or was until fairly recently, the determining factor in the social life of the people. Time and again this rather rigid classification based upon birthright and, therefore, liable to engender inequalities and divisional strife, has been repudiated both in the scriptures and by individual men of wisdom and insight. The principle itself has been upheld by them all, but it is interpreted in a spirit of a deeper understanding as is expressed, for instance, in *Vajrasūcika Upanishad*. Here the pertinent question is asked: 'Who is verily, the Brahmana? Is he the individual soul? Is he the body? Is he the class based on birth? Is he the knowledge? Is he the deeds (previous, present or prospective)? Is he the performer of the rites?' To all these questions, the answer given is 'it is not so'.

Then, who verily is the Brahmana? He who after directly perceiving, like the amalaka fruit in the palm of one's hand, the Self, without a second, devoid of distinction of birth, attribute and action ... becomes rid of faults of desire, attachment, etc., and endowed with qualities of tranquillity ... He alone who is possessed of these qualities is the Brahmana. This is the view of the vedic texts and tradition, ancient lore and history. The accomplishment of the state of the Brahmana is otherwise impossible. (IX)

The scale of transformation is not restricted to this present life, on the contrary, it reaches out to embrace both past and future existences. What could be more awe-inspiring and impressive to the mind of the seeker than the picture of the vast ladder of incarnation and reincarnations of which he forms part, and on which, so he is taught, he ascends or descends according to the fruits of his own deeds. It is the same scale of becoming described above, but here it is not restricted to man's inner development, nor to the way he journeys through life, but it includes all life from its lowest to its highest manifestations.[7] Life in all its forms, whether within or without, whether past, present or future, is seen as one vast hierarchy of states breathtaking in its scope and all-inclusiveness. Here lies the destiny of man, as India sees it, and here is played out the drama of the individual human life.

Where is the origin and where the termination of this stairway of all existence, this perpetual process of transformation upwards, downwards, always in motion and always changing? One movement gives birth to another, one process arises out of another, and state follows state. To ask the question of an absolute beginning[8] postulates the necessity of a break in the continuity of existence itself. This, to the Indian mind, is unthinkable and indeed, impossible; for it runs counter to two of the most fundamental experiences embodied in all Indian religion; the manifold but absolute unity of life, and the upward and downward movement, evolution and involution, inherent in it. It is the synthesis of these two ideas that decisively determines India's religious thought, a synthesis that is largely independent of any specific beliefs and doctrines.

Hinduism, Buddhism and Jainism alike are imbued with it and for that very reason reject questions regarding an absolute beginning of this vast process of integration and dissolution, ever rising and falling on the scale of becoming.

Not an easy thing it is, monks, to find a being who during this long many-a-day has not at one time been a mother, a father, a brother, a sister, a son, a daughter. How is this? Incalculable is the beginning, monks, of this faring-on. The earliest point is not revealed of the running-on, the faring-on of beings hindered by ignorance, fettered by craving.

Samyutta Nikaya II, 178 f

Through this ceaseless 'faring-on of beings' runs as a connecting link 'that which lives' as the Jains call it, the unity behind the myriads of different states of existence. Out of the realization of this hidden unity flows compassion.

Not to cause or tend to cause pain or destruction to any living being by thought, speech or conduct (*Ahimsa*) is symptomatic of this manner of thinking. The man who sees the one life rise and fall through all its multitude of manifestations necessarily adopts non-injury as his guiding principle; for he realizes that, all life being one, any injury done to any living creature means self-injury.

No living things should be slain anywhere;
Nor ordered forcibly this way or that,
Nor put in bonds, nor tortured in any way,

Or treated violently otherwise;
Because ye are that same which ye would slay,
Or order here and there against his will;
Or put in prison, or subject to pain,
Or treat with violence; ye are the same;
The Self-same Life doth circulate in all.

Acārāṅga Sutra

If the beginning cannot be seen where is the end? Within this scale of becoming there is no end. The end can only be reached by going beyond, in the sense that man must penetrate to that hidden realm of unity which knows no change; this is 'Brahma-faring' leading to the freedom of Nirvana. All questions regarding the nature of this goal are futile.

Nirvana is the repository of freedom. But if you ask what is the repository of Nirvana, this question goes too far and is beyond the compass of an answer.

Samyutta Nikaya III, 189

At this point ceaseless becoming reveals itself as eternal being, the ladder of perfection has served its purpose and is left behind. In the words of the Buddha

The stopping of becoming is Nirvana.

Samyutta Nikaya II, 117

NOTES FOR CHAPTER 4

1. *Māndūkya Upanishad.* See J. Mascaro, *Himalayas of the Soul*, pp. 65–6.
2. *Vinaya pitaka* I, 1.
3. Jainism is equally preoccupied with the idea of an ascending ladder of transformation. The Path, as taught there, is composed of two main categories, purification with all its diverse requirements, and absorption, the gateway to higher states of existence. The teaching speaks of fourteen rungs which stand for the gradual conquest of one state of awareness after another. All have to be transcended because only the completely free man can find peace.
4. *Life Divine*, p. 937f.
5. The techniques and disciplines designed to give guidance on this graded ascent are in themselves regarded as forming a hierarchy of 'ways' or 'vehicles'. Just as in our days Sri Aurobindo sees in the integral yoga the highest form of yoga, so the ancient traditions speak of Raja yoga as the kingly yoga, in the same way as many Buddhists regard the Diamond Vehicle (Vajrayana) as standing at the summit of all spiritual disciplines. The progressive stages on the ladder of perfection thus produce their

own progressive techniques. (See *The Middle Way*, vol. XXXIV, No. 3; Nov. 1950, p. 99.)

6. *Lankavatāra Sātra*, 96.

7. Also included is a heavenly hierarchy of celestial beings and their respective realms which correspond to the various grades into which the higher states of consciousness and absorption are divided. What is experienced in the depths within appears projected into the heights of a transcendent world without. See the parallel teaching in both Christian and Islamic mysticism.

8. i.e. creation *ex nihilo*.

5

The Linear View

... There is the *circular* movement, by which a thing
moves uniformly round one point as centre, another
is the *straight* movement by which a thing goes from
one point to another; the third is *oblique*, being
composed as it were of both the others.
Consequently, in intelligible operations, that which is
simply uniform is compared to *circular* movement;
the intelligible operation by which one proceeds from
one point to another is compared to the *straight*
movement; while the intelligible operation which
unites something of uniformity with progress to
various points is compared to the *oblique* movement ...

The discoursing of reason from sensible to intelligible
objects, if it be according to the order of natural
reason, belongs to the *straight* movement; but if it be
according to the divine enlightenment, it will belong
to the *oblique* movement.

THOMAS AQUINAS: *Summa Theologica*

It is tempting to speculate on the question why a culture feels drawn to
one aspect of the Way rather than to another and what the factors are
which determine such preference. We have here one of those problems
which allow of no simple solution, and it is doubtful whether the
intricate play of tendencies responsible can ever be uncovered and
traced sufficiently to supply a satisfactory explanation. It seems,
however, likely that here, too, compensatory trends are at work evoked
by exclusive attitudes persevering for too long. Once such a situation is
reached in any one tradition, it appears that an altogether different
tradition is likely to take the lead, and in doing so, to promulgate a novel
approach to the Way and to explore this, in all its possibilities, over the
centuries.

Seen from the point of view of religion as a whole, a fresh stimulus is
thus given, a new vista opens and, on an inter-cultural scale,
onesidedness is once more rectified. In the long history of religion, this
is what appears to have happened repeatedly, and it certainly happened,

in a revolutionary manner, when the Near East became the cradle of the great monotheistic faiths, Judaism, Christianity and Islam.

As regards their conception of the Way to God, a common bond unites all three. They see the dynamics inherent in the pilgrim's progress primarily as a continuous, linear motion, proceeding in one of two directions, forward towards an end or goal, or backwards towards a beginning, or point of departure. The first is labelled development and progress, the second, retrogression and degeneration. In this motion is included the development from the more primitive to the more complex as well as the reversion from a balanced differentiation of relationships to a merely instinctual equilibrium of forces. The ideas of development and regression thus appear in immediate opposition, and the question presents itself whether this is not the same opposition inherent in the twofold movement which India knows under the terms of evolution and involution.

Both these terms belong, of course, in equal measure, to the East and West, but this common usage must not be allowed to veil the fact that the meaning attached to them is different where eastern and western religion is concerned. We have seen, that in the Indian view the two-fold movement of evolution and involution is one which proceeds from state to state or, in other words, ladder-like, from one level of significance to another. It is essentially discontinuous in character and, what is more, seen as a whole it partakes of the circular movement of world cycles in which beginning and end are identical.

In the interpretation of the near eastern religions, on the other hand, the terms evolution and involution stand above all, for continuous movements taking place on one and the same plane of existence. To explore this plane, which is identified with the world as it is seen and experienced through the senses, and to seek to understand its laws, is the great challenge to humanity, as western man sees it. He measures, compares and establishes intricate systems of relationships in order to canalize life's multifarious and multidimensional motion into an uninterrupted and orderly flow which, whether approached as a totality or in parts, is always envisaged as linking two extreme points arbitrarily chosen, and acting as limiting agents for the abundance of data to be investigated. The great tools in this search for knowledge are analysis and synthesis used freely in all fields of thought. Here again, there may be detected a twofold movement, one tending towards an increase in particularization, the other towards an increase in unity. Dissection is balanced by integration, the method of deduction by that of induction and man's search for the individual law ruling the part is as intense as his search for the general law ruling the larger whole.

The governing agent behind such an outlook is the acceptance, as an absolute and exclusive truth, of the linear sequence of events fixed in time and space. Its only knowledge is that of passing time in which the present is non-existent and man is only aware of an ever-receding past and an unreachable future, as well as of an exclusive space in which everything and every happening takes place either inside or outside, either here or not here. This is the world in which all events are irretrievable and their sequence in time irreversible; in which change is synonymous with either progression or regression, and in which the before gives meaning to the after.

Such a view can only be held on the basis of a continuous linear time pattern, it does not conform with either the gradual or the cyclic view of life. In the former the higher grade can never be explained in terms of the lower preceding it, for what is involved is transformation which always presupposes discontinuity, that is, a break with what has gone before. Likewise, both aspects, that of scale and cycle, do not exclude the recurrence of events; in the one it takes the form of the repetition of a rhythmic pattern, in the other that of repetition of experiences on different grades of existence.

Both views are impossible in a world ruled by passing time and three-dimensional space. Here temporal and spatial co-ordinates determine every event unalterably to one particular point in space-time and it is this fixation and its attending relationships with other equally fixed events which bestows on it its unique significance. The clear determination of this point of intersection together with the sequence of happenings surrounding it, becomes the main concern of man. His investigations are concentrated upon both duration and position of every occurrence, for in his view it is this alone which makes things real; without it the world loses its concreteness, it becomes illusory and ephemeral. In other words, only those events are accorded reality whose place in history is established beyond doubt. The linear and the historical view reveal themselves not only to belong together, but to be identical.

In the field of religion, such a view of life necessarily leaves its unmistakable imprint. The question of the historicity of a faith, as a whole or in parts, becomes crucially important, for unless it can be proved to be based on historical data its 'story' is regarded as myth or legend and is rejected as unreal. For what ultimately separates myth and, in a lesser degree, legend from history, is the fact that neither are wholly dependent upon, and thus not limited to, the time and location of their occurrence. The same or a similar myth can and does appear in various guises in different places and at different times. This in no way affects its essential features, nor does it reduce its potency. Not so an event which, in some way, is linked to history. It can neither be shifted in time nor space, nor can it repeat itself without loss of significance. It demands to be accepted as essentially unrepeatable, as having happened once for all times.

'In Israel all religion is history';[1] although these words are eminently true of the Jewish faith as a whole, it is equally true to say that in the Old Testament there are preserved the records not only of the 'old order' but also of the gradual shift away from it towards a religious orientation that was openly historical in character. A telling example is afforded by the change of interpretation which the central figure of the Jewish faith, the Messiah, has undergone. In pre-exilic times the figure of the Messiah appears in a form which bears the clear imprint of the cyclic aspect of the Way. The emphasis is on cyclic repetition of an eternal pattern of events.

> The Israelite king must be understood as a Saviour actually present in the people assembled in the Sanctuary to repeat and 're-live' the great fundamental events of God's victory over Evil. The king is a present Messiah, no eschatological figure ... He is the fighter in the ritual combat of the Creation Drama, the Bearer of Salvation, present in full actuality in the 're-living' of the saving facts in the New Year Festival.[2]

Here past and future are annihilated in the eternal Now of which the individual partakes in and through the ritual. The determining factor is the 'eternal return' and therewith the eternal presence of the saviour, made manifest and relived ever anew, *ad infinitum*.

This pattern of ideas underwent a radical change during the days of the exile. 'The realities of history did not confirm the faith, nourished by the experiences of the enthronement festival, that Israel's happiness was secured through the presence of the anointed of Yahweh.'[3] What is witnessed here, is the entering into the Jewish religion of 'the realities of history' demanding recognition and prescribing their own laws. What are these laws?

History is concerned first and foremost with the transient aspects of life. It searches for the track of events left in the temporal order of things and the eternal aspects are only accepted in so far as they impinge upon that order. Such a view is the outcome of a situation in which man's urgent concern is the life here and now, its stark reality, its impermanency and its burden of evil and suffering. This is what, after the exile, the people of Israel experienced in unequalled measure; and out of this experience grew a new religious attitude.

No longer is the Messiah seen as a kingly figure, but he has become the suffering servant of Yahweh and as such partakes of the world's travails. He is the Messiah of the second Isaiah who 'is despised and rejected of men; a man of sorrows, and acquainted with grief'. (53, 3.)

In describing this change, the term 'demythologizing' has been used. This is, indeed, what happened, if we interpret the term in its broadest sense, namely as the turning to, and acceptance of, the historical view of life, and the giving up and denial of, the metaphysical view as expressed in myth. This is, too, what happened to the religion of Israel, for we find that the idea of the suffering servant is transferred from the Messiah to his people, the people of Israel. They become the servants of their Lord, and take upon them the darkness and wretchedness of their historical existence on earth. By this act of acceptance, they become the chosen ones of God, but it was this same acceptance, too, which made Israel shift its hope of salvation away from the painful presence to redemption in the future. 'Israel passes from experience to hope'[4] and with this the figure of the Messiah passes from one present amongst his people to the coming Saviour. It is the vision of the Messianic kingdom as described in Daniel which from now sustains Israel.

> I saw in the night visions, and, behold, one like the Son of Man came with the clouds of heaven, and came to the Ancient of days, and they brought him near before him. And there was given him dominion, and glory, and a kingdom, that all people, nations, and languages should serve him: his dominion is an everlasting dominion, which shall not pass away, and his kingdom that which shall not be destroyed.
>
> Dan. 7; 13/14[5]

The significance of this change, in this context, lies in the fact that, with the adoption of the Messiah as an eschatological figure a projection into the future has taken place of an experience which previously had been sought in the eternal now, that is, beyond the dividing of time. Whether this future is envisaged as referring to an earthly or other-worldly existence is only of secondary importance here; for, as subsequent developments have shown, both alternatives represent but different stages in this transformatory process; they constitute the inevitable result of an ever increasing emphasis on the historical point of view, with its exclusive concern with the continuous and linear nature of evolution.

In this way, religion and history tend to become identified, a fact which is amply proved by the holy book of Judaism. The Old Testament is first and foremost, the historical record of a people, telling of their intercourse with the lord of history, Jehova, their God. The medium in which He reveals Himself is historical existence, that is to say, the revelation is granted to an individual person at a particular time and place. Such a revelation is in its very nature exclusive in character in spite of the fact that it may claim universal acceptance and application. Here belong the great revelations recorded in the Old Testament, first through Noah and Abraham leading up to the central event in Judaism, when the God of Sinai showed himself to Moses, His servant, and to the people of Israel as a whole.

It was at this point in Jewish history that the Torah, the divine law, was transmitted bestowing on the Jewish faith its unique character and investing it with meaning and authority. With this is touched the heartbeat of Judaism for it is the law, whether written or oral, which was to guide Israel on its tortuous path through the centuries. The Torah is the word of God in historical manifestation, given once for all and revealing the divine will. This the people are charged to follow in faith, and to implement it in their lives, for obedience to, and conformity with, the Torah is identical with the living of the holy life as it is taught in the Old Testament. It is an approximation to the divine norm enacted in history, the complete consummation of which, however, is only realizable in the fullness of time heralded by the coming of the Messiah.

What is envisaged here are two orders of existence, the divine and the human, which in the holy life are made to harmonize and, like two parallel lines, have their point of coalescence in the infinite future. Such a parallelism is the outcome of a one-sided emphasis on the reality of historical existence for, the moment the aspect of continuous linear development is given prominence over other processes of growth, the need for the supposition of a 'supra'-historical plane asserts itself, and the dualism of this world as against that world created. The Jewish answer to this challenge is the ideal of a perfect synchronization and harmony between the two planes as it is expressed and made manifest in the holy covenant between God and His people.[6]

The question which arises is whether unity can in any measure be realized by treading this path. Institutional Judaism would reply that the holy life in its complete adaptation to, and conformity with, the divine law, is as far as we can go in the pre-Messianic world.[7] An intimate personal communion between the two worlds is admitted but any idea of oneness or identification is rejected. Thus fundamentally, dualism remains, at least as far as the orthodox view is concerned. What is taught is a unity based upon the ideal of two existential orders, the divine and the human, working in perfect unison, an ideal eminently characteristic of Judaism and giving it much of its beauty and fervour.

With history entering the domain of religion a great challenge is thrown up for man. It is the challenge inherent in that particular type of dualism which the historical approach inevitably creates, and which consists of the dichotomy of history on the one hand, and 'supra-history', celestial history or metaphysics, on the other. The latter, whatever the term used, always refers to that which is 'beyond' and refuses to fit into the framework of passing time and three-dimensional space but which, at the same time, represents man's hope of redemption from the tragic reality of historical existence. We have seen the way in which Judaism meets this challenge and it is against this background that the answer of Christianity must be understood. The challenge is essentially the same yet the response is different.

Christianity, too, sees the Way predominantly as a linear process determined by the temporal and spatial co-ordinates of historical existence. Like Judaism, it accepts the inescapable reality of the vicissitudes of that existence, an acceptance which lies at the very core of its teaching. As has been shown, it was this standing face to face with the tragedy of human life which sent the Jewish people on their fateful path 'from experience to hope', and therewith from the ability to partake directly in the presence in the sanctuary of their king and saviour, to the belief in the future Messiah. In this view, the Messiah does not enter into historical existence, as it presents itself day by day, but the historical fate of the individual, as well as that of the people as a whole, is regarded as preparing the way for, and as finding its fulfilment in, the coming Messianic reign. With Christianity, this process is carried a stage further, indeed it may be said that the turn of the spiral development closes and a new level is reached. Here the Messiah enters history and, what is more, he identifies himself with it. A synthesis thus takes place which opens the possibility for unification of previously diverging aspects of the Messianic idea.

To the Christian, the coming of Christ is the central event of all existence, it is the pivotal point whence true history is created and around which history henceforth revolves. Furthermore, the Christian story, as related in the gospels, is presented as history, and it is this fact which is of crucial significance, a fact which must not be confused with the question of the actual historicity of the events. Whether what is related has, in fact, taken place or not, the chosen medium is history and not myth, legend, allegory or parable, although elements of all these are present. With this total identification of the divine revelation with history, the gospel events become part of the unrelenting process of passing time which flows from the present to the future in never ending motion. Each event becomes a point of intersection, representing one specific moment in a specific place, and as such, it is irreversible, unrepeatable and final. This uniqueness and finality is emphasized clearly in the New Testament and what is more, it is put in opposition to the old order in which the divine pattern is re-actualized through repetition.

For Christ is not entered into the holy places made with hands which are the figures of the true; but into heaven itself, now to appear in the presence of God for us:
Nor yet that he should offer himself often, as the high priest entereth into the holy place every year with blood for others;
For then must he often have suffered since the foundation of the world; but now once in the end of the world hath he appeared to put away sin by the sacrifice of himself. And as it is appointed unto men once to die, but after this the judgment:
So Christ was once offered to bear the sins of many; and unto them that look for him shall he appear the second time without sin unto salvation.

Hebrews, 9, 24–28[8]

If the Christian drama is re-enacted again and again in the liturgy of the Church, this is done 'in remembrance' of the events which took place 'once for all' at a certain time and place in the historical past. It is not done, as is the case in renewal rites of the old order, so as to shake off the burden of history and find an escape in the timelessness of divine oneness, but it is a constant reminder of the fact that at a certain point in passing time a fusion between terrestrial and celestial history occurred, thereby transforming historical existence as a whole. Because this is so, all events attending the entrance of the Messiah into history acquire universal significance. They belong to both realms, the eternal and the mundane. Their re-enactment, therefore, in the liturgy has a triple function. Besides being a reminder of a unique pattern of events firmly anchored in history, it is the channel for an eternal presence and eternal actuality. Human life, otherwise chained to time's relentless flow, is here, according to Christian teaching, transformed and redeemed through the blending of the two realms.

Does this mean the gift of renewal open to man again and again whenever he is in need of it? For the redemptive 'once for all' act to become repeatable another fusion must take place. Both the divine pattern and the irreversible process of history must become one with the cyclic rhythm of nature. In the liturgy this triple synthesis is realized, for it is not only a record and reactualization of the divine revelation in history, but the framework in which the drama unfolds is that of nature's progress through the year, leading from birth, growth, and bearing fruit to decay, death and rebirth. It is here that the cyclic aspect of the Way manifests itself and it is through this fusion alone that periodical renewal becomes possible.

Thus every event in the Christian story has three aspects; the historical which makes it unique, the divine which gives it universal significance, and the natural which represents the aspect of cyclic repetition. Seen from this angle, the birth of the saviour, the central event in Christianity,[9] combines in itself the birth of Jesus the man, the birth of the Christ and with it the contact of the divine with the mundane level, and the rebirth of life and light, the winter solstice. This experience of regeneration, together with that of an immediate presence gradually transforming human life, has found its expression in the collect for Christmas Day:

Almighty God, who has given us thy only-begotten Son to take our nature upon him, and as at this time to be born of a pure Virgin; Grant that we being regenerate, and made thy children by adoption and grace, may daily be renewed by thy Holy Spirit; through the same our Lord Jesus Christ who liveth and reigneth with thee and the same Spirit, ever one God, world without end.

This collect of the nativity is said continually from Christmas Day until New Year's Eve.

The daily renewal here prayed for can become reality at one point only, the point of the present moment, the eternal now, for it is here and here alone that the synthesis of the three orders of existence, the natural, the human and the divine, can take place. Passing time and its power over man becomes annihilated at this point, and historical existence redeemed; what Eliade has called 'the terror of history' fades away and is seen for what it is, the figment of a mind which seeks escape from the present in a dead past or an imaginary future.

If it is thus true to say that the way of Christianity frees man of the 'terror of history', it is equally true, as the record of the Christian religion exemplifies, that time and again in the course of its growth, this terror could not be stayed. Whenever this happens it is a sign that man has thrown in his lot with a view which sees life predominantly under the aspect of linear development. The immediate result is, as has been indicated, that the unity of the three realms experienced in the 'now-moment' is broken. History appears as an antithesis to the natural and, above all, to the divine order. Man, instead of co-operating spontaneously with nature, fights against her and, instead of striving to transform every moment of earthly life through contact with the divine, sets out to bridge imaginary gulfs which divide him from the world of God. The only tangible reality known to him is history, as it is played out in every day life, which thus becomes fraught with tragedy for is it not itself but a bridge connecting the unknown with the unknowable?

> History is in truth the path to another world. It is in this sense that its content is religious. But the perfect state is impossible within history itself; it can only be realized outside its framework. This is the fundamental conclusion of the metaphysics of history and the secret of the historical process itself ... For to situate the Kingdom of God as a solution of human destiny within the historical process itself is tantamount to excluding its realization and even its preparation.[10]

Such reasoning, which seems to be conclusive, is yet based upon a fallacy. For if, as Berdyaev points out, the problem of history is determined by the nature of time, if, in fact, the historical process and linear time cannot be separated but are identical, does this not mean that the world beyond history must necessarily also be beyond passing time? By regarding an event like the Messianic kingdom or the second coming of Christ as belonging to the future, it is by no means lifted out of the historical process and raised to a supra-historical level but, on the contrary, the historical interpretation of time is maintained and used to invest with all the characteristics of 'historicity', an event which by definition stands outside history.

One such characteristic is the emphasis upon the impossibility of realizing the Kingdom of God here and now and its transference to an unknown future. For in the historical approach the immediate yet eternal presence is non-existent, past and future take its place. The expectation in the distant hereafter of the second coming of Christ, seen from this point of view, reveals itself as an outward sign of an inner failure to live the transformed life, as exemplified by Christ. For, as Berdyaev has said himself, and as many seekers know from immediate experience:

> The coming of Christ put an end to the cleavage between the metaphysical and the historical which became united and identified in Him.[11]

The religion of Islam was revealed, in its totality, to one man, the Prophet Muhammad. In this way, the divine erupted into history, opening a channel for Allah's message to flow through, and celestial and historical existence became insolubly linked through the divine proclamation, the Word made manifest.

Both Judaism and Islam are based on revelations of this type and it is significant that both faiths passionately reject the idea of the incarnation, the Word made flesh, that is, of a point in history where a fusion or union of the human and the divine took place. In Islam, just as in Judaism, the reason for this rejection is clearly and repeatedly stated. It is maintained that the acceptance of such a fusion necessarily impairs the belief in the transcendent and undivided unity of God (*tauhīd*), for, within the divine Monad, it postulates a division (*shirk*), of whatever nature this may be or whatever the interpretation it receives, and this, according to Muslim teaching, is one of the most grievous iniquities.[12]

Here the paradoxical situation arises that a teaching which upholds the absolute unity of the one and wholly transcendent God is forced to perpetuate the separation of the two worlds and to reject the possibility of union. By the same token, a religion like Christianity, which embraces such a union, is driven to give up the idea of the absolute transcendent oneness of God and to admit, instead, a unity in diversity.

The Koranic revelation, unlike both the Judaic and the Christian, partakes of the full light of remembered history. This fact is of the utmost importance for here, in the eyes of Muslims, lies one of the main reasons for the superiority of the Islamic over previous revelations. Its historicity[13] cannot be doubted, and it follows that it is more complete, purer and therefore more to be trusted. For is it not a fact that the line of history can be traced back, step by step, to that unique event when Muhammad became the mouthpiece of Allah? According to Muslim teaching, the Koran verifies, corrects and completes the previous revelations as they have been preserved in the Torah and the Gospels, both of which have suffered mutilation and distortion in the course of time.

Here too, it is passing time in its linear motion which bestows on the divine revelation its mark of certainty and trustworthiness. Wherever such an attitude prevails, the vital question arises of how to invest the historical event with a timeless validity without which the religion could not endure. The answer Islam gives shows a close relationship to that of Judaism. Just as the Torah is regarded as pre-existent from all eternity, so is the Koran. The Book, the Word of Allah, has its heavenly blueprint, as it were, and because the tablet of the divine proclamation is preserved in heaven, it is eternal and ultimate in its supreme authority.

Beneficent God!
By the Book that makes manifest!
Surely we have made it an Arabic Qur'ān that you may understand.
And it is in the Original of the Book with
Us, truly elevated, full of wisdom.

Sura, 43, 1–4

At one particular period in recorded history the pages of the Original were opened for all mankind to read, and it is this event which brought about the birth of a new religion. In the words of a believer:

The veil (was) lifted from the Preserved Tablet
And the content began to be transferred to the Tablet of his mind (the
    Prophet's)
To be proclaimed to the world, and read and studied for all time.
A fountain of mercy and wisdom, a warning to the heedless, a guide to
    the erring, an assurance to those in doubt, a solace to the suffering, a
    hope to those in despair—
To complete the chain of Revelation through the mouths of divinely
    inspired Apostles.[14]

The Koran, then, is Man's true friend, leading him into Allah's Way which is the right and the straight path. It is significant that the Koranic verses which contain exhortations to follow the way of God, more often than not, end with a reference to punishment and reward awaiting man in the hereafter. It is there that justice will be given and it is there, beyond history, that hell and paradise are located, whether these are regarded as abodes which the soul enters after death or as after-life states of consciousness.

The historical view of the Way thus, once again, produces out of itself a supra-historical world. All hopes are directed towards a life to come and the possibility of a new life in the here and now is replaced by the promise of eternal bliss—or punishment—in a future existence.

Benignant, Hearing God!
These are the verses of the Qur'ān and the Book that makes manifest:
A guidance and good news for the believers,
Who keep up prayer and pay the poor-rate, and they are sure of the
    Hereafter.
Those who believe not in the Hereafter, We make their deeds fair-
    seeming to them, but they blindly wander on.
These are they for whom is an evil chastisement, and in the Hereafter
    they are the greatest losers.

Sura, 27, 1–5

The hereafter, according to Muslim belief, begins with the resurrection or the last day, the latter term clearly pointing to the end of passing time. This belief is one of the most fundamental in Islam, in fact it forms one of the five principles of faith.[15]

The Koran contains many colourful descriptions of the paradisical life awaiting the blessed. 'Verily, amid gardens and rivers shall the pious dwell. In the seat of truth, in the presence of the potent King.' (*Sura* 54, 54–55.) Then will 'man come forth unto God' and a new earth and a new heaven will appear (*Sura* 14, 48). God and His creation will become unified, the split between them will be healed and the divine law, preserved eternally in heaven, will fuse with its manifestation in history. When this happens the 'Messianic Age' of Islam will have dawned.

Until such times, man's concern must necessarily be twofold. It must be directed towards the immediacy of historical existence and, at the same time, it must be held by the hope of the hereafter. The first presents a field for investigations and reasoned expositions, the second a distant goal, appealing to the imagination and the inner life of the spirit. The linear view, wherever it is held, opens the doors to historical research and to intense preoccupation with the events of the past, as they line up to reach, and give meaning to, the present and the future. Men like Philo, St Augustine, are only possible within the sphere of the predominance of the linear view of life.

To the great historians of the Hebrew-Christian tradition can be added Arab names, first and foremost Ibn Khaldun of Tunis. Arnold Toynbee compares him with Thucydides and Machiavelli, and others see in him a forerunner of Bodin, Vico, Comte and Curnot. There can be no doubt that in him, standing at the apex of a line of Arab historians, the 'new' approach based upon the idea of continuous development, closely knitted together by a linear series of cause and effect, has borne rich fruit. His investigations into the nature, philosophy and theories of history are unique in their depths and vision, but they lead him, as indeed they must do, to the conclusion that there are two incompatible worlds, one dark and full of vice, the other light and blissful. The first is with us now, the second is promised us in a future existence. 'Men have not been created solely for this world, which is full of vanity and evil and whose end is death and annihilation. And God himself has said "Think you that We have created you in vain!" Rather, men have been created for their religion, which leads them to happiness in the after life, and this is the path of God who possesses heaven and earth.'[16]

From what has been said, it appears that in most orthodox teaching, whether Jewish, Christian or Islamic, the possibility of a union of the historical and the metaphysical world, in the present, is not contemplated, on the contrary, the 'not here and not now' of such an event is fervently upheld. A barrier is thus erected between the human and the divine realms, and it is exactly this barrier which the mystics of any of the three great monotheistic faiths have always been unable to accept, and this in spite of the fact that they have realized that by this refusal they take serious issue with the official teachings. Whatever their individual allegiance, their manner of overcoming the barrier is fundamentally the same. They do not abandon the historical approach, for this is much too deeply ingrained in their hearts and minds, but they infuse it with new meaning by merging it with vital elements of the other aspects of the Way, the cyclic and the gradual. It is by this means that the onesidedness of the orthodox view has again and again been rectified and balance has been restored.

Wherever such a restoration of balance takes place, however, it is found that certain tenets which stem from an overemphasis on the linear aspect can no longer be upheld. Here belong the belief in an absolute beginning of historical existence, the postulation of a supra-historical world divorced from the present and only to be attained in a future 'beyond', and, closely related to both, the insistence on a type of divine unity, so pure and transcendent that it excludes the divine creation, that is, the phenomenal world.

To trace in detail the manner in which these ideas were modified by the mystics of the great monotheistic faiths would exceed the scope of this study; but because what happens is so remarkably similar a broad outline will be attempted.

We find that wherever the vision of the Way in its wholeness has been granted there the idea of 'creation ex nihilo', of an absolute beginning of the created world out of nothing, is rejected and the idea of emanation takes its place. As has been indicated, this is the view taken in India and the Far East, where it is mostly coupled with the idea of a rhythmic out- and in-breathing of the divine potencies. To Jewish, Christian and Muslim mystics such an idea would be, in essence, entirely acceptable. Muslim devotees speak of the journey of the ocean towards the drop and of the journey of the drop towards the ocean, and in the language of Christian mysticism, 'this world is an out-birth out of the eternal ... and it must all return into the eternal essences'.[17] Such views, in which the cyclic nature of the cosmic drama finds expression, have been accorded the most elaborate treatment certainly in Islamic, but perhaps even more so in Jewish mysticism. What the Sufis call the gradual veiling of the divine light, the Kabbalah and later, Chasidism, knows as the progressive self-limitation of God.

This divine self-limitation is seen as a downward movement, as a voluntary going into exile of the *Shechinah*, the divine effulgence. The counter-movement is the in-gathering of the scattered sparks and their ascent towards reunion with God.

To prepare the way for this in-gathering and make possible the homecoming of the *Shechinah* or, in other words, to effect the reversal of direction so that the cycle of creation, which has its beginning and end in God, may find completion, this is man's charge and privilege. Every word, every action, every thought must be put in the service of this task, as it is said in a Kabbalistic text:

> In every deed or transaction a man performs by his own free will, be it matter of precept or of option, let the name of God be ready in his mouth ... let him say with his mouth and utter with his lips: 'This thing I do, for (the honour of) the union of the Shechinah with the Holy One—blessed be He.'
>
> *Kitzur Sh'lh.* fol. 8, col. 1[18]

Here historical existence has become an integral part of a cosmic process in which, as Martin Buber has pointed out, the event of reunion in man means the ever new binding together of the divine and worldly spheres, the ever new marriage of the 'Majesty' with the 'Kingdom' through man.

All true mystics know of this marriage and they know, too, that through it the coming of the heavenly kingdom loses its purely eschatological character. History is not seen merely as an indispensable preparation for the supra-historical event of the descent of the kingdom, but as an integral part of that kingdom whose advent does happen in a multitude of ways here and now, indeed, as we have seen, this is the only place where it can happen. In the words of a modern Christian writer:

> Since human life is lived out in time and space, man's encounter with God can only be a specific event here and now, ... our being questioned, judged and blessed by him, is what we mean when we speak of an act of God.[19]

Such an encounter means fusion and therewith unity of the world above and below. This unity, so dear to the mystics, is, however, not the transcendent and inviolable unity of which so many doctrines speak which excludes the multiplicity of the created world, but an all-embracing unity that includes all existence. The distinction between these two types of unity is one of which pilgrims of the Way have always been aware; what is perhaps its most cogent exposition comes from Sufi teaching. To the mystics of Islam it became clear at an early stage, that the doctrine of divine unity (*tauhīd*), the corner stone of Muslim belief meant, in fact, a cleavage between God and His creation. They saw in it 'the separation of the eternal from that which was originated in time,'[20] and this in spite of the fact that, according to Koranic teaching the unity of God implies the oneness of His person, His attributes and His works. In the eyes of the Sufis this doctrine was incomplete because it did not include, but expressedly excluded the unity of God and man.

The crucial question which sooner or later presents itself to all believers in the oneness of God is how the divine unity can be maintained and yet made to embrace the human world of time and space. The answer, whether it is that of Jewish, Christian or Islamic mysticism, is always based on the twin ideas that separation from God is the most painful experience which can happen to man and that there is only one way to overcome it; man must change and become new so that his divine essence is made to shine through and transform his earthly existence in such a way that he himself becomes not only the bridge-builder but the bridge itself.

The change aimed at is that gradual transformation symbolized by the Scale of Perfection which is an ascent and a return in one. The divine light which has gradually veiled itself, the spark which has sunk more and more into the darkness of matter, God entering the human world, is resurrected, the veils are lifted one by one, matter is gradually redeemed and man rises, through more and more exalted states of being, to become god-like himself. In the words of Ruysbroeck, the fourteenth century Flemish mystic:

Transcending ourselves, we return towards our origin that we may be absorbed in the abyss, source of every perfection.[21]

With this, separation is no more, the unity of God and His creation is restored in and through man and the Messianic kingdom is seen as belonging, not to an ever receding future, but to a new order of existence, potentially present in every man.

NOTES FOR CHAPTER 5

1. M. Buber, *Chassidische Botschaft*, p. 215.
2. A. Bentzen, *King and Messiah*, pp. 73–7.

3. A. Bentzen, *op. cit.*, p. 73.
4. A. Bentzen, *op. cit.*, p. 73.
5. Also: Dan. 7, 27; 2, 44; Is. 9, 6; 45, 17; 59, 20.
6. This applies to all strata of human activities for the Law is all-embracing and therefore supplies man with the blueprints of life, as it were. Applied to the sacred temple, for instance, such 'blueprints' were given to Moses on Mount Sinai (Ex. 25, 9 and 40) and again to David who hands this divine pattern to Solomon for the building of the sanctuary. (I. Chronicles 28, 19.)
7. See also Lev. 11, 44; 19, 2; 20, 7–8; Ex. 19, 6; and M. Eliade, *The Myth of the Eternal Return*, pp. 6–7.
8. See also Hebrews 10, 9–14, and Romans 6, 9–10.
9. G. Heard in *Is God in History?* (p. 196) has the following to say:
   No wonder then that the Church, to mark for ever this supreme historical fact (i.e. the appearance of the Redeemer) made the birth of Bethlehem a datum line, a focus point on which all past history has converged and away from which all history is to expand. Christianity does not take the Crucifixion or the Resurrection as the centre. For if history began anew, it began when the new life of Redemption of all life was begun ... This was a coming, an Advent. (See also C. G. Jung, *The Integration of the Personality*, p. 234.)
10. N. Berdyaev, *The Meaning of History*, p. 198–9.
11. N. Berdyaev, *op. cit.*, p. 59.
12. *Sura*, 31, 13.
13. 'Historical attestations' (asnād) has played an all-important part in Muslim tradition; it is applied not only to Koranic researches but also to the rules laid down for the acceptance of Hadīth or sayings. There rule No. 1. was that no reported saying must be accepted if it was opposed to recognized historical facts.
14. A. Y. Ali, *The Message of Islam*, pp. 20–1.
15. *Sura*, 2, 2–4.
16. C. Issawi, *An Arab Philosophy of History ... Ibn Khaldun*, p. 64ff.
17. Jacob Boehme, *The Threefold Life of Man*, VI, 40. In: W. Kingsland, *An Anthology ... p.* 50.
18. M. H. Harris, *Hebraic Literature*, p. 278.
19. A. Bultman. See H. W. Bartsch, *Kerygma and Myth*, p. 196.
20. Al-Junaid. See A. J. Arberry, *Sufism*, p. 57.
21. 'The Adornment of the Spiritual Marriage.' *Flowers of a Mystic Garden*, p. 31.

II
THE GOING FORTH

Purification

In the preceding chapters, the emphasis has been on the outer dynamics
of the Way; in what follows, we shall endeavour to lay open its inner
rules of action and to penetrate to those transformatory experiences
which result in a new birth within and which, simultaneously, remould
the external life as it is lived day by day.

To do so, however, it is essential to realize that the deeper meaning
of this inner pilgrimage will only reveal itself if the Way is seen, not in
isolation, but as movement within movement, nourished by what has
gone before and reaching out towards new and unknown fields of
experience.

There appears to be a threefold rhythm basic to life's inherent
motion which applies in equal measure to the various aspects of natural
growth, spiritual development and cosmic evolution. Its starting point is
oneness and non-differentiation, whence it leads through differentiation
and multiplicity to re-union and re-integration.

In the religions of the world there is preserved the story of this

threefold rhythm of growth. They speak of a paradisical state of
undivided oneness, oneness with the world and with the powers beyond,
a state which modern research has labelled 'primitive'; they speak
furthermore of a breaking away from this original oneness, of the
appearance of the divider, and of issuing forth into the world of
opposites coupled with a loss and a fall. They tell of yet another realm
where this loss is made good and unity regained, and it is made clear
that this third phase does not stand for a mere going back to the
beginning but for a venturing forth in search of a new life in which the
thousand things of the world are not denied but integrated, and the
opposites not rejected, but transcended in a new whole.

Higher religion is primarily concerned with the passage from the
second to the third phase, from the dualistic to the unitive state of being.
This is 're-ligio', the rebinding of that which has become divorced, the
restoration of wholeness, and this is the 'Pilgrim's Path', occupying a
central position in a greater dynamic and as such holding the key of
both the before and after. For its point of departure faces in two
directions, backwards towards a state of undifferentiated oneness and
forward towards re-integration and synthesis. By the same token, there
are two ways leading from it: one is the way of retrogression, back into
the embrace of the Great One, the *uroboros*, the round, and, what
Levy-Brühl has called *'participation mystique'*, the world of non-
differentiation. The other is the way of progression, leading to re-
integration, the synthesis of opposing forces, to manifold unity and
wholeness.

This picture of the two ways must, however, not lead us to suppose
that once the right orientation has been chosen, continued progression is
assured. The opposite is true. The lure of the *participation mystique*,
and therewith the danger of retrogression, looms at every point of the
Way, however far the pilgrim has advanced. It confronts him in a
thousand different guises, and detection becomes increasingly difficult.
More and more the state of undifferentiated oneness seems to resemble,
or even be identical with, the longed for goal of synthesis and union and
therefore appears desirable.

Keeping in mind that the intrinsic motion of this process of growth
appears to be that of the spiral, the reason for this becomes clear. The
beginning and end of any one turn of a spiral lie closest together and,
indeed, many of the characteristics of the *participation mystique*, and of
what mysticism calls union through a return to the source, are
seemingly the same. What matters vitally is the question how this return
is accomplished; by retrogression which means ultimate dissolution and
extinction or by a progressive and creative process which leads to a

transcendent and more abundant life. The criterion lies in the choice between negation and acceptance. Retrogression is the result of a shrinking away from, and a negation of, the world as it presents itself in all its diversity and contradictions; whereas the hallmark of integration and assimilation is acceptance, for only that which is fully accepted can be transformed. This is the choice which has to be faced again and again on the Path and it proves the only sure guide for man to know whether his journey will lead to new life or to death.

Such then is the point of departure for the great venture, a point of which C. G. Jung has said 'At this point begins the path travelled by the East since the beginnings of things' and, it may be added, by every religion coming out of the East, and that is every major religion known.

It is at this point, too, that man becomes aware, in some measure at least, of the seemingly senseless manner in which life tosses him about between opposing forces and of his own helplessness in the face of it. Often there is no more than a vague feeling that something is wrong and that life is in some way incomplete and is lacking in purpose and meaning. As part of a natural development in adult life, such feelings indicate that man has reached that threshold or gateway of which the spiral and labyrinth symbolism speaks and which, as has been shown at length, acts as a place of selection. Do we remain on the threshold and eventually turn back, or do we accept the challenge and enter the 'straight gate', thereby venturing forth into the unknown? In the first case, the natural growth of our being will be arrested and we surrender to 'the endless round of things', thus forfeiting the possibility of attaining to another dimension, that of depth. New explorations of the world around us, great inventions, or even the most elaborate structures of pure thought reaching to unique heights and subtlety, all these will not alone help us to pass through that gateway. On the contrary, taken in isolation, they tend to distort our view and thus hinder our progress. Beyond the gate stretches what appears at first sight to be virgin land; only gradually will it become apparent that identical problems, situations and experiences have been described by seekers of all times. We find ourselves at the beginning of a venture whose goal we cannot see, neither do we possess the knowledge of the road leading to it. However, as Chuang Tse has said: 'The foot treads the ground in walking; nevertheless it is ground not trodden on which makes up the good walk. A man's knowledge is limited; but it is on what he does not know that he depends to extend his knowledge to the apprehension of God.'[1]

What this translation renders God, others have called truth, the ultimate, the kingdom of heaven or unity. At this point names matter little, for the goal is unknown and may, indeed, reveal itself to be unknowable; what matters is the compelling urge to set out in search of something which transcends the individual's own small world, something which will quench his thirst for a deeper meaning and purpose of life.

The man who, by inclination, feels attracted to the way of devotion will see in that something, which is greater than himself, his lover and beloved. He will say in the words of a Sikh psalm:

> I wandered through the whole world calling out for my Beloved, yet my thirst departed not.[2]

This is the keynote found in all Bhakti texts whether of the east or the west. When Kabir sings

> My heart cries aloud for the house of my lover

his words seem to be echoed by St John of the Cross in the opening lines of his *Song of the Soul and the Bridegroom*

> Where hast thou hidden Thyself,
> And abandoned me in my groaning, O my Beloved?[3]

The follower of the path of knowledge calls the goal he is seeking truth or enlightenment and whatever the tradition to which he belongs, he will hear the call as the people of the Old Testament heard it:

> ... Incline thine ear unto wisdom, and apply thy voice for understanding,
> Yea, if thou criest after knowledge and liftest up thy voice for understanding;
> Then shalt thou understand the fear of the Lord, and find the knowledge of God.
>
> Proverbs 2, 2–5

The Buddha called it the limb of wisdom, the searching into things and promised that, so long as this was practised amongst his followers, his teaching would not decline.

The man of action sees the pilgrimage in a different light. To him the goal can only be one thing, the establishment of the kingdom of heaven on earth; and he goes forth to prepare the road for the coming of the golden era of peace and brotherly love, the promised land of bliss, the

Messianic age. He is convinced that only through action, here and now, can the Good Life be found and the fulfilment of the divine law be perfected. His prayer, in whatever language, is that of the Ahabah, the Jewish prayer:

O our Father ... put it into our hearts to understand, to discern, to mark, learn and teach, to heed, to do and to fulfil in love all the words of instructions in the Law ... O bring us in peace from the four corners of the earth, and make us go upright to our land; for thou art a God who worketh salvation.

It is not primarily the desire for union with the beloved nor thirst for truth which he offers but perfect service, for he feels, as Ruysbroeck did, that 'every good deed, however small, if it be directed to God by simplicity of intention, increases in us the divine likeness, and deepens in us the flow of eternal life.'4 This is also the way of Krishna in the Gita where it is taught that whatever the action, so long as it is done in a spirit of dedication to the Lord, it will lead to the highest abode.

The many and different epithets which man uses to describe the high goal of his journey have often been called so many aspects of that which is by definition always beyond man and beyond his powers of description. Whether love, truth or goodness are, in fact, attributes or aspects of the More we cannot say; one thing, however, seems clear, that such terms are likely to elucidate, not so much the nature of the unknowable, as the attitude of the individual who chooses and employs them. When man first sets out in search of an ideal he naturally follows the promptings of his own nature, and he orientates himself accordingly, towards love or truth in their highest manifestations, or towards the perfect act and the holy life. Thus he goes forth full of determination and enthusiasm, and whatever his ideal, its fascination will carry him with ease over the initial steps of the Way. The new world beyond the spiral gate lies open before him, his to explore, his to transform and to be enriched and transformed by it. There is a freshness, joy and inherent promise in that first venturing forth which grips deeply and cannot be easily forgotten.

Why then does this not last, why must there follow first a slowing down and a halt and then a turning back? The initial drive does not so much spend itself as it is checked by a counter movement, at first hardly discernible but gradually gathering momentum. Optimism and fervour is met by a dawning realization of one's own impotence. The traveller who is thus brought to a standstill is he who prays:

Lord, I know what virtue is, but I cannot practise it; I know what vice is, but I have no power to desist from it.

Prapanna Gita, 57[5]

Almost identical words were uttered by St Paul:

For the good I would I do not; but the evil which I would not, that I do.

By way of explanation, St Paul goes on to say:

For I delight in the law of God after the inward man:
But I see another law in my members, warring against the law of my mind, and bringing me into captivity to the law of sin which is in my members.
O wretched man that I am! who shall deliver me from the body of this death?

Romans, 7, 22–24

St Paul here puts his finger on the main cause of our impotence, the war which goes on between our conscious will and unconscious forces, between the within and the without or, in Goethe's words, between the two souls living in the breast of every one of us. Whatever the path man chooses, sooner or later he will be confronted with this dualism of the two laws, one under his control, the other eluding it, one appertaining to the outer, the other to the inner man. It is thus that the world within reveals itself and through its opposition demands attention. An impasse bars further progress and seems inaccessible of any solution. For the first time, the realization dawns that the two laws, which manifest themselves in an almost endless variety of ways, are of the very fabric of life itself and that an escape from their diametrically opposing demands is therefore impossible.

Time and again, the demands coming to us from our immediate environment, or from society in general, reveal themselves to be incompatible with our individual inclinations and inner convictions. We adopt certain standards of behaviour, whether they be social, ethical or religious, only to find that there exist inner forces beyond our control which constantly render fruitless our attempts to live up to, or even come anywhere near, an implementation of our ideals. The result is a feeling of frustration which deepens with deeper penetration into the labyrinth of the spiral way where the demands on our conduct grow and our standards become more exalted.

The need for remedial action becomes apparent; without it further progress cannot be made or, if man pushes on regardless of the danger signs confronting him, he will find that it was at that precise point that he has strayed from the path and lost his way. For it is here that another threshold has to be passed, the threshold leading to what the Sufis, and with them all other religious aspirants, each in their own terminology, have called the valley of purification. The 'Via Purgativa', as the Christians have named it, is not a prerogative of any one religion, age or country; it is universally recognized as constituting the first lap of the journey towards perfection, and there is not a holy scripture in existence which does not contain ample proof of this, finding further enhancement by the testimony of those who have embarked on this venture, the devotees and holy men, the mystics and saints of all times. To prove the universal validity of the call to purgation seems therefore superfluous; the question, however, which we shall attempt to answer is, what are the overall characteristics of the Via Purgativa?

It appears that it consists of a series of phases, the number of which varies in the different traditions and which roughly divide into two main groups. The first is concerned with the general application of certain basic ethical and moral demands. The devotee is admonished to refrain from evil deeds, not to harm but to help others and, by so doing, to purify his inner self. This may be summarized in Buddhist terms:

Cease to do evil, learn to do good; cleanse your own heart; this is the teaching of the Buddha,

or, in the Zoroastrian precept, to cleanse one's own self with good thoughts, words and deeds. This call to strive for the good and shun evil, standing as it does, at the very beginning of the quest, addresses itself to man's conscience and does not cease to do so until the very end. It accompanies the seeker on his journey into the unknown, ever reminding him that it is here, in the good and pure life, where both the beginning and consummation of his endeavours are to be found.

The second group deals with more detailed and more specific demands. If the language used in the first is very much alike in the different religions, that of the second is remarkably varied. The terms used have to be considered carefully in their context and then only can the attempt be made to discover their meaning.

In the Bible the term most frequently used for the man in need of purification is 'hypocrite'. According to the Old Testament, the hypocrites in heart heap up wrath, their life is among the unclean and they shall not come before God.[6] This line of thought is taken over into the New Testament where it gives rise to such well-known passages as are found in Luke (11) and Matthew (23). Here the Scribes and Pharisees are denounced as hypocrites because they show a false mask to the outside world, thereby hiding the depravity of their true selves within. In so doing they go against God's will for, as the Psalmist says, 'Behold thou desirest truth in the inward parts' (51). The hypocrite, then, is he in whom the outer and the inner world are in opposition and whose answer to this cleavage is the false compromise of what C. G. Jung has called the *persona*. He defines it as 'a complicated system of relationships between individual consciousness and society', 'a secondary reality, a product of compromise', and calls it a kind of mask 'designed on the one hand to make a definite impression upon others, and on the other to conceal the true nature of the individual'.[7]

It is exactly this dichotomy which is stated in such strong and unmistakable terms in Matthew 23, 25–28.

Woe unto you, Scribes and Pharisees, hypocrites! for you make clean the outside of the cup and of the platter, but within they are full of extortion and excess. Thou blind Pharisee, cleanse first that which is within the cup and platter, that the outside of them may be clean also ... Even so ye also appear righteous unto men, but within ye are full of hypocrisy and iniquity.

Purification which only affects the outer man inevitably leads to a cleavage, a fatal separation of the inner and outer world, and there is no escape from it, unless the process of purification is allowed to enter the 'inward parts', until the 'secret faults' (Psalm 19, 12) are brought to light or, in other words, until man is prepared to drop the pretence of the mask, the false face shown to the world.

The need for adaptation to the demands of society and environment cannot be doubted; it is ever present and the answer to this need is the *persona* which, however, must not be taken so much as an expression of man's individuality but rather as a product of the demands of the collectivity. It is by its means that we hope to overcome the opposition between ourselves and the world and to reach out towards integration. It appears that at a certain point in this process the danger of identification threatens. We forget that the face shown to the world, which originated from the need for adaptation, is a temporary expedient, a compromise at best; we identify ourselves with that ideal image, created in response to the dictates of our environment. From that moment further growth towards unity and wholeness is thwarted. The mask acts like a wall plunging the 'inward parts' into darkness by preventing the light of day to enter. Everything not conforming with the chosen personality is excluded and hidden behind the *persona* and thus banned to the shadow realm of the unseen.

When this happens, man has two faces, one shown to the world, the other, invisible to the eye, yet potent in its influence; he has become double which in the terminology of the Bible is opposed to singleness, standing for wholeness. It is significant that in the same chapter in which the Scribes and Pharisees are denounced for their doubleness the paramount need for singleness is also stressed. The symbolism used is that of light and darkness denoting the split within man. He who is double is the man in whom the light is prevented from illumining the whole being.

> Take heed therefore that the light which is in thee be not darkness,
> If thy whole body therefore be full of light, having no part dark, the
> whole shall be full of light, as when the bright shining of a candle
> doth give thee light.
>
> Luke 11, 35–36

How very closely this teaching is paralleled in Buddhism is at once made clear by the following verses from the *Dhammapada*:

> A man does not become a Brahman by his matted locks or his lineage
> or his birth; in whom there is truth and righteousness, he is blessed,
> he is a Brahman.
> What is the use of thy matted locks, O fool! Of what avail thy
> raiment of antelope skin? Within thee there is ravening but the
> outside thou makest clean.
>
> 393/394

Again, the remedy for the split between the within and the without is purification, the only gateway leading to wholeness and unity.

Of the man who has crossed that threshold, the Buddhist scriptures say:

> He joins the divided, he rejoices in agreements, his words unite.
>
> *Digha Nikaya* I, 1, 8

Not only the teaching itself but also the symbolic image accompanying it is closely related to that of the Bible, although it is not primarily that of light being obscured by darkness, but of a perfectly unspotted white garment that alone can be dyed the desired colour and can become purely and wholly that new colour. In order to achieve this unspottedness throughout, Buddhism speaks of the necessity of an 'inner washing' or of the need to be cleansed in every limb.[8]

This is synonymous with striving for singleness of heart and just as the Old Testament insists that a hypocrite shall not come before God, so the Buddhist scriptures teach that only the true man can pass 'unto the further shore', in the same way as Krishna reminds Arjuna, in the *Bhagavadgita*, that those with corrupted selves, who are full of hypocrisy and engage in action with impure intention, can never attain union with the Lord.[9] Their destiny is sealed, for they remain divided.

In the *Chandogya Upanishad* a most forceful illustration of the perils and the glory of the two ways is given. The test described is that of the heated hatchet and it is said of him who is a liar 'Being given to untruth, covering himself by untruth he takes hold of the heated axe and is burnt. Then he is killed'. The man however whose conscience is clear 'Being given to truth, covering himself by truth, he takes hold of the heated axe he is not burnt. Then he is released'. The first will go the way of the *Asuras*, the way of untruth, the second that of the *Devas*, of light and truth, the way which leads to 'fitness for vision of the *Atman*' and eventually to union with the *Atman*.

This teaching of the intimate relationship between purity and union on the one hand and impurity and division on the other, runs like an ever-recurring theme through all religious texts. They show unanimously that union and, ultimately, identification is only possible where on both sides there is absolute purity. 'As pure water raining on pure water becomes one and the same, so becomes ... the sage who knows'[10] or, in the words of the Koran, the purifiers are loved by Allah and it is they and they alone who are fit to enter the Garden of Bliss where separation is no more and the faithful live for evermore in the presence of God.[11]

NOTES FOR CHAPTER 6

1. H. A. Giles, *Chuang Tzu*, p. 333.
2. Guru Amar Dās. D. Field, *The Religion of the Sikhs*, p. 93.
3. *Spiritual Canticle*: The Mystical Doctrine ..., p. 141.
4. 'The Adornment of the Spiritual Marriage', *Flowers of a Mystic Garden*, p. 9.
5. *Universal Prayers*, p. 169, No. 213.
6. Job 13, 16 and 36, 13–14.
7. *Two Essays* ... pp. 151 and 190.
8. *Majjhima Nikaya* VII, 37–8.
9. 16, 10. Compare Ephesians 6, 5.
10. *Katha Upanishad* II, 1, 15.
11. *Sayings of Muhammad*, No. 219, 370, 401.

7

The Wilderness

To what land shall I flee? Where bend my steps?
I am thrust out from family and tribe;
I have no favour from the village to which I would
   belong,
Not from the wicked rulers of the country:
How then, O Lord, shall I obtain thy favour?
ZOROASTER Hymn

As I walked through the wilderness of this world, I
lighted on a certain place where was a den, and I laid
me down in that place to sleep: and, as I slept, I
dreamed a dream. I dreamed, and behold, I saw a
man clothed with rags, standing in a certain place,
with his face from his own house, a book in his hand,
and a great burden on his back. I looked, and saw
him open the book, and read therein; and, as he
read, he wept, and trembled; and, not being able
longer to contain, he brake out with a lamentable cry,
saying, *What shall I do?*
JOHN BUNYAN The Pilgrim's Progress

How can the necessary purification be achieved? Is a resolution of the
conscious will sufficient to bring about the inner catharsis without which
integration and wholeness become impossible? In most cases the
answer is that it is not, even if the need for purification is realized and
fully accepted. The reason for this appears to lie in the very nature of
the *'persona'* itself which, as has been shown, is the product of a typical
attitude that is primarily turned outwards towards society and its
demands. In other words, the flow of psychic energy proceeds one-
sidedly in an outward direction seeking ever new relationships and thus
spinning a fine web of external ties, making the individual more and
more subservient to the dictates of his immediate environment and of
society as a whole. With this the need for the *persona* grows and any call
to stop doing 'eye service as man-pleasers' cannot be followed until this
over-activity directed outwards is rectified.

What all religions ask of the seeker at this point is, therefore, a partial
reversal of orientation, a turning inwards and, at the same time, for one

cannot be done without the other, a loosening of the fetters which tie him to his surroundings. It is not a denial of the world that is asked, but a partial and temporary withdrawal from it, not a complete stopping of the outflowing energy which, indeed would be impossible, but a restoration of balance. In the language of the sacred scriptures the seeker is told, on the one hand, to pray and meditate, to look within, to practise silence and, on the other, to learn non-attachment, to withstand worldly temptations, and to forgo transient pleasures. Both these demands belong together, for they are but the different expressions of the same phenomenon: the need for a new orientation.

Seen in the context of man's life as a whole, this change of outlook is an entirely natural event belonging to later life and coming at a point when the necessary outgoing activities of youth and early manhood should have come to fruition, and secured for the individual his rightful position as a member of whatever tradition and society he happens to belong to. Life seems to demand that the phase of establishing relationships with, and finding one's place in, outer life and the world at large should be followed by another whose goal is the assimilation, the drawing in and making one's own, of the experiences and values encountered during the first phase. Only thus can life's motion be completed and integration be achieved. Without it, life remains incomplete. If it is true that life's motion is spiral in character, then it follows that this reversal of direction is a necessary occurrence, inherent in the first impetus as well as all subsequent stages.[1] It is not a freak event vouchsafed only to the chosen few, but an integral part of human development and thus, in theory at least, the birthright of every man.

This process of disengagement from the thousand things of the world has been compared to the movement of a tortoise.

He who draws away the senses from the objects of sense on every side as a tortoise draws in his limbs (into the shell), his intelligence is firmly set (in wisdom).

Bhagavadgita II, 58[2]

What is referred to here is, in the language of Indian Yoga, 'tapas', the technique of conserving energy and directing it one-pointedly to the desired goal. In China it is known as the backward flow of psychic energy and it is maintained that without it the self lacks nourishment from the inner source, its energies are wasted by a gradual seeping away, a trend which, if not halted, eventually leads to spiritual death. Only by the establishment of a circular course of energy can this be avoided; then the out-going movement is supplemented by an indrawing movement and instead of gradual exhaustion there is regeneration and renewal. This is what in Taoism is called the 'circulation of the light' or 'breath' and it is said: 'When the Light is allowed to move in a circle, all powers of Heaven and Earth, of light and dark, are crystallized.'[3]

The idea of a withdrawing and backward flowing motion is equally known in other traditions. Always it is recognized that unless attention is directed inwards, and thus a contrary movement effected, progress on the Way is barred. C. G. Jung has seen this clearly, and he has insisted that the inner development which he calls integration or individuation, demands at its outset a complete *volte face*, a facing in a new direction. To the familiar world of conscious activities has to be added the invisible world within; the light of day has to be left for the darkness of a shadow world, where the outgoing senses cannot help, unfamiliar, as they are, with the task of attuning themselves to the world within. What is called *metanoia* in the Bible, repentance, the reversal of man's whole attitude, is therefore followed by the 'dark night of the senses' or 'the state of ghostly sorrow' as Christian mystics have described it. What happens, is stated by one who should know, St John of the Cross.

During the aridities of the night of sense—when [... the soul is drawn out of the way of sense into that of the spirit ...] spiritual persons have to endure great afflictions, not so much because of aridity, but because they are afraid that they will be lost on this road; thinking that they are spiritually ruined, and that God has forsaken them.

To this the following plea is added:

O spiritual soul, when thou seest thy desire obscured, thy will arid and constrained, and thy faculties incapable of any interior act, be not grieved by this, but look upon it rather as a great good, for God is delivering thee from thyself.[4]

Entering this night world of the senses means bewilderment; with the senses dulled and blindfolded, as it were, one feels lost and afraid. Dante went through such an experience and portrays it in inimitable words in the opening of the *Divina Commedia*:

> In the midway of this our mortal life,
> I found me in a gloomy wood, astray
> Gone from the path direct: and e'en to tell,

It were no easy task, how savage wild
That forest, how robust and tough its growth,
Which to remember only, my dismay
Renews, in bitterness not far from death.

When Dante speaks of the savage witness of that forest,[5] of the sleepy dullness which came over him, of the fear which had gripped him during the long night and, finally, of the sunrise which rekindled the promise of light in his heart, he is using images which are as unique in their compelling beauty as they are universal in their application. For the passage through the wilderness is an indispensable phase of the Way, wherever it is trod; in the language of the Old Testament, it is part of God's plan for His people. By sending them through the wilderness with its terrible drought, its fiery serpents and scorpions, he taught them that by external food, by bread alone, they cannot live, but that it is the still small voice in the human heart which has to be discovered and which alone can give true life.

The various texts, concerned with the passage through the wilderness, make it clear that its effect is mainly twofold. First, as Dante has expressed it, a feeling of sleepy dullness and inertia prevails. Monks, and recluses in general, seem liable to be afflicted by this and so, apparently, are many others. In fact, we have here a well-known phenomenon of which the Christian Church for one, has always been aware. In the middle ages it went under the name of *accidie* (*acidia*) and its inherent dangers were extolled at length, indeed, it was ranged as one of the seven deadly sins. The reason for this is obvious; for if a man is thus afflicted and does not realize what is happening to him, he easily succumbs and refuses to move any further, waiting inertly for a miracle to happen, unwilling to face, and actively tackle, the difficulties which halt his progress.

According to Hindu teaching, he gives way to *tamas*, denoting darkness, ignorance, insensibility, and inertia, and constituting one of the three basic qualities (*gunas*) which form the very substance of all that exists. Unless this is counterbalanced by the second basic quality, *rajas*, standing for will-power, drive and dynamic action, there is no hope.

In Christian terms the one sure remedy for *acidia*, so the parson in the *Canterbury Tales* informs us eloquently, is fortitude. The sleepy dullness must be followed by its exact opposite, the determined search for a way out, whatever the cost, and the willing acceptance of the hardships involved. As Chaucer has said, 'This fortitude can endure, by long suffering, the toils that are fitting'. Both reactions belong together and form part of that state of mind variously known as 'the state of self-accusing' (Koran),[6] when everything we do turns against us, 'the state of the great doubt' (Zen) that sears and burns like a ball of red-hot fire, 'the valley of detachment' (Sufism), or 'the cloud of unknowing' (Christian mysticism), when we cannot see clearly, because all our acquired knowledge and learning is of no avail. This twofold experience is the pre-condition for the attainment of the third basic quality *sattva*, representing clarity, purity and enlightenment. Indeed, it has been said,

> The greater the doubt, the greater the awakening; The smaller the doubt, the smaller the awakening; No doubt, no awakening.[7]

If this is so, it follows that the great seers and prophets must have gone through, to us, unimaginable depths of doubt and dread. This is indeed born out by the scriptures. Jesus was driven into the wilderness, not forty years as the Children of Israel, but forty days and there he was 'tempted of Satan; and was with the wild beasts; and the angels ministered unto him'. (Mark, I, I3.)

When Gautama the Buddha related his early struggle for enlightenment to Sariputta, he described his sojourn in the wilderness vividly:

> Then Sariputta, I plunged into a fearsome forest thicket and dwelt therein. Such was the fearsome horror of that dread forest thicket that anyone whose passions were not stilled and entered there, the very hairs of his body would stand on end ... So that, Sariputta, these verses never heard before, these curious verses, occurred to me:

> > Scorched, frozen, and alone,
> > In fearsome forest dwelling,
> > Naked, no fire to warm,
> > Bent on the quest is the Sage.[8]
> > *Majjhima Nikaya* I, 166

What is portrayed here refers undoubtedly, not only to the extreme asceticism Gautama practised at that time, but to an inner state of confusion and darkness. He had turned from the world's entanglements and had subdued and stilled the desires binding him to the world, and he was now facing, what he himself describes as the panic, fear, and horror which the dread forest thicket created in him. He had not yet reached enlightenment and, like other seekers, had to pass through the night of the senses. It is related how, at the moment of complete deprivation through fasting in the woods, angels (*devatā*) appeared, first begging him to end the fast and then pledging heavenly sustenance in order to defeat death.

Later, when the Buddha had begun his ministry, the sojourn in the wilderness is often referred to and, in fact, becomes an integral part of his teaching. The Buddhist scriptures use various images in its portrayal, for instance, a man in search of the true path is likened to a man in a forest walking along a mountain height and finding 'an ancient road, an ancient track'. Another simile often used is that of the ocean or stream to be crossed.

> Just as a man, brethren, who has started on a long journey sees before him a great stretch of water, on this side full of doubts and fears, on the further side safe and free from fears; but there is no boat to cross in, no causeway for passing over from this side to the other side.
>
> *Majjhima Nikaya* I, 134

In the same way as the traveller through the wilderness is threatened by fearful beasts, so the follower of the Buddha's teaching, if he wants to cross to the further shore, has to brave the 'monster-teeming sea, with devils and fearsome waves impassable'. The place of the ladder or path discovered in the desert or forest is here taken by the necessity 'to find a boat', or 'fashion a raft' or 'build a ship'. Without path, boat, raft or ship, without the norm, the teaching of the Enlightened One, there can only be despair and hopelessness, or as one of the texts calls it 'gross darkness, the darkness of bewilderment'.

It is related that one of the chief disciples of the Buddha, the venerable Tissa, when finding himself in a state of sloth and torpor, and deriving no joy from the religious life, turns to the master for help. The reply of the Buddha is in two parts. First, he makes clear the paramount need for non-clinging to all that is impermanent. Then he tells a parable; he tells of two men, one skilled the other unskilled in wayfaring. The unskilled man asks the way and is told by the skilled man that, after a little stretch, the road will divide. The left-hand one is to be avoided, the one on the right is to be followed. This will lead successively to a thick forest, a marshy swamp, a steep precipice, and eventually to a delightful stretch of level ground. The meaning is immediately explained by the master himself. The man unskilled in the way stands for the great mass of people, the man skilled in wayfaring represents an enlightened being; the divided way is the state of wavering; the left-hand path is the wrong way of life; the right-hand path is the Eightfold Path taught by the Buddha; the thick forest is ignorance, the marshy swamp lust and desire, the steep precipice doubt and despair, the delightful stretch of level ground is *nirvana*, the journey's goal.[9]

The important fact which is conveyed here is that just because the wayfarer has chosen the right path he enters upon a period of trial. In other words, this phase of perplexity and distress must not be shunned because it is here that purification of the inner man takes place. Once this is understood, as the Buddha makes Tissa understand, then the wayfarer 'attempts the steep'[10] and having done so he turns in disgust from everything hindering his progress.

The imagery employed in the great religious traditions to convey this experience of entering the wilderness, varies considerably and yet, once the deeper meaning has been discovered, the images become eloquent, yielding their hidden message. The great Hindu classic, the *Bhagavadgita*, chooses for its setting not indeed the desert, the thick forest or the impassable ocean, but an equally telling scenery, the battlefield. In the opening chapter we find Arjuna assailed by doubts, deeply confused and in despair. Values which, up to that point had guided him securely, suddenly appear meaningless. His appointed task is to lead the battle against the hostile armies which, however, are composed of his own kinsfolk. Do they not form part of his very life, the life he knows and is familiar with? Should he go forward and fight and thus cause distress and death to his own flesh and blood, or go back to that world of accepted values, he knows so well? Here we are given a picture, in a highly dramatic form, of that same crisis which brings with it the need to fight inimical forces within and to lose one's way in order to find it. Arjuna voices all the haunting doubts which assail him who has chosen the 'right' path, as well as the bodily symptoms which go with it:

My limbs quail, my mouth goes dry, my body shakes and my hair stands on end.
(The bow) Gāndīva slips from my hand and my skin too is burning all over. I am not able to stand steady. My mind is reeling.

I, 29/30

The colophon added to this chapter calls it 'Arjunaviṣādyoga'[11] the Yoga of dejection and sorrow of Arjuna. This title tells us in the clearest possible manner that the phase of doubt and melancholy, too, is a form of yoga and, like all other types of yoga, it is concerned with a bodily and spiritual discipline. In the words of the modern Indian Sage Sri

Aurobindo 'it is a night and a negation' which, however, is 'not the punishment of a fall, but the condition of a progress'.[12]

The texts quoted or mentioned so far reveal several important aspects of the wilderness. One is, what has often been called, the dividing of the ways. Near the entrance to this experience we are faced with a crucial choice; with the broad and the narrow way, or the wide and the straight gate of the Bible; the right and left-hand paths or the two highways of many traditions; thus, for instance in the Koran where it is said

> What! have we not made him eyes,
> And tongue and lips,
> And guided him to the two highways?
> Yet he attempted not the steep.[13]
> And who shall teach thee what the steep is?
>
> XC, 8–12

The choice is ours, but if we care to listen to the advice of all those who have gone before, the recognition of the two paths should be possible.

We have seen that he who chooses the right-hand path chooses danger. In the symbolic language of many scriptures destructive creatures bar his way; sea monsters in the Buddhist text quoted above, scorpions and serpents in the Bible, crocodiles in Egyptian imagery[14] and wild beasts and creatures of wrath in many other traditions. What do these signify? It is a well-known phenomenon that almost immediately we set out on the religious quest inimical forces, from without and within, suddenly appear. When Christian in John Bunyan's *Pilgrim's Progress* found his path flanked by two roaring lions and when, trembling, he halted, he was asked: 'Is thy strength so small?' and was told

> Difficulty is behind, Fear is before,
> Though he's got on the hill, the lions roar;
> A Christian man is never long at ease,
> When one fright's gone, another doth him seize.

The explanation modern psychology has to offer is that these monsters are mostly of our own making, whether they appear outside as maleficent forces or entities, or inside as aggressive attitudes or evil tendencies; and this is exactly what has been taught throughout the history of higher religion. They are the 'unclean spirits' that lodge in our own house.

This is clearly hinted at in the lines spoken by the Buddha, quoted above. Only he can survive the horrors of the wilderness who has conquered lust and desire; in other words, only the purified man can conquer the wild beasts; the unpurified is overwhelmed by his own impurities. Perhaps the most forthright as well as interesting recognition of this fact is found in the *Tibetan Book of the Dead*. At the point when the wrathful and fear-inspiring deities appear, the plea is uttered again and again: 'Fear not, be not terrified, be not awed whatever fearful and terrifying visions may appear, recognize them to be the embodiments of thine own intellect'.

Yet another aspect of the wilderness demands our attention. It is that of temptation. At such moments of dire peril, the temptation is clearly and naturally, to give up the venture, to return to the familiar world where it is possible to live 'by bread alone', and to resume the old life, one-sidedly turned outwards towards the external world with all its attractions and promises. This is the nature of the temptation which confronted such high beings as the Buddha, Jesus, and Muhammad and,[15] in a minor degree, confront every man who follows this path of inner development. The evil one, Mara, the slinking devil, Satan, appears, conjuring up visions of 'mountains of gold'[16] and of 'the kingdom of the world seen in a moment of time'[17] tempting us to abandon the journey into the unknown, and to give way to inertia and fear and return to the well-trodden highway of the left hand, we know so well.

It is clear that unless the voice of the tempter can be silenced, and silenced again and again, *metanoia*, or in the Arabic tongue, *tauba*, true repentance, the facing in a new direction, cannot take place. Al-Ghazzali, the Muslim mystic, bears eloquent witness to this. In his *Confessions* he tells of agonies of doubt and despair and how he was torn between the still small voice within crying 'Up! Up! thy life is nearing its end and thou hast a long journey to make. All thy pretended knowledge is nought but falsehood and fantasy. If thou dost not think now of thy salvation, when wilt thou think of it? If thou dost not break thy chains today, when wilt thou break them?'—and the voice of the tempter assuring him that all this is but a passing mood and that it would be folly to renounce his high position in the world. Thus torn between opposing forces, standing at the cross-roads, Al Ghazzali went through months of utter bodily and mental misery. He was inflicted with loss of speech and could neither eat nor drink. At the point of total darkness, dawn broke.

The enfeeblement of my physical powers was such that the doctors despairing of saving me, said: 'The mischief is in the heart, and has communicated itself to the whole organism; there is no hope unless the cause of his grievous sadness be arrested'. Finally, conscious of my weakness and the prostration of my soul, I took refuge in God as a man at the end of himself and without resources. 'He who hears the wretched when they cry' (Koran, XXVII, 62) deigned to hear me.[18]

This could be paralleled in many traditions and in many ways. An eloquent example is contained in the Old Testament. When the Children of Israel were driven out of Egypt their flight through the wilderness was halted by the Red Sea. At that crucial moment, when all hope of survival seemed futile, the voice of the tempter spoke. Serfdom now appeared to them preferable to perishing in the desert. They said: 'For it had been better for us to serve the Egyptians, than that we should die in the wilderness.' To this Moses replied: 'Fear ye not, stand still, and see the salvation of the Lord'. (Ex. 14, 12/13.)

Here yet another aspect of the great doubt reveals itself dramatically. To find oneself in a wasteland, surrounded by danger and temptation, also means nearness of God. For it is at this point that the realization dawns that, in the words of St John of the Cross, 'the loss of the former ways means the gains of a new way, and the loss of all possessions means the gain of much greater possessions'. The moment doubt and frustration take on such proportions that a solution appears impossible, true insight becomes possible, for only then can the hold be broken which the old way, the purely outward turned life, has upon us.

This fact has been recognized by many teachers of religion and they use this knowledge in order to bring about or hasten the desired change. What is known to modern existentialist theologians as the 'readiness for dread' (*Angstbereitschaft*) 'which man has to accept by an act of resolve', has always formed part of any genuine religious instructions; because it has been realized that the divine encounter can only take place 'at the point where the human aspect is nothingness and only at that point'.[19] Indeed it may be said that, seen from this angle, to enter upon the path of religion is identical with the readiness for dread.

Many spiritual disciplines are designed deliberately so as to take us to that point of nothingness. For instance, there is the discipline of relentless questioning much practised in the East; 'whence do I come', 'wither do I go', 'what is the purpose of life', 'why am I here', and, perhaps the most potent of all, 'who am I?' Layer after layer of what appears to be concrete reality is thus torn away, often a rather unpleasant process. Everything is questioned and everything is found wanting. This relentless self-questioning is, in far-eastern practice, often intensified by the use of seemingly senseless statements and questions that not only baffle, and thus challenge the mind, but whose primary purpose it is, as Zen masters have said, to arouse the doubt-sensation and increase the doubt-mass. Here belong many Zen *koans* and *mondos*, ranging from such questions as 'what is the Buddha nature', 'how can I escape from the triple world', to others such as 'what is my original face which I had even prior to my birth' or 'all things are said to be reducible to the one, but where is the one to be reduced?'

To pursue these questions inevitably means becoming entangled as in a thicket where intellect and reason cannot guide us. We are driven to the conclusion that unless we penetrate to the centre of the thicket where it is densest, to that point where we have, at last, to admit that we are helpless as we are, the way out cannot be found. To admit the failure of one's own cherished ways, however, cannot be done without humbling oneself; in fact these two things are identical.

It is this particular aspect which the monotheistic faiths have stressed and used in their method of instruction. In the Old Testament we read:

And thou shalt remember all the way which the Lord God led thee these forty years in the wilderness, to humble thee and to prove thee, to know what was in thine heart, whether thou wouldst keep his commandments, or no ... (Deut. 8, 2–3).

To a Christian, true humility means the denial of ourselves inwardly and outwardly, as St Francis of Sales has defined it: 'To make it our glory to be nothing'. Here, just as in eastern techniques, the discovery of our own nothingness is preceded by a gradual realization that

No knowledge and no conception in this mortal life can serve as proximate means of this union of the love of God. All that the understanding may comprehend, all that the will may be satisfied with, and all that the imagination may conceive, is most unlike unto God, and most disproportionate to Him.[20]

If, in this quotation, we substitute 'ultimate enlightenment' for 'union with God', it would make an admirable commentary to the aim and purpose of the Zen technique.

The man whose 'soul melteth for heaviness'[21] finds the quickening of God's word nigh unto him because the point of nothingness gives access to realization and enlightenment. It is at this point, too, both in the development of the individual and of mankind, that the figure of the

Way-shower, the guide, the friend, appears. Of him the Buddha has said:

> He it is who doth cause a way to arise which had not arisen before; who doth bring about a way not brought about before: who doth proclaim a way not proclaimed before: who is the knower of a way, who understandeth a way, who is skilled in a way. And now, brethren, his disciples are wayfarers who follow him.
>
> *Samyutta Nikaya* III, 66

Through him is kindled in man that one faculty without which he would never begin his pilgrimage nor maintain sufficient strength to see it through. That faculty is faith in what, as yet, is beyond comprehension, faith in the existence of a world which is here yet cannot be grasped, and faith in the possibility of growth and attainment to a higher level of being.

The new way thus discovered is the Way of the Lord, it is that ladder which joins earth and heaven as it was seen in a vision by Jacob when he too was in a wilderness. On it the angels were ascending and descending, and above it stood the Lord God; and Jacob recognized, when he awoke, that the place which made him afraid and which he called dreadful, was yet the house of God, the very gate of heaven.

> And Jacob rose up early in the morning and took the stone that he had put for his pillows, and set it up for a pillar, and poured oil upon the top of it. And he called the name of that place Beth-el (house of God).

Thus the stone found in the desert and worth nothing becomes the pillar, the cornerstone of the new temple.[22] What the Old Testament describes symbolically as the worthless stone that is yet beyond price, other texts see in terms of darkness and light.

> Night and day—day in comparison with unbelievers, night in comparison with the Angels ...
>
> In this then which is now day, but yet night, night in comparison with the future day for which we yearn, day in comparison with the past night which we have renounced; in this night, I say, let us therefore seek God with our hands. Let not work cease; let us seek God; let there be no idle yearning.
>
> St Augustine. Ps. LXXVI, 4

The same teaching is embodied in Krishna's words in the *Bhagavadgita*.

> What is night for all beings is the time of waking for the disciplined soul; and what is the time of waking for all beings, is night for the sage who sees. (II, 69.)

Here, two levels of experience meet and even clash; night becomes day, and day night; seeing becomes not seeing and not seeing seeing. All values are reversed which is another way of saying that everything is made new and wholly other. How does this miracle happen? What is the ransom asked for the wilderness to turn into the land of bliss, for despair to be drowned by joy, and for the burning pain of the great doubt to be swept away by *satori*, the breakthrough into certitude?

NOTES FOR CHAPTER 7

1. E. Neumann, *The Origin and History of Consciousness*.
2. See also *Katha Upanishad* II. 1. St Theresa uses almost identical imagery.
3. R. Wilhelm, *The Secret of the Golden Flower*, p. 34.
4. *The Dark Night of the Soul*. In: *The Mystical Doctrine* ... p. 83–106.
5. The holy forest was a well-known symbol in the Renaissance and later; for example, the holy forest in Ariosto's *Orlando Furioso* which was thought to be labyrinthine, and Shakespeare's forest in the *Tempest*. The close connection between mazes and the wilderness is borne out by the fact that, to this day, some outdoor mazes are called 'wilderness'. (G. R. Hocke, *Die Welt als Labyrinth*, pp. 88 and 109, and W. H. Matthews, *Labyrinths and Mazes*, p. 88.)
6. *Lawwama* of which a Muslim writer says: 'Our breasts become an arena of struggle; temptation allures, conscience chides, we stumble'. Kamal-ud-Din, *Al-Islam*, p. 15.
7. Chang Chen-Chi, *The Practice of Zen*, p. 78.
8. Compare this with the twentieth chapter of Lao-Tse's *Tao Te Ching* where a similar state of mind is portrayed.
9. Samyutta *Nikaya*, III, 106.
10. See p. 86.
11. S. Radhakrishnan in his commentary on the Gita says:
    The distress of Arjuna is a dramatization of a perpetually recurring predicament. Man, on the threshold of higher life, feels disappointed with the glamour of the world and yet illusions cling to him and he cherishes them. ... Arjuna passes through a great spiritual tension. When he detaches himself from his social obligations and asks why he should carry out the duty expected of him by society, he gets behind his socialized self and has full awareness of himself as an individual alone and isolated. He faces the world as a stranger thrown into a threatening chaos. The new freedom creates a deep feeling of anxiety, aloneness, doubt and insecurity. If he is to function successfully, these feelings must be overcome. (p. 95f.)

12. *Life Divine*, p. 48.
13. '*Aqabah*', here rendered 'steep', means a mountain-road, or a path in the higher reaches of a mountain, or a mountain that bars the way. On it walk those who have chosen the right course (*Sura* II, 157) and who, for that reason, are tried 'with something of fear and hunger and loss of property and lives and fruits'. (Koran commentary *Sura* II, 155.)
14. See also the *Egyptian Book of the Dead*, Chapter XXXII–XLI.
15. A very similar story is told of the founder of the Sikh religion Guru Nanak:
    ... It is said that Nanak went into the wilderness, where he was severely tempted by Kaljug, the devil. He resisted every attack, however, and afterwards was granted a special vision of God, during which he held converse with Him, and received instruction for his mission. During this experience, he composed an important part of the Japji, which has since become the keynote of Sikh doctrine. (D. Field, *The Religion of the Sikhs*, p. 13.)
16. *Samyutta Nikaya* II, 10; also *Mara Samyutta* I, 1, and *Sutta Nipata*.
17. Luke 4, 5.
18. *Confessions*, p. 43ff.
19. R. Bultmann. See H. W. Bartsch, *Kerygma and Myth*, p. 205.
20. St John of the Cross, *Ascent of Mount Carmel*. In: *The Mystical Doctrine* ... p. 21.
21. Psalm 119, 28.
22. Genesis 28, 18. Bethel becomes, in the Koran, *Al-Bait*, The House, or *Al-Bait al-Haram*, the sacred house, i.e. the Ka'ba. It is the goal of the holy pilgrimage which is a period of trial, leading across the desert of the scorching sands, as well as the desert of the senses, when all worldly attachments are severed and man follows the age-old call of surrender to God. See also *supra* pp. 109–10.

8

Self-Renunciation –
Sacrifice in Indian Teachings

> Subdue your self, for the self is difficult to subdue.
> If your self is subdued, you will be happy in this
> world and in the next.
> Better it is that I should subdue my self by self-
> control and penance, than be subdued by others with
> fetters and corporal punishment ...
> Though a man should conquer thousands and
> thousands of valient foes, greater will be his victory if
> he conquers nobody but himself. Fight with your
> self; why fight with eternal foes? He who conquers
> himself through himself will obtain happiness.
>
> *Uttarādhyayana Sutra*

The *Katha Upanishad* relates how a youth, searching for the ultimate
meaning of existence, is initiated into the universal yet hidden truths
contained in the religious lore of his people. These truths can be
transmitted through one channel only, the channel of death, and thus it
is that it is Yama, death himself, who instructs the youth Naciketas, for
only he who passes through the gates of death can hope to fathom the
mystery of life and enter the promised land of immortality.

These gates are sacred, yet awe-inspiring, because it is here that
ransom is asked and that Yama kindles the Naciketas sacrifice. As we
have seen earlier,[1] there are various levels on which the sacrificial
offering can take place; at this point we are concerned with one
particular aspect only, the inner sacrifice of the 'I', claiming
independent selfhood. However, so as not to paint a false picture by
disregarding the evolutionary background, two tales, involving sacrifices
and belonging to different phases of development, will be told by way of
introduction. They are variations on the universal theme of the
regeneration of life through death or, seen from another angle, they are
two versions of that prototypal myth, the myth of Osiris, telling of his
death, his dismemberment, the scattering of his body over the land and
his resurrection.

The home of the first sacrificial rite is Bengal where the Khonds, a people of Dravidian stock, venerated the earth goddess Tari Pennu, to whom human victims were offered annually, so as to ensure the fertility of the field as well as protection from misfortunes. The Meriah, as the victim was called, was held in great esteem and often consecrated to the deadly, yet life-giving task many years before the actual sacrifice. His death was regarded as needful to the continuation of life on earth and thus was vicarious in character.

On the day before the sacrifice the victim, dressed in a new garment, was led forth from the village in solemn procession, with music and dancing, to the Meriah grove, a clump of high forest trees standing a little way from the village and untouched by the axe. There they tied him to a post, which was sometimes placed between two plants of the sankissar shrub. He was then annointed with oil, ghee, and tumeric, and adorned with flowers; and a 'species of reverence, which is not easy to distinguish from adoration,' was paid to him throughout the day. A great struggle now arose to obtain the smallest relic from his person[2] ...

On the day of the sacrifice, the Meriah was again anointed and he was shown to all the people of the village. One absolute rule was that, for the actual sacrifice, he must not be bound nor resist death in any way. Force or coercion would invalidate the offering. After death and dismemberment, portions of his, by now sacred flesh and limbs, were partly buried ritually in the soil as an offering to the Goddess of the Earth, and partly scattered in the fields to ensure fertility of the soil.

The second tale is that of Attis, the youthful god venerated in Phrygia, who was said to have been born miraculously of a virgin called Nana. He, like Adonis, was most likely a god of vegetation who, therefore, together with all that grows and gives food to man, stands for nature's cyclic rhythm of life-death and new life. According to one version, he died by self-mutilation under a pine-tree where he bled to death. Out of this mythical event grew the Roman spring festival of Attis and Cybele,[3] celebrated on March 22nd, when a pine-tree was erected in the sanctuary whose trunk, covered like a corpse with bands and wreaths, bore the effigy of the young god. After ritual feasting, which included the offering of blood, mourning and fasting from bread, the effigy was buried on the third day.

But when night had fallen, the sorrow of the worshippers was turned to joy. For suddenly a light shone in the darkness: the tomb was opened: the god had risen from the dead; and as the priest touched the lips of the weeping mourners with balm, he softly whispered in their ears the glad tidings of salvation. The resurrection of the god was hailed by his disciples as a promise that they, too, would issue triumphant from the corruption of the grave. On the morrow of the twenty-fifth of March, which was reckoned the vernal equinox, the divine resurrection was celebrated with a wild outburst of glee.

Anybody who has read Frazer's *Golden Bough*, knows that these two rites do not represent isolated cases but could, with many variations, be multiplied almost at will. So it is legitimate to regard them as representing two typical stages of development—amongst many others—in a process which, seen from the psychological point of view, can be called interiorization. In the first case a regeneration ritual is performed annually which involves the actual killing, dismemberment and burying of a human (or animal) victim which comes to life again in the newly fertilized soil, the womb of the new season's crop, thus ensuring continued existence and prosperity to the people.

In the second case, the ritual re-enactment of the self-sacrifice of Attis, in which the symbolic representation of the event plays an important part, is regarded as sufficient to bring about the desired renewal in both nature and man. This only becomes possible if and when it is recognized, consciously or unconsciously, that the rite performed corresponds to a process in man himself, which it is thought to be desirable to initiate and repeat. The worshippers mourn the death of Attis and therewith participate in it; they likewise rejoice at the resurrection of the god because through it they themselves are assured life after death.

This process of interiorization or, as modern psychology would call it, the process of withdrawing unconscious projections and thus making them conscious, is going on all the time just as is its counterpart, the process of exteriorization, or the projection of unconscious psychic contents on to the outer world. But so far as the phenomenology and history of religions is concerned, this two-way traffic, as it were, is seen to form part of an overall movement which is directed mainly towards greater interiorization, linking the so-called primitive cults to the higher religions. The adherents of the latter regard their religion as something primarily happening in the invisible and inward domain of consciousness, the secret chamber of the heart or mind, and this is true even in those cases where the inward-turned orientation is counterbalanced by the belief in a transcendent, as against an immanent, deity. Such a process of gradual withdrawal of projections, and therewith of identifications with external phenomena, necessarily brings in its wake a changed outlook on life.

The attitude of man to what is perhaps the most vital of all religious practices, sacrifice, is manifestly deeply affected by such a new orientation, and the question arises if the types of sacrificial rites, as described above, are expressive of the same basic notions as is the teaching of death and resurrection found in the higher religions. The answer is that both levels undoubtedly share certain vital traits yet they are separated by a clear breach, in the same way as any process of growth is discontinuous in which different levels of development are involved. Sacrifice in the higher religions, as will be seen, denotes something entirely different from that performed within the framework of a lower cultural stratum, just because it addresses itself to another grade of awareness which bestows different meaning and creates different values. In spite of this, however, the essence is not touched, and this fact is revealed in certain fundamental pre-conditions which all forms of sacrifice must fulfil, although they also are interpreted according to the level which they serve.

Perhaps the most essential of these conditions is that the sacrifice must be voluntary; behind the sacrificial act, there must be free choice and an untrammelled will. Furthermore, what is offered must be of man's very own, it must be something which, in relation to the situation out of which the need for the sacrifice arises, is of the highest value to the sacrificer and to which, therefore, he feels the greatest possible attachment. Again, in the sacrifice there must be included, in some form, total renunciation, total loss and an offering even unto death. Something has to disappear and die in one realm of being in order to be reborn in another. Here a basic feature of any genuine sacrifice is disclosed. Sacrifice is the point of contact between the lower, human, and the higher, divine, worlds, a fact which stands out clearly in both the Khond and the Attis sacrifice. The human victim, the Meriah, is venerated like a god from the moment he has entered in the rite and, therewith, in the sacrifice itself. Attis, too, the fair youth who tended the herds, becomes a god through his self-sacrifice, in the same way as Osiris, the king, is worshipped as a god only after his death and resurrection.

These traits are universally valid, yet with a growing interiorization their points of reference change and they appear in a new light, both as regards outward appearance and inner meaning. Thus the condition that the sacrifice must be voluntary is, in the case of the Khond people, clearly recognized. It is stated that there must be no resistance and for this condition to be fulfilled, the victim is drugged or made otherwise acquiescent. This in the high religions becomes an act of free decision which, however, is often arrived at by compelling despair and frustration; furthermore, one of the many effects of incense-burning, or similar practices which often accompany the sacrificial act, is undoubtedly a slight drugging of the senses. In this context, however, by far the most important shift of meaning, together with an almost total change in the ceremony attending it, occurs in the nature of the offering itself. More and more the realization dawns, as the withdrawal of identification with external objects proceeds, that what is sacrificed must be something residing within; it is this realization which the great religions seek to awaken in every one of their followers and it is this, more than anything else, which distinguishes higher from lower religion.

Amongst the wealth of myths and legends of the Hindu people, there is one which, in content, is closely related to the Osiris myth and which, in all probability, belongs to a similar cultural stratum. It is the myth of Shiva and his consort, Satī.

The adversary of Shiva in this story is Daksha, the father of Satī and leader of the gods. At a great sacrificial feast, he reviles the absent Shiva, whereupon Satī, the devoted spouse, following an old tradition, surrenders her life at the feet of her spiteful father. She is consumed by self-engendered inner fire.

Shiva, in his wrath and sorrow, bestrides the earth, causing destruction wherever he treads. All vegetation perishes and all creatures face starvation and death. On his back Shiva carries the dead Satī for all the world to lament her passing. No creature can halt the god, and mankind seems doomed. It is Vishnu who comes to the rescue. He follows Shiva and, by throwing his discus fifty-two times, he dismembers Satī's body and her limbs are scattered over the earth. Where they fall, a temple in honour of the Mother Goddess is erected, a place of worship (Ptha-Sthāna), where the sacrifice of Satī, like a seed, bears fruit and her cult is perpetuated.[5]

In another aspect, too, this story is like a seed which bore fruit in a legend belonging to the great epic of the *Mahābhārata*, the legend of Prince Yudhishthira. As Coomaraswamy has pointed out, Hindu imagination has here 'reached a point where it can conceive of nothing in the universe transcending in greatness man's conquest of himself'.[6]

The self-conquest of Yudhishthira is the subject of the concluding chapters of the *Mahābhārata*, entitled 'The Great Journey' and 'The Ascent to Heaven'. As in the case of the prophet Elijah, a fiery chariot appears before Yudhishthira who, on his last journey into the high mountains of the Himalayas, the abode of the gods, is invited by the charioteer, Indra, to enter it so as to be taken up into Heaven. The prince replies that he cannot follow Indra unless his queen, as well as his dead brothers, are allowed to enter, too; he is ready to forgo eternal bliss for the sake of those he loves.

This is the first test involving a self-sacrifice; the second follows immediately after the god has granted the request. There is, accompanying the prince, a creature who has served him loyally and faithfully, his dog. Indra wants to send him away, but, even for the sake of the liberation of a dog, Yudhishthira renounces entry into the heavenly realm. 'To cast off one who has loved us is infinitely sinful.' He stands firm through all pleadings and arguments and when the final word has been spoken and the test consummated, the dog is changed into a radiant form, that of the god of Righteousness, Dharma. Triumphantly, Yudhishthira is taken up into heaven, only to be confronted with yet another trial and another sacrifice. After rejecting the abode of heavenly delights and pleasures offered to him, he is led to a realm of utter darkness and horror where pitiful voices can be heard, imploring his help and presence. With deep anguish he recognizes the voices; they are those of his own kith and kin, and he realizes that the place he has entered is hell. In anger and pity he calls to his guide and sends him back to the gods with the message that he will never return. 'Here with my friends in hell, where my presence aids them, shall I abide for ever.' Once again the supreme sacrifice proves the gateway to heaven. What was hell is transformed into heaven and the gods honour him saying:

> Thy trials are ended ... Here, in the Milky Way, put on the body of immortality and then ascend thy throne. Be seated amongst the gods, great thou as Indra, alone of mortal men raised to Heaven in this thine earthly form![7]

According to Hindu belief, the greatest of all sacrifices was the primordial sacrifice of creation, when the universe came into existence through what can be called the prototype of all human sacrifices, the dismemberment of *Purusha*, the cosmic man.[8] This idea goes back to the Vedas, where that first, in the true sense of the word, creative offering is described. We are told that the moon was gendered from *Purusha's* mind, the sun from his eye; the sky was fashioned from his head, and from his feet the earth; from the sacrificial oil arose spring, from the holy gift, autumn, from the wood, summer. Birds and all animals were made from the dripping and the holy scriptures were born from the ritual.

When the gods, offering sacrifice, bound as their victim, Purusha.
Gods, sacrificing, sacrificed the victim: these were the earliest holy
ordinances.
The mighty ones attained the heights of heaven, there where the Sadyas,
gods of old, are dwelling.

Rig-Veda X, 90

Here in this Vedic hymn it is clearly recognized that sacrifice is not
only the most potent act but the one and only means of creative
transformation. In it resides the elixir of life, in it man becomes divine.[9]
It is therefore rightly seen as the 'earliest holy ordinances' which in the
beginning created the world by a divine-human sacrifice and which
even now, by a human-divine sacrifice, raises man to the realms of the
gods.

With this the cycle closes; for what is a creative self-giving of the
divine, an externalization, involving a movement downward, as it were,
into ever greater density of matter, finds its culmination in man, whence
the reverse movement of self-giving sets in and, through increasing
internalization, man finally offers, as a supreme gift, himself. With this
ultimate sacrifice he becomes one with the divine creation. On a new
level he becomes *Purusha*, cosmic man, as *Purusha* became the
universe in the beginning. In the words of the great modern teacher of
Yoga, Sri Aurobindo:

This descent, this sacrifice of the Purusha, the Divine Soul
submitting itself to Force and Matter so that it may inform and
illumine them, is the seed of redemption of this world of
Inconscience and Ignorance.[10]

When this is realized, the macrocosmic sacrifice of *Purusha* acquires
a new meaning. In the beginning, his limbs and all parts of his body
created the manifold universe, including man. When this sacrifice is
repeated on the microcosmic plane of human life, all limbs and
functions of the human body are revealed as the seat of divine
indwelling. *Purusha* is seen 'in the faces, heads and necks of all'[11] and
this supreme person, the self, discloses itself as *Atman*, the divine self.

Now when the eye is fixed upon the ether, that is the spirit in the eye
(*purusha*) which sees; the eye is but a means to see. When one thinks
that he will smell a thing, it is the Self (*ātmā*) the nostril is but a
means to smell. When one thinks that he will utter a word, it is the
Self; speech is but a means to utterance. When one thinks that he

will think a thing, it is the Self; the mind is his divine eye; with this divine eye he sees these desires and rejoices therein.

Chandogya Upanishad VIII, 12, 4/5

This is the great secret teaching which Prajā-pati, the 'Lord of creatures', gave to Indra the god, and Virocana the demon. The latter took it to mean that it is the bodily senses, the bodily self that is identical with the highest person, the *Purusha*. He did not understand that only through self-giving, sacrifice and faith, can the truth be perceived. It is because of this ignorance that he was a demon, for we are told that precisely the non-giving and not offering sacrifices is the doctrine of the evil ones. Indra, on the other hand, after a lifetime of seeking, became, through the sacrifice of the limited and personal self, a perfected soul.

The great stumbling block then in the way of the seeker is his idea of a separate selfhood. This is what must be given up, together with all claims of the superiority of the 'I', the elusive yet powerful notion which is so precious and so dear to us and with which we identify ourselves. The very thing which we think, feel, and even seem to know we are, the sense of 'I', this we are called upon to forgo. What is needed, the *Bhagavadgita* calls freedom from the thought of 'I' and 'thinking not of mine, only this will make a man fit to become one with the highest'.[12]

For attachment to the 'I' is the prime cause of bewilderment and delusion. According to Patanjali, it leads to a state of wrong values and wrong judgments. The non-eternal is regarded as eternal, the impure as pure, the painful as pleasant, and the non-*Atman* as *Atman*. The real cause of such delusion is stated succinctly 'To identify consciousness with that which merely reflects consciousness—this is egoism'.[13]

This sense of 'I', always exclusive and possessive in its activities, must be controlled and its supremacy broken, for it is this which creates wrong views in the mind of man by making him believe in a 'false identification of the experiencer with the object of experience'.[14] The man who is thus deluded thinks 'I am the actor' and he identifies himself with the senses, the feelings, and all activities of his mind and body, whereas for the man who has renounced, the contrary applies. Thus the teaching which the bewildered Arjuna receives on the battlefield is:

The man who is united with the Divine and knows the truth thinks 'I do nothing at all' for in seeing, hearing, touching, smelling, tasting, walking, sleeping, breathing; in speaking, emitting, grasping, opening and closing the eyes, he holds that only the senses are occupied with the objects of the senses.

He who works, having given up attachment, resigning his actions to God, is not touched by sin, even as a lotus leaf is untouched by water.

Bhagavadgita V, 8–10

What is here called false identification of the experiencer with the object of experience, or in the language of the *Gita*, the need for breaking the identification of the 'I' with the activities of the senses, is part of that process which seeks to bring up into consciousness more and more of those contents of human experience which, because they are largely unconscious, hold sway over us. We do not realize our subservience, and by this ignorance of the true facts, we create what is called the great illusion, whose perpetrator and maintainer is the ego. To shatter this illusion involves a sacrifice, a dying to self, a passing through the spiral gate of death, which reveals itself to be the very gate of heaven.

This is the keynote reverberating through the *Upanishads*, the *Gita* and the *Sutras* as well as through the teachings of the great seers India has produced throughout the ages. Needless to say, they differ in their approach, for here, too, there are the three main streams of devotion, knowledge and works, all leading to, and feeding, the ocean of the transformed life. Those who enter the stream of knowledge are called upon to dissolve the false sense of I by analysis and a constant questioning. As Sri Ramakrishna asked:

What is my ego? Is it my hand or foot, or flesh or blood, or muscle or tendon? Ponder deep and thou shalt know that there is no such thing as 'I', as by continually peeling off the skin of an onion, so on analysing the ego it will be found that there is not any real entity corresponding to the ego. The ultimate result of such an analysis is God. When egoism drops away, Divinity manifests itself.[15]

Those who tread the path of devotion pour out in love all they have and all they are at the feet of their divine master; they joyfully offer themselves for they see in the death of selfhood the end of separation and the pre-condition of union with their beloved.

In our own time, Sri Aurobindo adds to the way of knowledge and devotion that of works when he expounds, in his system of integral yoga, a process of self-giving which embraces all levels in man, all his activities from the humblest to the most exalted. This 'great world-rite', as he calls it, must be performed in full consciousness and full acceptance and awareness of its meaning, only then can the miracle of the resurrection take place.

> The one entirely acceptable sacrifice is a last and highest and uttermost self-giving ... for the soul that wholly gives itself to him, God also gives himself altogether. Only the one who offers his whole nature, finds the Self. Only the one who can give everything, enjoys the Divine All everywhere. Only the sublimation by sacrifice of all that we are, can enable us to embody the Highest and live here in the immanent consciousness of the transcendent Spirit.[16]

The first part of Sri Ramakrishna's questions and answers, quoted above, can be said to be Buddhist in character, for it contains the idea of arriving by analysis at the realization that there is no such entity as the ego, that, in fact, it does not exist. The call of the Indian sages to 'know thyself' was followed by the Buddha to the very end; and its elaboration and practical application forms the core of early Buddhism. Buddhist, too, is the idea found in the story of the Prince Yudhishthira, who refuses entry into heaven for the sake of his dog. This, in essence, is the Bodhisattva ideal, for he, too, forgoes the bliss of Nirvana out of compassion with all living creatures.

Buddhism, like Hinduism, repudiates the false identification of what we call self with the constituents of the personality or, in Buddhist terminology, with the five groups of grasping, i.e. material shape, feeling, perception, the impulses and consciousness (*skandhas*). What is needed, the texts call 'uprooting false view of self' and they make it clear that the thing to forgo utterly is that which says I and 'mine' to the constantly changing, and therefore impermanent, modes of existence, within as well as without.

> If one does not behold any self or anything of the nature of self in the five groups of grasping, one is an Arahat, the outflow extinguished.
> *Samyutta Nikaya* III, 127/8

This quotation reveals two important tenets. The first is, just as the Hindu scriptures maintain, that only by a renunciation of the sense of 'I' can Brahma, the highest be known, so the Buddhist canon reiterates constantly that the fundamental condition for 'crossing to the other shore', that is, for becoming an enlightened being, is the giving up, once for all, of the false notion of 'I'.

The second is the clear assertion that the dominance of the self is synonymous with the 'outflow' and all it stands for. This is the outward-going movement, the running after the attractions of the external world, followed by the identification of the self with what is erroneously regarded as possessing permanency and abiding values. The result is a vicious circle in which the momentum of 'the outflow' is heightened through false identifications and these are increased, in their turn, through the search of the self to satisfy its newly-formed attachments by investing them with increased energy, made possible by an increased 'outflow'. In Buddhist imagery, it is like an everspreading fire, consuming everything in its wake, always hungry for more fuel.

Buddhism presents to its followers the paramount need for the rooting up of the false notion of self, which forms part of the *an-attā* doctrine, not as an article of faith, nor as an ethical maxim, but as a statement of fact which is arrived at and developed by way of analysis, by reasoning and the elimination of erroneous beliefs. At the base of this method lies ceaseless questioning and a thirst for deeper understanding. The root question put before the Buddhist novice, providing a most potent stimulus for delving ever further into the mystery of existence, is the question 'What am I?', which the Buddha himself put repeatedly and answered dispassionately, convincingly, and at great length. He showed, by flawless reasoning, what the 'I' is not, what it cannot be, thereby leading the disciples step by step from wrong imaginings and ignorance towards enlightenment. His is a slow process by which the notion of a separate and independent self is gradually dissolved, as continuous drips of water slowly dissolve a hard lump of salt.[17]

The following is characteristic of the Buddha's way of instruction:

All matter, all feeling, all perception, all formations, all consciousness, past, present or future, internal or external, gross or subtle, low or high, far or near, all should be considered, in conformity with reality and with perfect wisdom, thus: 'This is not mine, this am I not, this is not my self'. Thus considering, the wise, noble disciple does not identify himself with materiality, does not identify himself with feeling, does not identify himself with perception, does not identify himself with the formations, does not identify himself with consciousness. Not identifying himself, he is detached. Being detached, he is freed.

Majjhima Nikaya XXII; CIX

The man who has thus gained liberation from the bonds of 'I' and 'mine' is the *Arahat*, a being who walks the earth egoless, having performed on himself the sacrificial rite of self-annihilation. The shadows of identification with the world are dissolved and he is filled with the light of knowledge, ready to pass the threshold into *Nirvana*.

The annihilation of self is a term with many meanings in Buddhism and there are instances where it borders on, or actually stands for, the voluntary surrender of life. From the body being regarded as repellent and even futile, because of its transient nature, as it is in some schools of thought, there is only a short step to the desire for death and the destruction of what is regarded as a burden.[18]

The next step was taken, not by Buddhism but by Jainism where the annihilation of the body, and the wilful ending of one's life, is taught as the highest discipline to be followed by the chosen few. Here the sacrifice of one's life, as an act of deliberate self-destruction, becomes the logical corollary of the realization of the non-existence of a separte self (*an-attā*). As it is the 'I', and the 'I' alone, which hankers after and provides the desire for life, the seeing of the truth becomes synonymous with a disgust for life.

Although the Buddha does not present the *an-attā* doctrine in the form of an ethical precept, there is yet inherent in it a moral law which is both fundamental and common to all genuine religious teaching. For he who has rejected false views of the 'I', is detached and has gained insight, and will, as a result, cease from spite, hatred and malice, as he will also, at the same time, be freed from grief and suffering. This the texts make abundantly clear.[19]

Selflessness in early Buddhism, as in much of Hinduism, is therefore not primarily a term denoting a certain ethical attitude, but it stands for one particular type of insight which is arrived at by reasoning and analysis rather than by the adherence to a moral code. It is this insight, however, which transforms men and results in the adoption of what amounts to a moral code.[20] The great Buddhist virtues of harmlessness, of love, compassion and sympathetic joy are based upon the abandonment of attachment to the false identification of the self with all that is impermanent and subject to change. As the *Brahma Viharas*[21] clearly show, the cultivation of these virtues is of vital importance in the process of gaining illumination, but it is insight in the doctrine of the not-self which imbues them with meaning and makes possible their implementation in everyday life.[22]

To us in the West, it is difficult to follow this line of thought and to divorce selflessness from its ethical connotation. Our natural reaction is to reverse the order and uphold the priority of the moral code which, if applied in the proper way, will result in the giving up of self; seen from this point of view, selflessness, having been drawn into the ethical sphere, must be regarded as synonymous with the virtues of love and charity. Here analysis and reasoning hardly play any part; on the contrary, they are often rejected as a hindrance.

The Mahayana schools of Buddhism elaborated the idea of love and compassion as found in Theravada texts and made it to bear fruit in profusion. Thus in a Tibetan treatise on the yoga of non-ego the yogin is instructed to 'think that now thou art about to transfix the Elements of Self with spears'. The names of these spears are the four *Brahma Viharas*, all-embracing love, great compassion, great affection, great impartiality, to which is added the spear of the Bodhisatvic mind. The aim is always sacrifice of self which expresses itself in utterances like the following:

> I will cease to live as self, and will take as my self my fellow-creatures. We love our hands, and other limbs, as members of the body; then why not love other living beings, as members of the universe?[23]

What is perhaps the most exalted expression, this idea has found within Buddhism, or any other religion, is that voluntary sacrifice for the good of others of him who stands at the gates of heaven, the enlightened or divine being, the leader and teacher of men, about to enter the abodes of the Elysian Fields. As Yudhishthira refused to enter, so does the *Bodhisattva* who, in his initiation, utters the vow that he will not enter *Nirvana* before all creatures of this earth have reached enlightenment. Until that day, his high office has only one purpose; to console the unconsoled, to rescue all living beings from the ocean of existence, and to be a refuge and resource for all in need.

The offering of one's life in service or in death, out of compassion with the suffering of the world, this is the hallmark of the Buddha-to-be; as one of them has said 'For a Bodhisattva to surrender life and limbs in aid of others is the keenest joy.'[24] By such an act of loving self-sacrifice, which must be as spontaneous as it must be complete, the mystery of the transformed life is revealed, and the seeker breaks through to a new existence. At that moment, according to some Buddhist sects, *Nirvana* is entered:

> One of the meanings of Nirvana is the death of the false self, and this is called in Zen the Great Death. It is different from ordinary death. Immediately after the Great Death we give birth to a new self. This awakening of the new self means that body and mind have dropped off. Sudden awakening means the awakening of the Buddha-nature when the true self is liberated from bondage. It is like the rising sun.[25]

NOTES FOR CHAPTER 8

1. See Labyrinth chapter.
2. J. G. Frazer, *The Golden Bough*, p. 435.
3. According to some sources, Attis was Cybele's son; according to others, her lover.
4. J. G. Frazer, *The Golden Bough*, p. 348ff.
5. According to another version, it was Shiva himself who scattered the limbs of the dead Satī. See S. Nivedita and A. Coomaraswamy, *Myths of Hindu and Buddhists*, pp. 286ff, 295.
6. A. Coomaraswamy, *op. cit.* p. 215.
7. A. Coomaraswamy, *op. cit.* p. 215.
8. The identification of the creation of the world with the sacrifice of a primeval creature, representing the universe, occurs in many traditions; for instance, the creation of the world from the body of Ymir, the leader of giants, figuring in Teutonic mythology or, in Babylonia, the killing of the monster Tiamat by Marduk. (See M. Eliade, *Patterns of Comparative Religion*, p. 96ff.)
9. 'He is made holy', which is the literal meaning of the word sacrifice (Sacra-facere).
10. *The Synthesis of Yoga*, p. 98.
11. *Svetasvatara Upanishad III*, 11. In the *Egyptian Book of the Dead* which is a guide, both for the departed and those seeking initiation, the same teaching is found. The seeker, whether in this life or the next, 'his foes defeated by the divine protection, the body raised to incorruption, acquires in every limb and every feature the seal of God' (Chapter XLII).
12. II, 71, also XVIII, 53.
13. *Yoga Aphorisms* II, 5, 6.
14. Patanjali, *Yoga Aphorisms* II, 17.
15. *Sayings of Ramakrishna*, No. 385.
16. *The Synthesis of Yoga*, p. 102.
17. A phrase often used in Buddhist meditations is 'I am not', the idea being that, through repetition and the contemplation of its meaning, this statement will eventually be accepted by the mind as expressing a true fact and will thus liberate man from his chief and most cherished illusion.
18. See, for instance, Suvarnaprabhasa, *Buddhist Scriptures*, pp. 25–6.
19. See, for instance: *Dhatu-Vibhanga Sutra*, 240–5; *Majjhima Nikaya* I, 8; *Samyutta Nikaya* III, 19.
20. The same relationship is taught in Mahayana Buddhism. We read in the *Prajnaparamita-Sutra*:
    When this body is regarded as mine body-*karma* is produced; when this speech is regarded as mine speech-*karma* is produced; when this mind is regarded as mine mind-*karma* is produced. Whereupon covetousness follows, the precepts are violated, anger arises, and indolence, distraction, and an evil way of thinking ... (B. L. Suzuki, *Mahayana Buddhism*, p. 130.)
21. The four sublime abodes or states: loving kindness, compassion, altruistic joy and equanimity.
22. In certain schools of Mahayana Buddhism, as also in Taoism, the *an-attā* teaching is further developed and becomes the doctrine of the void. A pictorial representation of this is found in the ten oxherd pictures, where the 'forgetting of the Ox' (the self) leads to an empty circle: 'Both the man and the animal have disappeared, no traces left. The bright moonlight is empty and shadowless with all the ten-thousand objects in it.' As the Taoists would say, to embrace all is to be self-less. (D. Suzuki, *Manual of Zen Buddhism*, p. 127ff.)

23. SantiDeva, *The Path of Light*, p. 88.
24. B. L. Broughton: *The Vision of Kwannon*, p. 120.
25. *Middle Way*, XXXIII, No. 2. August 1958. Dr Shinichi Hisamatsu.

9

Self-Surrender –
Sacrifice in Near-Eastern Teachings

Lo in the Cross is all, and in dying is all; and there is
no other way to life and true inward peace: but the
way of the holy Cross and of daily mortification.
Walk where thou wilt, seek what thou wilt; thou wilt
find no higher way above, nor safer way below: then
the way of the holy Cross ...

Turn thyself upwards, turn thyself downwards;
turn thyself outwards, turn thyself inwards:
everywhere thou shalt find the Cross; and
everywhere thou must needs keep patience: if thou
wilt have inward peace, and earn an everlasting
crown.

THOMAS Ā KEMPIS, *The Imitation of Christ*

When the moment has come to draw its last breath,
the Phoenix spreads out its tail and its feathers and
thereby a fire is kindled and the flames spread swiftly
to the heaped-up wood and it blazes up with vigour.
Soon both pyre and bird become a glowing red-hot
mass. When the glowing charcoal is reduced to ashes
and but one spark remains, then, from the ashes, a
new phoenix arises into life ...
Become a bird of the Way to God and develop your
wings and your feathers. Nay, rather, burn your
wings and your feathers and destroy yourself by fire,
and so will you arrive at the Goal before all others.

FARID AL-DIN'ATTAR

In the great monotheistic faiths, Judaism, Christianity and Islam, the
call to surrender, and sacrifice of self, cannot be separated from the call
to love God, for it is out of the love of God that devotion and submission
to His commands flow, together with the desire to end separation by the
loving sacrifice of independence and all selfwill. Judaism demands from
its followers complete obedience to the word of God, an obedience
which affects human life as a whole in all its aspects. Such obedience is
only possible through and by self-surrender, by a sacrifice in the heart

of man. This is of the very fabric of the Jewish faith, so much so that it is often implied in the texts even where it is not explicitly stated.

The *Shema*,[1] the recital of which goes back to the ritual as practised in the Temple, and which forms part of the daily prayers in both synagogue and home, expresses this call to surrender in a most impressive and authoritative way. The basic tenets of the religion of Israel are here given in a nutshell, the oneness of God, and the command to love Him, and to devote one's whole being to Him. It opens with the holy words known and revered by all Jews:

Hear, O Israel: The Lord our God is one Lord: And thou shalt love the Lord thy God with all thine heart, and with all thy soul, and with all thy might.

It closes with a call to give up self-centredness, and to turn to the Lord, and to keep all His commandments.

In the Jewish view, man's innermost being, his very soul, is God's; it is given by God, it should live in God, and it will return to God. The realization that our hearts, our eyes, our souls, are not our own but are God's, pre-supposes a sacrifice of the ego and its claim to leadership; this is beautifully rendered in the *Adon Olam*, one of the best known of Jewish hymns, the last verse of which reads:

My soul into His hands divine
Do I command: I will not fear
My body with it I resign,
I dread not evil: God is near.

The Jew who can truly say this of himself has followed the call of the *Shema* to 'be holy unto the Lord'. This idea of holiness, so vital to the understanding of Judaism, has a two-fold connotation. First, it denotes the turning away from 'whatever urge of Nature that makes self-gratification and self-serving the essence of human life', and second, it means self-giving which finds expression in the love and service of God, as well as in charity towards all men.[2] Without this there cannot be undertaken the *'Imitatio Dei'*, which, in the Jewish version, is proclaimed in those unforgettable words in Leviticus on which, ultimately, the whole of Jewish ethics and religious laws are based 'Ye shall be holy; for I the Lord your God am Holy' (XIX, 2).

The highest form of self-surrender, as taught in Judaism, is the *Kiddush Hashem*, the sanctification of the name of God. It includes the giving of one's life in the service of God, which may end in martyrdom, and it embraces 'every act of self-denial, self-restraint, and self-sacrifice' undergone as a loving servant of the Lord.³ Judaism teaches that these acts of self-abnegation must be performed in the spirit of humility and total submission to God's will.

Many of the most beautiful passages in the Psalms were inspired by this searching of the soul for the holy life and the living implementation of the sanctification of the name of the Lord (Psalm XXXI). But the Psalms are not the only bearers of this message. In the Old Testament, at its very heart, there is told the story of Abraham and Isaac.

And it came to pass after these things, that God did tempt Abraham, and said unto him, Abraham; and he said, Behold, here I am.
And he said: Take now thy son, thine only son Isaac, whom thou lovest, and get thee into the land of Moriah; and offer him there for a burnt offering, upon one of the mountains which I will tell thee of ...
Genesis, 22, 1–18

This story contains all the characteristics of a true self-sacrifice. What is offered is the one thing beloved, flesh and blood of one's own flesh and blood. It is offered as a total loss, for it is first to be killed, and then burnt. But this very act, done in the wilderness, at the central point of the labyrinth, becomes a channel for God's grace and blessing. New and more abundant life is promised for generations to come, and the very place where the deed of death was to be performed, becomes *Jehova-jireh*, the place where the Lord will provide.

One of the judgments of the Lord is to render selfless service to those in need, to draw out the soul 'to the hungry, and satisfy the afflicted soul': for then obscurity and darkness will be changed into the light of the noon-day.⁴ This is the divine call which is heard on the highest festival of the Jewish Year, the Day of Atonement, the day of repentance and self-dedication. It reminds every Jew what the holy life entails, and it shows him the way towards '*metanoia*', repentance and therewith renewal. The words of the service of the Day of Atonement bear witness to the fact that it is not physical death that is asked of the faithful but a complete change in heart and soul through self-naughting and self-giving:

O my God before I was formed I was nothing worth, and now that I have been formed I am but as though I had not been formed. Dust am I in my life: how much more so in my death. Behold I am before thee like a vessel filled with shame and confusion ... As it is said, Say unto them, As I live, saith the Lord God, I have no pleasure in the

death of the wicked; but that the wicked turn from his way and live:
turn ye, turn ye from your evil ways; for why will ye die, O house of
Israel?

The age-old symbol of this act of dying and renewal is the bath of
total immersion. It was taken over into Jewish mysticism where such
epithets of the Lord as 'the fountain of living waters'[5] was, in
accordance with Talmudic teaching, interpreted as meaning that to
Israel the Lord God is that bath. According to the Chassid Rabbi
Mendel of Kozk it is, however, only effective as a means of renewal, if
one is immersed in it wholly, and not a single hair is showing; for it is
thus that man should be immersed in God. This symbolic act was
practised by the Chassids with great fervour; in their eyes it stood for
the readiness to enter the realm of nothingness, or in the words of Rabbi
Sussja 'the Zaddikim must first throw away their lives, so as to receive a
new spirit'.[6]

In illustration of this, it is related that once the need and distress of
the young Rabbi Jissachar Bär was so great that he gave up all hope. He
felt that he had come to the point of death, and he resolved to go to the
bath once more, before he would be too weak to move. This bath was
sixty to seventy steps deep. He undressed down to his shirt and
descended the flight of steps. Whilst doing so he heard strange noises
from below which grew in strength. A draught coming from the depth
extinguished the light he was carrying. The utter darkness surrounding
him was filled with fearsome and tumultuous voices and he realized that
they belonged to beings intent on barring his progress. In haste he took
off his shirt and jumped into the water. Silence descended, only a
clicking noise was heard as though someone was smacking his fingers in
order to indicate that the game was up. The Rabbi dived time and time
again then finally ascended the steps, dressed himself and went home.
In front of his house stood a wagon laden with sacks of flour and other
food. The driver asked 'Are you Rabbi Jissachar Bär? I have been sent
to deliver these goods, they are yours.'[7]

There is close kinship between the Old Testament and the Koran,
and this in spite of the host of contrasting features which could be, and
indeed have repeatedly been, cited. One of the points of intimate
contact is found in the idea of sacrifice; for not only is the teaching of a
very similar nature but the actual event, related as history, which is
regarded as the living example and prototype of the sacrifice asked of
the faithful, is the common property of both religions. This event is
God's call to Abraham to sacrifice his son, and the father's willing
obedience in submission to God's command. In the Koranic version,

and according to Muslim belief, it was Ishmael, not Isaac, who was the chosen offering.

> And he (Abraham) said: Surely I flee to my Lord—He will guide me.
> My Lord, grant me a doer of good deeds.
> So we gave him the good news of a forbearing son.
> But when he became of (age to) work with him, he said: O my son, I have seen in a dream that I should sacrifice thee: so consider what thou seest. He said: O my father, do as thou art commanded; if Allah please, thou wilt find me patient.
> So when they both submitted and he had thrown him down upon his forehead,
> And We called out to him saying, O Abraham,
> Thou hast indeed fulfilled the vision. Thus do we reward the doers of good.
> Surely this is a manifest trial.
> And We ransomed him with a great sacrifice.
> And we granted him among the later generations (the salutation),
> Peace be to Abraham.
>
> *Sura* 37, 99–109

The Abraham of the Bible was shown a ram caught by his horns in the thornbushes and this, he understood, was God's ransom for his only son. Ishmael of the Koran was also ransomed by Allah with the sacrifice of an animal, a 'cattle quadruped' as it is named in the holy book. This event has grown into the very fibre of Islamic tradition. It is commemorated in the rites attending the holy pilgrimage, and, at the same time, perpetuated in one of the two great religious festivals of Islam, the 'Id' festivals. The second of these is the *Id al-Adzha*, literally meaning the recurring happiness (Id) of the sacrifice (Adzha). On that occasion, if he is in a position to do so, every Muslim throughout the world is asked to sacrifice an animal; in so doing, he is linked in a world embracing bond of sacrifice to his brethren who are at that very moment engaged in the holy pilgrimage, in conclusion of which an animal is slain. As it was Abraham's, so it is every pilgrim's, and with him every Muslim's symbolic act of total submission to their Lord. The god of Abraham and Isaac condemned blood offerings, vain oblations, and incense burning because these sacrificial acts had ceased to stand for a changed heart and soul.[8] Allah, too, rejects mere outward acts of worship, for, concerning sacrifices, it is said,

> Not their flesh, nor their blood, reaches Allah, but to Him is acceptable observance of duty on your part. Thus has He made them

subservient to you, that you may magnify Allah for guiding you aright. And give good news to those who do good (to others).

Sura 22, 37

The animal sacrificed represents, to the faithful, the lower, the animal nature, and furthermore it reminds him that as a 'Muslim', that is, as 'one who submits', he must be willing to offer up his life at the command of his creator and master, just as the sacrificial animal is made to do at the command of his human master. Sacrifice in Islam, therefore, 'signifies the sacrifice of the sacrificer himself, and becomes thus an outward symbol of his readiness to lay down his life, and to sacrifice all his interests and desires in the cause of truth ... And one day, and one particular moment on that day, is chosen so that all Muslim hearts from one end of the world to another may pulsate with one idea at a particular moment, and thus be led to the development of the idea of self-sacrifice in the community as a whole'.[9]

The killing of the flesh, and the silencing of the demands of the animal within, constitute the essential pre-condition of spiritual growth. Islamic texts speak of seven stages of inner evolution which are mainly concerned with the attainment of a higher morality made possible by progressive selflessness. The 'I' identifies itself at the lowest stage with the flesh and advances through sacrifice to identification with the individual, the family, the tribe, the race, the species, to a cosmic awareness of a divine omnipresence which expresses itself in such words as are found in the Koran: 'My prayer and my sacrifice, my life and my death are surely for Allah, the Lord of the worlds.'[10]

The man who can truthfully say this, is he who gives to others of that which he loves and which, therefore, contains part of his own self and he 'is he whose bosom Allah has expanded for the Surrender unto Him' and he is a follower of one who said of himself 'I am the first of those who submit'.[11]

The moth which, enamoured with love for the candle's light, is consumed by the flame, and in so doing becomes itself radiant with light; the phoenix which gathers fuel for its own pyre, and sets it alight with its wings and feathers so as to become one with the glowing flames, only to rise out of the dead ashes to a new life; the nightingale which, intoxicated by the rose, drives a thorn into its heart and thus bleeds to death in love—these are some of the images which the mystics of Islam use to portray that inexpressible experience which they know is the one and only gateway to union with the Beloved. For the way most Sufis choose is that of devotion and love and the stage on which their sincerity

is tested to the utmost and, at the same time, on which all depends, is
the stage of self-annihilation.

> He that would prosper here must from him strip
> The World, and take the Dervish Gown and Scrip:
> And as he goes must gather from all sides
> Irrelevant Ambitions, Lusts and Prides,
> Glory and Gold, and sensual desire,
> Whereof to build the Fundamental Pyre
> Of Self-Annihilation: ...
> Then, all the Pile completed of the Pelf
> Of either World—at last throw on Thyself,
> And with the Torch of Self-negation fire: ...[12]

Some Sufis go as far as equating Sufism as a whole with this 'dying from
self' in all its phases, basing their contention on the famous verse in the
Koran 'Everything is perishing, except His face'. These mystics have
given us passages of intense beauty, describing both the agony and bliss,
the torture of separation, and the exaltation of union which accompany
this station of death and rebirth. All Sufi systems, however much they
may differ otherwise, make mention of the narrow gate of annihilation,
whether it is called poverty (*faqr*), renunciation (*zuhd*), servanthood
(*ubidiya*) or, denoting the highest grade, passing away (*fana*). Such is
the path of love leading to Him who both slays and bestows life, and of
whom a *hadith* says:

> Who seekest Me findeth Me.
> Who findeth Me knoweth Me.
> Who knoweth Me loveth Me.
> Who loveth Me, him I love.
> Whom I love, him I slay.
> Whom I slay, him must I requite.
> Whom I must requite, Myself am his Requital.
>   Attributed to Ali ibn Abi Talib

The pendulum of change swings between opposing views which
follow each other like the mountain and trough of a wave. Thus it is that
within the overall movement, extending from the sacrificial act as a
mainly external affair to its interpretation as an inner act of
renunciation, there can be detected a swinging to and fro from one
extreme position to the other, and this is borne out both by the history
of any one religion and the comparative history of the various faiths.
The framework in which these fluctuations occur is different in every
case so that the observable phenomena vary almost endlessly.

It may be said that interiorization had reached its consummation with early Buddhism; yet it was precisely this fact which gave birth to a great swing back towards exteriorization. The inner sacrifice of the 'I' was matched by the *Bodhisattva* figure, the divine being, who sacrifices himself for the good of mankind. The first, strictly speaking, is imageless or tends towards such an ideal, for images, so it is argued, feed the senses, and so ultimately the ego, and are therefore a hindrance. In the second, images abound, the process of giving up selfhood becomes a dramatic sequence of events in the world at large, for all to see and for all to partake. What happened within Buddhism, and what could equally well be shown for Hinduism, also happened regarding the great monotheistic faiths. Seen in the context of historical development, Christianity stands between the two great imageless religions, Judaism and Islam. The timeless myth and its attending imagery of the dying and resurrected god, the divine being, plays no part in their official teachings; it cannot do so, if only for the obvious reason that their God is wholly transcendent and wholly invisible, and for man to attempt even forming a tentative image of Him carries the stigma of idolatry. This transcendent Lord, Jehova, Allah, demands of man the sacrifice of his very being in the same way as He demanded it from Abraham, whose act of self-negation becomes the great symbol of sacrifice in both religions. God Himself is not directly involved in this sacrifice. The age-old ritual of animal sacrifice which, as the story of Abraham seems to suggest, had taken the place of human sacrifices, is interiorized and, although still performed as in the case of Islam, now stands for the inner 'sacrifice of the sacrificer'.

Between these two faiths, closely related in this particular aspect, stands Christianity at the opposite end of the pendulum's swing. It is as though the commandment 'Thou shalt not make unto thee any graven image, or any likeness of anything that is in heaven above, or that is in the earth beneath, or that is in the water under the earth',[13] after it had been revered for centuries, had produced out of itself its exact opposite. The soul of man yearned to prostrate itself once more before the living image and visible proof of God's participation in, and identification with, the world. Such participation and identification, always and everywhere, involve a divine sacrifice and appear as such in mythological and religious lore. The area where the cradle of Christianity stood, the Mediterranean Basin, had also been the cradle for one particular type of the myth of the dying and resurrected god of which we have here mentioned two outstanding versions, that of Osiris and of Attis.

Parched soil soaks in the water from on high and out of it springs new life. This myth, pregnant with meaning, was absorbed, probably mainly in its Greek version, by the fertile soil of Jewish tradition and, in its Christian rendition, once again erected the image, for all to see, of the cosmic tree at the centre of the world on which hangs the dying god, offered himself to himself, who, through his sacrifice, brings salvation to mankind. Christianity teaches that, at this point, myth became history and that, with this, not only mankind but the world, entered into a new phase. It may well be that with this, too, a circle was completed for, in the dim past, it seems likely that certain historical events became myth. This study is not concerned with the investigation into the origin of myths. It is important, however, to note this relationship between history and myth.

It appears that between external happenings and certain basic contents of the human psyche, whether inborn or acquired, an intimate interchange takes place, one engendering the other; this can happen in the outward direction, when these contents project themselves on to outer events and, in a sense, create them and inbue them with meaning, or in the reverse direction, when the psyche reacts to outer events, and an enlargement of consciousness takes place. The first process is intimately connected with 'myth-making', history becomes myth, the second with 'demythologizing', in the sense of a realization of the inner meaning of the myth, and its translation into life, myth becomes history.

Both these processes must have been operative at the birth of Christianity and this can perhaps nowhere more clearly be demonstrated than in the way the idea of the divine and human sacrifice was 'christianized'.

The mere fact that the primordial symbol of the sacrifice of the god was once again made to occupy the very centre of a religious cult, coupled with that intense upsurge of image-making and image-worship, which accompanies the birth and all subsequent development of Christianity, points to a re-activization of the outward directed process of the human psyche which projects dynamic inner contents, too long deprived of the external language of symbol and image, and identifies them with outer events. The myth was created anew in all its potent powers.

At the same time, however, Christianity stands and falls with the contention that this very myth of the dying God in Christ became dramatic reality. Earthbound human life becomes the stage for the great sacrifice and man's everyday activities its proving ground. The myth is seemingly dissolved by becoming identified with the suffering and sin of humankind, thus opening a way towards redemption. This process appears to be a vital pre-condition for revitalizing the myth, both in the sense of keeping it alive and transforming it into life. The myth, too, must die in order to be reborn on a new level of significance.

To the followers of Christ, this transformation of the timeless myth into transient life opens the way towards the *Imitatio Christi*, for the words of the epistle, read on Holy Saturday, apply to everyone 'You have undergone death, and your life is hid away now with Christ in God'.[14] This is the new life entered through sacrificial death, an event that perpetuates itself for ever in the ritual of the Church. It is re-enacted in every Eucharist celebrated, and its annual re-enactment relives, with intense participation, the stages of this, both cosmic and inner-spiritual drama, which is one of darkness and light, of night and the rise of the new sun in all his splendour. It is not the gentle night of Christmas, when the infant spark takes birth, but the dramatic night of Easter of which we read:

> This is the night of which it was written: And the night shall be enlightened as the day: And the night is my light in my enjoyments ... the night in which the things of heaven are joined to those of earth, the things of God to those of man.
>
> Roman Missal, Holy Saturday

The *sine qua non* of the *Imitatio Christi*, therefore, is self-naughting, for in this act is found the point of contact with Calvary, which is the spiral gate of death on which is mounted the Cross of Christ. Only 'nought' can pass through it, for, as Eckhart has said, to become one with the divine unity 'one must be dead—quite dead—no longer himself—beyond comparison because unlike anyone else—and then he is like God'.[15]

In a letter to a Religious, J. P. de Caussade, the great teacher of the spiritual life, speaks of the best preparation for Holy Communion:

> Approach then, with confidence, with complete abandonment to the state of poverty and deprivation in which it has pleased God to place you. Remain in it as though sacrificed, annihilated and unseen like Jesus Christ in His Sacrament, because He is there in a kind of annihilation. Unite yours to His. Where there is nothing left that is created, or human, there is God.[16]

As we have seen in the case of other religions, all-out endeavours to eradicate all sense of a separate selfhood often engender a tendency to reject and even hate everything that is normally associated with life in its fullness. Such an attitude can claim scriptural support from such passages as John 12, 25:

> He that loveth his life shall lose it; and he that hateth his life in this world shall keep it unto life eternal.

Moreover, the history of Christianity shows that here, too, this type of self-denial tends to become identified with the purely negative aspects of life which are then deliberately sought and even courted. To take upon oneself the trials and tribulations of human existence is seen as the highest means to attain to the desired goal, the sacrifice of the self.

St Thomas à Kempis is following this line of thought when he says:

> If I abase myself, and reduce myself to nothing: and shrink from all self-esteem, and grind myself to the dust that I am: thy grace will be propitious to me and Thy light near unto my heart.
>
> *Imitation of Christ*, Bk. IV, Ch. VIII

In the same vein, St John of the Cross even identifies the choice of the repugnant and disagreeable with our love of God; this, to him, is 'the sum and root of all virtue'.

Here again the opposites meet; hate of the world means love of God and to be persecuted, holds the promise of attainment. Just as, in the words of St Paul, Baptism means participation in the death of Christ, and Crucifixion holds the promise of newness of life. This, however, only holds true for him who does not stop at the gate of self-naughting but passes through it; only then is the Old Adam transformed into the New Man and there are surely no words more apt to be written over this gateway than those coming from the author of the *Imitation of Christ*:

> In dying is all; and there is no other way to life and true inward peace.
>
> Bk. II, 12, i

NOTES FOR CHAPTER 9

1. Deut. 6, 4–9; 11, 13–21; Numbers 15, 37–41.
2. Holiness, Hebrew: *Kadosh*, 'expresses a quality consisting negatively in "separation from" and positively in "dedication to".' Applied to the charge laid upon Israel, holiness entails negatively a separation from all that is opposed to the will of God, and positively a dedication to His service. (I. Epstein: *Judaism*, pp. 15 and 23.)

3. I. Epstein, *Judaism*, p. 33ff.
4. Isaiah, 58, 10.
5. Jeremiah, 17, 13.
6. M. Buber, *Erzählungen der Chassidim*, p. 784, and *Chassidische Botschaft*, p. 111.
7. M. Buber, *Erzählungen* ... p. 682.
8. Isaiah, 1, 10–11.
9. Muhammad 'Ali, *The Religion of Islam*, p. 444.
10. Sura 6, 163.
11. See also Sura 3, 91.
12. Farīd Al-Din'Attār, in M. Smith, *The Sufi Path of Love*, p. 93.
13. Ex. 20, 4.
14. Col. 3, 3.
15. Sermon 21. R. B. Blakney, pp. 195–6.
16. Letter to Mme de Lesen, in Sir J. Marchant, *The Way to God*, p. 133.

III

TRANSFORMATION

The Cave of the Heart

For you there is an advent of the soul towards the Divine Light, therefore shall your heart and soul in the end attain to union with that Light. With your whole heart and soul, seek to regain Reality, nay, seek for Reality within your own heart, for Reality, in truth, is hidden within you. The heart is the dwelling-place of that which is the Essence of the universe, within the heart and soul is the very Essence of God. Like the saints, make a journey into your self; like the lovers of God, cast one glance within you. As a lover, now, in contemplation of the Beloved, be unveiled within and behold the Essence. Form is a veil to you and your heart is a veil. When the veil vanishes, you will become all light.

FARID AL-DIN'ATTAR

Whither need I go to seek holiness?
I am happy here within myself at home.
My heart is no longer a pilgrim:
It has become tied down to itself.

Restlessly one day I did want to go:
I prepared sandal-wood paste,
Distilled aloe wood, and many perfumes:
I set out towards a temple to worship:
Then my Guru showed me God in my own heart.

Sikh Scriptures: V. RAMANAND

When it is said that at the nucleus of the spiral way resurrection and new birth follow crucifixion and death, it is another way of saying that here lies the point of passage from one order of existence to another. Those who go through that experience are the twice-born, for they have a second time crossed the portal of death and found entrance into another mode of existence. They are like little children in a world in which they have to orientate themselves afresh. It is a world of new dimensions, of new laws and new values. The limited field of ego-consciousness is taken up, as it were, into an enlarged sphere of awareness, whose pivotal point is no longer the ego, but a new centre which appears as the fount of all life and power. The moment of discovery of this new centre is one of humility in which the 'I', surrendering its superior position, bows down and says 'not I but Thou'; it is also one of awe for the new order of being revealed, carries the seal of numinosity and an all-inclusive unity. What is left behind is the one-level existence of an ego-centred life; what lies in front is a world of infinite dimensions, revolving around the new centre like the planets around the sun. Only the image of scale can express what is experienced. It is for this reason that the sacred texts here favour such metaphors as 'higher' and 'deeper' in order to convey the fact that the new source of life is as much above normal ego-consciousness as it is deep down and out of its reach.

Such expressions are symbolical and indeed they cannot be anything else, for, as the mystery of the second birth unfolds, the labyrinthine path is lost to view; the senses unaided cannot trace it any longer and their language cannot reach it. Symbols take the place of factual descriptions and the images and metaphors employed are as many-levelled in their meaning as is the world they depict. They are like complicated locks which will only yield to the key of actual experience, each turn of the key revealing new vistas and dimensions. This must be borne in mind, for a one-level interpretation will not only ignore the hidden wealth of meaning but, if upheld as exclusive of all others, distort and even falsify the truth conveyed by the symbol.

The field of action of the new centre is all-inclusive. It addresses itself to the whole of man's being, body, soul and spirit, as also to the world, in all its ramifications. Its place is both the within and the without and this is the great mystery which can only be unveiled in and through immediate realization. The depth and wealth of meaning pertaining to the whole complex symbolism of the new centre will become apparent in what follows, but so will the fact that, again and again through the ages, this manifoldness has been lost sight of, and interpretations offered which refer to one grade of significance only. Sometimes it is the bodily, sometimes the emotional, sometimes the spiritual level which is singled out for attention; at other times, again, concrete and abstract explanations cancel each other out, or the whole symbolic imagery is regarded as pure fantasy, poetic licence, or mystical reverie, and is thus denied any real substance.

There is yet another, even greater, difficulty. The experience of the new centre is nothing static; on the contrary, it is charged with a dynamic force which seeks expression in and through man in an ever changing form. Moreover, it is evolutionary in character, giving rise to a development which renews man as much as it transforms him. This

Jacket illustration. THE SHEPHERD'S LABYRINTH. Boughton
Green.

1. Butinone: CHRIST DISPUTING WITH THE DOCTORS. (See note 55, p. 31.) (Reproduced by kind permission of the National Gallery of Scotland.)

2. THE CHILD KRISHNA DANCING ON THE SNAKE.
(See note 13, p. 193.)

From the *Larousse Encyclopedia of Mythology*.
(Reproduced by kind permission of Paul Hamlyn Ltd.)

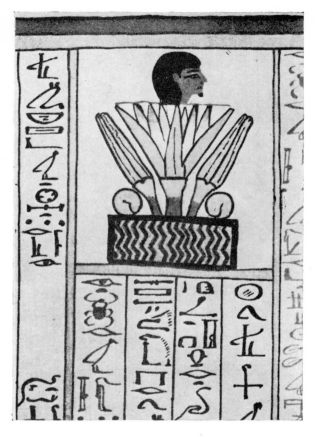

3. THE SOUL RISING FROM THE PRIMEVAL LOTUS (p. 177).
(Papyrus of Ani, British Museum.)

From R. T. Rundle-Clark, *Myth and Symbol in Ancient
Egypt.*
(Reproduced by kind permission of Thames and Hudson Ltd.)

4. AVALOKITA'S MANDALA. Tibetan Thang-ka (p. 176).
(Reproduced by kind permission of Berkeley Galleries Ltd., London.)

5. Graham Sutherland: THE CHALICE.

Detail from the Great Tapestry in Coventry Cathedral (p. 189).

(Reproduced by kind permission of the Coventry Cathedral Council from a Pallas Gallery postcard.)

6. SHAKA-NYORAI AND THE UNIVERSE-TREE—The Treasure of Yüten-ji, Diamond Mountain, Korea (p. 189).

From E. A. Gordon, *Symbols of the Way*—Far East and West.

(Reproduced by kind permission of Maruzen & Co. Ltd., Tokyo.)

dynamism, too, as will become apparent, expresses itself in images and symbols spontaneously produced and all paying witness to the unfathomable nature of the 'pilgrim's progress'.

When we speak of a change of heart, we mean that the whole attitude of a man has undergone a complete transformation. Language here expresses a deep wisdom, for it appears that from the remotest past to this day, the image of a new heart has been synonymous with the new and transformed life.[1] Indeed, the heart turns out to be one of those universal symbols which, in many variations, is the common property of all the great religious traditions, always standing for that place of contact with the More which we have here named the new centre. Because of its double nature of both human and divine, it is at once the secret and invisible core in man and the dwelling place of the god.

Thus of old, the Egyptian initiates, after having passed the last gateways to illumination, are 'received into the Sacred Heart of Rā'. This was the consummation of their quest which, however, could only be reached after many tests and trials of which the most vital was the weighing of the human heart against the feather of truth (*Maāt*).[2] When 'it hath been found true by trial in the Great Balance' it becomes the most precious possession of man and when he realizes this he proclaims:

> My heart is with me and it shall never come to pass that it will be carried away. I am the lord of hearts, the slayer of the heart, I live in right and truth (*Maāt*) and I have my being therein. I am Horus, the dweller in hearts, who is within the dweller of the body.[3]

The dynamic pattern underlying these practices and utterances, belonging to the dawn of recorded history, proves to be symptomatic for all subsequent development. Its main features have a timeless validity, for whatever the tradition, there will be found the knowledge of the manifold development leading from the purification of the heart to the discovery of the heart as the seat of divine influx and from there to the realization of the oneness of heart with Heart.[4] And thus it is that to be received into the Sacred Heart of Rā, the summit of Egyptian religious endeavours, for the Tibetan Buddhist is to be received into the heart of Vairochana, and for the Christian to be received into the Sacred Heart of Jesus, as we read in an ancient devotion, where the advice is given:

> ... frequently offer, give up, and cast your heart and soul into the most sweet Heart of our Lord Jesus Christ, your Creator, your Redeemer, your crucified Friend—into His Heart so full of love;

into His Heart the abode of the most Holy Trinity; into His Heart where 'dwelleth all the fulness of the Godhead corporally'; into His Heart, through which 'we have access both in one Spirit to the Father'; into His Heart, finally, which, in Its Infinite love, contains and embraces all the elect in Heaven and on earth.[5]

The Egyptian like the Christian, Indian or Chinese devotee seeks the 'heavenly heart' within himself. According to Upanishadic teaching, it is a hidden place which he must enter so as to make it his permanent abode.

Enter the lotus of the heart and meditate there on the presence of Brahman

so the *Kaivalya Upanishad* instructs him, and in the same vein the *Mundaka Upanishad* says,

Within the lotus of the heart He dwells, where the nerves meet like the spokes of a wheel. Meditate on Him as OM and you may easily cross the ocean of darkness. In the effulgent lotus of the heart dwells Brahman, passionless and indivisible. He is pure, he is the light of lights. The knowers of Brahman attain to him.

The secret dwelling place of the divine within has fired man's imagination and the imagery clustering around it is rich beyond words. It is the house or city of Brahman (*Brahmapura*), and it is the golden sheath of the Buddhi in which Brahma is encased; it is also the city of jade[6] in whose purple middle dwells the god of utmost emptiness and life, as it is described in a Taoist text, where we read:

The Confucians call it the centre of emptiness; the Buddhist the terrace of life, the Taoist the ancestral land, or the yellow castle, or the dark pass, or the space of former Heaven. The Heavenly Heart is like a dwelling place, the Light is the Master.[7]

To this array of epithets we may add others of Judo-Christian and Islamic origin which are equally colourful. Thus the image of the heavenly heart was also used by Jewish mysticism. It is said, for instance, that Rabbi Chanoch interpreted the passage in Deuteronomy (IV, 11) 'and the mountain burned with fire unto the midst of heaven' as follows:

The fire of Sinai burned its way into man until it created in him a heavenly heart.[8]

The Rabbi was one of the Zaddiks in whose eyes the heavenly heart was the shrine where the divine spark was hidden, waiting to be released and to be reunited to its maker.

The Christian mystics speak of the temple or tabernacle of God, thus St. Augustine, quoting the scriptures:

> Do thou all within. And if perchance thou seekest some high place, some holy place, make thee a temple for God within. For the temple of God is holy; which you are.[9]

St. Theresa's interior castle is composed of many rooms in the same way as in our Father's house in heaven there are many mansions which the seeking soul traverses in search of the sacred centre; for this realm within is none other than the Kingdom of Heaven, or the 'field' of the New Testament where the great treasure lies hidden. To the Sufis, also known as 'men of the heart', it is the mystic shrine, the temple or the *Ka'ba* of the heart of which Ansari says,

> On the path of God
> Two places of worship mark the stages.
> The material temple,
> And the temple of the heart,
> Make your best endeavour
> To worship at the temple at the heart.[10]

In the imagery of Omar Khayyām, the Persian Astronomer-Poet, the house of God is the tavern from whence a voice can be heard calling the faithful to worship at the inner shrine:

> Before the phantom of False morning died,
> Methought a Voice within the Tavern cried:
> 'When all the Temple is prepared within,
> Why nods the drowsy Worshipper outside?'[11]

The temple, the tavern, the castle or the house of God, then, is built like the human body with a hidden yet life-giving core at its centre. This is encased and protected by many layers:

> like the kernel of the palmito, from which seven rinds must be removed before coming to the eatable part.[12]

Essentially the same image is given in the *Chandogya Upanishad*, where it is said:

> Now, here in this city of Brahman is an abode, a small lotus flower; within it is a small space, what is within that, assuredly is what one should desire to understand. (VIII, 1, 1.)

This is the 'inner court inhabited by the king,' it is where the sacred stone of the Ka'ba of the heart is located, it is the centre in the midst of conditions as the Buddhists call it, and it is the secret chamber, the closet in the heart, or, in the lyrical poetry of St John of the Cross, it is the inner cellar, of which he sings,

> Let us enter into the heart of the thicket.
> We shall go at once
> To the deep caverns of the rock
> Which are all secret,
> There we shall enter in
> And taste of the new wine of the pomegranate.
> There Thou wilt show me
> That which my soul desired;
> And there Thou wilt give at once,
> O Thou, my life!
> That which Thou gavest me the other day.
>
>   Spiritual Canticle[13]

The hidden domain of the giver of new life is manifold as are the phases of purification, non-attachment and sacrifice leading to it. Apart from the metaphors shown above, this manifoldness finds expression in such images as the many veils with which the face of truth is covered, the various layers of skin which enclose the heart,[14] and the fields and the woods that surround the centre of the thicket or garden of the soul. These, undoubtedly, refer to stations on the journey to the hidden depths within which the seers and mystics of all lands have mapped out for all to follow.

What happens in the heart of hearts is, in Christian imagery, the spiritual betrothal and marriage of the soul to her divine lover, for it is in the most inward part of man's being that the union of the soul with God takes place.[15] There the divine presence is found, and there the yearning soul gives herself in love to the bridegroom. It appears that here three distinct phases are experienced. First the phase of the betrothal when, in the words of St John of the Cross, 'the soul has it now in its power to abandon itself whenever it wills to this sweet sleep of love.'[16] Then the spiritual marriage of union, which in itself is twofold, for in it the soul is born in God, and God is born in the soul. Both St John of the Cross and St Theresa know of this distinction, as do many other Christian, as well as non-Christian mystics. St Theresa shows that the first event takes place in the prayer of union when the soul, having renounced everything, even all striving, except towards total submission to God's will, dies and finds itself reborn more fully in God. By this death and rebirth, the soul is made ready for the consummate act of grace when God is born in the soul. To Eckhart this divine birth in man is the goal and the hidden meaning of all creation. A passionate conviction pulsates in his words:

If one asketh me 'wherefore do we pray, wherefore fast, wherefore do we perform all manner of good works, wherefore are we baptized, wherefore did God become Man?', I would answer 'For that God might be born in the soul and the soul again in God. Therefore is the Holy Script written. Therefore hath God created the whole world, that God might be born in the soul and the soul again in God. The innermost nature of all corn meaneth wheat, and of all metal, gold, and of all birth, man!'[17]

Eckhart sees the soul as the Kingdom of God where the pearl beyond price lies buried which is none other than the divine birth in man. The finding of it is a higher attainment than the life of the soul in God, for not until God is born in the soul can the soul become an image of God. Only then is discovered that spiritual principle within which is 'untouched by time and flesh!'

In this principle is God ever verdant, ever flowering in all the joy and glory of his actual Self. Sometimes I have called this principle the Tabernacle of the soul, sometimes a spiritual Light, anon I say it is a Spark. But now I say that it is more exalted over this and that, than the heavens are exalted above the earth.[18]

The experience which expresses itself in such images is above colour and creed. Wherever men have found their way through love to the inner sanctuary, there the symbol of the spiritual marriage appears. To Ibn al-Fārid, the great Sufi poet, the secret flame of love burns in the 'privy bridal chamber' of the heart, and Hāfiz, the Persian mystic, describes this inner rapture in essentially similar terms as does St John of the Cross:

My heart is the secret place where His love abides: my eyes hold the
mirror to His Face. I, who have not bowed my head to either world,
now bend my neck beneath the burden of His many favours ...
May my eyes never be without the Vision of Him, for this secret
place is the spot where He chooses to dwell apart with me ...
Look not at the outward poverty of Hafiz, for his inner self is the
treasure-house of the Divine love.[19]

What is referred to here is, in Sufi terminology, the vision of the heart
(*ru'yat al-qalb*) and, again, this vision has its gradations which equal
those of Eckhart's. Al-Hujwiri distinguishes between two divine
manifestations in the heart. One is of God's Majesty, the other of God's
Beauty. He says,

There is a difference between the heart which, from the sight of His
Majesty, is consumed in the fire of love, and that heart which, from
the sight of His Beauty, is irradiated by the light of contemplation ...
God, by the revelation of His Majesty, causes the carnal souls of His
lovers to pass away, and by the revelation of His Beauty gives
immortality to their hearts.[20]

The first is what Eckhart calls the soul being born in God, the
second, God being born in the soul, and this alone is the consummation
and the blessed state, or, in the words of Al-Hujwiri, this alone fills the
heart with pure joy.
Such is the twofold attainment standing at the apex of the quest of
love, what in Hindu teaching is called Bhakti Yoga, and where indeed is
found the classical formula,

He whose self is harmonized by yoga seeth the Self abiding in all
beings and all beings in the Self; everywhere he sees the same.

                                        Bhagavadgita VI, 29

The gravitational point towards which a system is orientated and
around which it rotates, in this case the new centre within, the heart of
man's integrated being, is of no dimension, it is quantitatively non-
existent and yet it supports and maintains the whole.
It can be likened to

thirty spokes in one nave, and because of the part where nothing
exists we have the use of a carriage wheel.[21]

At the circumference there is motion and it is, indeed, here that the purpose of the wheel is revealed; for the source of the motion, however, we must look to the motionless centre from which the spokes radiate and in which they are united.

In Buddhist teaching there exists a still centre in the depth of the being which is in contrast to the perpetual agitation and restlessness of the surface mind. It is 'one's own inwardness', void because materially non-existent, yet it is the seat (*citta*) of *bodhi* or *panna*, that element of truth innate in man the realization of which is the aim and purpose of the Eightfold Path. The attributes of this element enumerated in Mahayana texts, are closely reminiscent of those given in relation to the *Atman* in the *Upanishads* or the divine indwelling in the monotheistic faiths.

> Just as space, essentially indiscriminate, reaches everywhere, just so the immaculate Element which in its essential nature is Thought, is present in all. It pervades as a general mark, the vicious, the virtuous and the perfect; just as ether is in all visible forms, be they base, intermediate or superior.[22]

The immaculate element is *Buddhata* or *Dharmata*, the essence of Buddhahood within, the ultimate point where man and Buddha are not two but one and which the Zen master Takakusu, in a well-known poem, like innumerable seers before and after him, calls the heart,

> To trust in the Heart is the Not-Two, the Not-Two is to trust in the Heart.
> I have spoken but in vain; for what can words tell
> Of things that have no yesterday, tomorrow or today?[23]

Here 'the heart' means our fundamental Buddha-nature, as it means the Brahman-nature in Hinduism, the Christ-nature in Christianity, the holy soul (*Neshamah*) in Jewish mysticism and the indwelling spirit of Muhammad in Sufism. Everywhere this point of contact and unification of the two worlds is seen as the smallest of the small, and the greatest of the great,[24] as invisible and yet manifesting itself everywhere, as in man yet utterly transcending him. Some have likened it to the apex of an inverted triangle, touching the human heart, whose base, however, embraces the cosmos.

The discovery of this truth is the most precious heritage of mankind. It is essentially independent of tradition and belief, for it appears to be innate in the human psyche and wherever higher religion has spoken and whatever the imagery used, the experience is basically the same throughout. Always it is based on the fact that the barriers of separation vanish at that point, or, in the words of St Paul, 'the middlewall of partition has broken down and what was two has become one'.[25] For in the place of the Heart man can recognize himself in the universe as much as he can find the whole universe within. Thus when the question is asked: 'What then is that which dwells within this little house, this lotus of the heart? What is it that must be sought after, inquired about, and realized?', the answer is: 'Even so large as the universe outside is the universe within the lotus of the heart. Within it are heaven and earth, the sun and the moon, the lightning and all the stars. Whatever is in the macrocosm is in the microcosm also. All things that exist, all beings and all desires, are in the city of *Brahman*.'[26]

To him who has attained to this realization the words of the Lord's Prayer, 'Thy Kingdom come on earth as it is in heaven', have become reality. This unity of the two kingdoms, or in language of the Koran, the meeting of the two seas, was seen and experienced by such men as St John the Divine[27] or the Sufi poet 'Attār who, in rapture, calls out:

The heart is the dwelling place of that which is the Essence of the universe, within the heart and soul is the very Essence of God ... Tear aside the veils of all you see in this world and you will find yourself apart in solitude with God. If you draw aside the veils of the stars and the spheres, you will see that all is one with the Essence of your own pure soul.[28]

One is inclined to dismiss such imagery, as we have encountered here, as 'merely symbolical'. If that were so, it would mean that by using the heart as a picture of the new-found centre within all one wishes to indicate is that, just as the organ of the heart is the life-source of the body, so the new centre is the giver of new life to the soul. This is undoubtedly one of the meanings of the heart symbolism, but is it the only one? The answer of the scriptures is emphatically in the negative; whatever tradition we turn to there is preserved, often only vaguely or in a garbled form, the knowledge of an altogether different meaning.

There is a tendency today towards emphasis on literal exegesis of the scriptures, towards attempting to understand the concepts presented at their face value, to interpret them exoterically and not esoterically. When it is said in the Bible that the sun stood still, could it not be that, through some cosmic constellation, this is just what happened? An investigation of this type can be of immense value, so long as it is regarded as a gateway to new levels of meaning hitherto neglected, and not as a proof of the validity of one theory to the exclusion of all others. Could it be, then, that by speaking of the heart as the seat of the indwelling deity, in some way, the bodily heart is referred to or some point related to it?

Bhagavan Sri Ramana Maharshi, the Hindu sage of recent times, instructed his devotees to meditate by pinpointing the attention on the heart and, at the same time, asking the question 'who am I?' By 'heart' he meant not, indeed, the physical organ but, what he called the spiritual heart on the right side of the chest. In accordance with what has been said above, he taught that there is located the 'place of Union'—where self and Self meet.[29] To this he attached the greatest importance and the following question and answer is reported:

Devotee: Sri Bhagavan has specified a particular place for the Heart within the physical body, that is in the chest, two digits to the right from the median.

Bhagavan: Yes, that is the Centre of spiritual experience according to the testimony of the sages. This Spiritual-Heart-Centre is quite different from the blood-propelling, muscular organ known by the same name. The Spiritual-Heart-Centre is not an organ of the body. All that you can say of the Heart is that it is the very core of your being, that with which you are really identical (as the word (i.e. *hridaya*) in Sanskrit literally means) whether you are awake, asleep or dreaming, whether you are engaged in work or immersed in *samadhi*.[30]

This teaching of the bodily location of the 'heavenly heart' can be traced in all great traditions and it has come down to us mainly in two ways. First in allusions contained in the sacred scriptures, and secondly in a much more elaborate form, in instructions of spiritual disciplines and practices as well as in description of actual experiences, showing what happens when theory is put into practice.

The *Upanishads*, as quoted, speak of the lotus of the heart; this, according to Vedantic teaching, is eight petalled and, as the vital centre in man, corresponds to the smallest ventrical of the heart (*hridaya*). The finding of this vital point within the body through yoga discipline is the goal of all striving.

Realizing through self-contemplation that primal God, difficult to be seen, deeply hidden, set in the cave (of the heart), dwelling in the deep, the wise man leaves behind both joy and sorrow.

Katha Upanishad, I, 2, 12

We are told that this centre must not be confused with the *chakra* of the heart of Tantrism (*anahata chakra*), which is one of the six chief nodal points of the subtle forces residing in, and pulsating through, the body. The *hridaya* centre is in addition to the *anahata chakra*, although this fact is only stressed in certain schools of Yoga, whereas others only speak of one heart centre. Patanjali, the author of the classic text on Yoga, the Yoga-Sutras, refers to this lotus as the Inner Light on which concentration should be fixed, or, again, he recommends meditation on the heart of an illumined soul with the object of making it fuse with one's own centre.

One of the early commentators elaborates on this.[31] He locates it between abdomen and the thorax, and says that its petals point downward and that it is the task of the spiritual discipline to make the lotus point upward, open towards the throat and the head.[32] As will become apparent later, this is significant, for it foreshadows an intrinsic movement directed upwards. The same is implied by the teaching that it is here in this centre where the *susumma*, the main nerve channel (the *nadi* of *Brahman*), takes its origin, which rises from there to the crown of the head.[33]

The instructions concerning this particular type of meditation are clear and precise:

> Retire into solitude, seat yourself on a clean spot in an erect posture, with the head and neck in a straight line. Control all sense organs, bow down in devotion to your teacher. Then enter the lotus of the heart and meditate there in the presence of Brahman—the pure, the infinite, the blissful.[34]

Other methods are to visualize one's guru, or the chosen deity, or again the sacred syllable OM, as placed in the middle of the lotus of the heart. Such a meditation, often combined with the repetition of some holy word, will, in time, effect the desired union with *Brahman*.

Shorn of its typically Indian apparel, the basic pattern behind this practice applies universally. The precise knowledge, however, of its bodily associations is often lost or so heavily overlaid as to be almost unrecognizable. Yet this teaching has survived and it appears, often in a new garb, in different parts of the world, and is always advocated passionately by its practitioners as the one sure road to liberation. It is not the place here to trace its entire history or put on record all its many versions. Only a few outstanding examples of its application can be mentioned.

When Taoist scriptures refer to the inner heart they use the term *ming* 'Gate of Heaven' or *hsin* 'heart'.[35] The ideograph of the latter appears to depict a bodily organ, probably the heart, and it has been said that 'when a Chinese speaks of the *hsin* he will often point to the centre of his chest, slightly lower than the heart'.[36]

According to both Taoist and Zen teaching it is highly desirable to be able to enter this central domain in contemplation and thus make possible the discovery of 'the deepest seat of consciousness'. This is the practice of *dyana* which the Master Szu-hsin Wu-hsin refers to when he says,

> Retire within your innermost being and see into the reason of it. As your self-reflection grows deeper and deeper, the moment will surely come upon you when the spiritual flower will suddenly burst into bloom, illuminating the entire universe.[37]

The spiritual flower, in Taoist teaching, is the Golden Flower whose germ lies hidden in 'the creative point' within. The method of reaching it, is that of 'fixation contemplation' taken over and adapted from the Buddhist *T'ien T'ai* school. The underlying idea is to steady and still the heart and hold it 'to the centre in the midst of conditions', through rhythmical breathing. Thus the heart as the centre of the ego dies and becomes the birthplace of the divine light.[38]

> When a man let his heart die, then the primordial spirit wakes to life. To kill the heart does not mean to let it dry and wither away, but it means it is undivided and gathered into one. Buddha said: When you fix your heart on one point, then nothing is impossible for you.[39]

The main feature of this whole imagery, the deity, the holy syllable, the lotus imagined residing in the heart, the gathering together of one's whole attention on that bodily point, and the influx of a new force, all these belong to the common vocabulary of the practising devotee. Thus it must not surprise us that we read the following in a detailed description of the various phases of meditation written by a Jewish mystic of the thirteenth century, who, as an aid to deep meditation, uses the 'science of the combination of letters', a Kabbalistic device.

> Be prepared for thy God, oh Israelite! Make thyself ready to direct thy heart to God alone. Cleanse thy body and choose a lonely house where none shall hear thy voice. Sit there in thy closet and do not reveal thy secret to any man ... Cover thyself with thy prayer-shawl and put *Tefillim*[40] on thy head and hands that thou mayest be filled

with awe of the *Shekhinah* which is near thee. Cleanse thy clothes, and, if possible, let all thy garments be white, for all this is helpful in leading the heart towards the fear of God and the love of God. If it be night kindle many lights, until all be bright. Then take ink, pen and a table to thy hand and remember that thou art about to serve God in joy of the gladness of heart. Now begin to combine a few or many letters, to permute and to combine until thy heart be warm. Then be mindful of their movement and of what thou canst bring forth by moving them. And when thou feelest that thy heart is already warm and when thou seest that by combination of letters thou canst grasp new things which by human tradition or by thyself thou wouldst not be able to know and when thou art thus prepared to receive the influx of divine power which flows into thee, then turn all thy true thought to imagine the Name and His exalted angels in thy heart as if they were human beings sitting or standing about thee ... Having imagined this very vividly, turn thy whole mind to understand with thy thoughts the many things which will come into thy heart through the letters imagined.... And be thou ready at this moment consciously to choose death, and then thou shalt know that thou hast come far enough to receive the influx.[41]

The teaching of the *Kabbalah* has here come to life, for in a commentary on Psalm 51, 10, it is said:

Know thou that the heart is the source of life, and is placed in the centre of the body as the Holy of holies, and as stated in the Book Zohar, is the central part of the world ...[42]

One more instance of this practice will be given, taken, yet again, from an altogether different background. It is the Prayer of the Heart, known and practised since early times in the Eastern Church, and still in use today. It constitutes the essence of the teachings found in the *Philokalia*, that collection of texts by fathers of the early Church, dating from the fourth to the fourteenth century. What is the Prayer of the Heart or the Prayer of Jesus, as it is traditionally called?

Outwardly, it is a discipline, a way which uses as its sole tool never ceasing repetition. This is done in two alternative ways: 'with the lips' or 'with and in the mind'. Both have to be practised, for if the one cannot be maintained, the other has to take over. This, in the words of the fathers, is the art of arts and the science of sciences, leading to the highest goal open to man. Here, too, there are certain stages of development. The texts speak of the search within, the need for constant attention, and watchfulness, and of the resulting possibility of uniting oneself with the unceasingly repeated prayer and 'together with the prayer, to descend into the heart and to remain there'.

The instructions of St Gregory of Sinai to his monks, regarding the preliminary discipline of searching within, speak of the need to remain in solitary prayer according to St Paul's precept 'Persevere in prayer, with mind awake and thankful heart' (Col. 4, 2), to concentrate on the heart and from there to send out the 'mental cry to our Lord Jesus, calling for his help and saying: "Lord Jesus Christ, have mercy upon me".'

Whilst doing so, attention and watchfulness are of the highest importance. The mind must be held in the heart uninterruptedly and faint-heartedness and laziness fought, for 'this attainment demands severe labour and spiritual struggle'. In the end, the mind will be given 'to taste the Lord' within the heart, then it will say the words of the apostle Peter: 'It is good for us to be here' (Matt. XVII, 4) and will always look inwardly into the depth of the heart and will remain revolving there, repulsing all thoughts sown by the devil. Out of this 'unceasing silence of the heart' arises atonement with the Prayer of Jesus; what Eckhart calls 'the soul being born in God and God in the soul' is here met with once again in the words 'the heart swallows the Lord and the Lord the heart, and the two become one'.[43]

What is perhaps the most moving and at the same time illuminating description of the effects and methods of the Prayer of the Heart is preserved in a little book written by a humble Russian pilgrim who, after hearing the bidding of St Paul 'Pray without ceasing' (Thess. I, 5, 17), made it his life's purpose to discover the way to this ideal. A holy father, a *starets*, instructed him in the practice of the prayer as taught in the *Philokalia* and impressed upon him the necessity of looking into his own heart and carrying his mind from the head down to the heart, where rhythmically with every in- and out-breathing the sacred formula should be imagined to enter and reside. So here, as in other traditions, the initial movement is downwards from the restlessness of the surface mind, located in the head, to the calm depth of the heart. The pilgrim followed his *starets'* instructions faithfully and in time discovered what other fellow pilgrims had discovered before him and will do so wherever the 'Silence of the Heart' is practised. His words may stand for those of many other seekers who have, like him, found the Kingdom of Heaven within.

So I began by searching out my heart in the way the New Theologian[44] teaches. With my eyes shut I gazed in thought, i.e. in imagination upon my heart. I tried to picture it there in the left side of my breast and to listen carefully to its beating, I started doing this several times a day, for half an hour at a time, and at first I felt nothing but a sense of darkness. But little by little, after a fairly short time, I was able to picture my heart and to note its movement, and further with the help of my breathing I could put into it and draw away from it the Prayer of Jesus in the manner taught by the saints, Gregory of Sinai, Callistus, and Ignatius. When drawing the air in I looked in spirit into my heart and said, 'Lord Jesus Christ', and when breathing out again, I said, 'have mercy upon me' ...

When about three weeks had passed I felt a pain in my heart, and then a most delightful warmth, as well as consolation and peace. This aroused me still more and spurred me on more and more to give great care to the saying of the Prayer so that all my thoughts were taken up with it and I felt a very great joy ...

After spending five months in this lonely life of prayer and such happiness as this, I grew so used to the Prayer that I went on with it all the time ... My soul was always giving thanks to God and my heart melted away with unceasing happiness.[45]

Several saints of the Christian Church have, as their attributes, the heart, either broken, flaming, pierced, winged, crowned by thorns or holding it up as an offering to their Lord; St Teresa, for instance, is often depicted in ecstasy with an angel piercing her heart with an arrow. Remembering, however, the fervour and dedication with which holy men, especially of the Eastern Church, have sought union with Christ in their hearts, does it not fit beautifully into the picture we have drawn here when we are told of St Ignatius of Antioch, greatly venerated in the East, that after his martyrdom the image of Christ was found imprinted in his heart. In the literal sense of the word, the Prayer of Jesus had become flesh.[46]

NOTES FOR CHAPTER 10

1. See note 38, p. 139.
2. *Egyptian Book of the Dead.* Introd. Chapter XXIX B.
3. *op. cit.* Chapter XXIX B. This explains why in ancient Egypt the heart, regarded as immortal, was not interred with the rest of the body, but kept separate.
4. In Christian terms: syntheresis.
5. *Ancient Devotions to the Sacred Heart of Jesus*, pp. 6–7.
6. See below, p. 172..
7. R. Wilhelm, *The Secret of the Golden Flower*, p. 24.

8. M. Buber, *Erzählungen* ... p. 840.
9. In Joan. Evang., XV, 25, in E. Przywara *An Augustine Synthesis*, No. 25.
10. S. Singh, *The Invocations of ... Ansari* ..., p. 35.
11. *Rubaiyat* 11.
12. St Theresa, *Interior Castle* II, 8.
13. *The Mystical Doctrine* ... p. 148.
14. Jerem. 4. Hesychius of Jerusalem, for instance, interpreted this saying in the way indicated. See Philokalia, p. 313.
15. St John of the Cross, St Theresa, the Blessed Henry Suso, Jacopone da Todi, and Thomas à Kempis were the main exponents of this imagery.
16. Spiritual Canticle. *The Mystical Doctrine* ... p. 166.
17. Quoted in C. G. Jung, *Psychological Types*, p. 311.
18. From the sermon: Intravit Jesus in quoddam castellum.
19. Diwan, in M. Smith, *Readings from the Mystics of Islam*, No. 126.
20. Kashf al-Mahjub, in M. Smith, *Readings from the Mystics of Islam*, No. 62.
21. *Tao Te Ching* 11.
22. *Ratnagotravibhaga* I, in *Buddhist Texts*, p. 182.
23. *Takakusu* XLVIII, 376, in *Buddhist Texts*, p. 298.
24. For instance: *Chandogya Upanishad* III, 14, 3, and Matthew 13, 32–33.
25. Eph. 2, 14.
26. *Chandogya Upanishad*, also *Svetasvatara Upanishad*. Compare Jacob Boehme: And as you find man to be, just so is eternity ... All is in man, both heaven and earth, stars and elements ... all creatures, both in this world and in the angelical world, are in man ... O Man! seek thyself and thou shalt find thyself. (W. Kingsland, *Anthology of Mysticism*, p. 95.)
27. 10, 5.
28. Jawhar al-Dhat, in M. Smith, *Readings* ... No. 96.
29. *Katha Upanishad*: 'There are two selves that drink the fruit of Karma in the world of good deeds; both are lodged in the secret place (of the heart), the chief seat of the Supreme. The knowers of Brahman speak of them as shade and light.' (I, 3, 1.)
30. A. Osborne, *Ramana Maharshi*, p. 149f.
31. Vacaspatimisra, ninth cent. See M. Eliade, *Yoga*, p. 70ff.
32. This is still practised by various schools of Yoga today, for instance, by an Indian Order of Siddha Yogis which teaches the necessity of turning the downward-pointing lotus flower of the heart upwards, so as to make it face the head.
33. *Chandogya Upanishad*, VIII, 6, 6. See p. 152.
34. *Kaivalya Upanishad*, 5–6.
35. The Japanese equivalent is *Kokoro* of which Lafcadio Hearn says: 'This word also signifies mind in the emotional sense, spirit, courage, resolve, sentiment, affection, and inner meaning—just as we say in English, "The heart of things".' *Kokoro*, London, 1905.
36. A. Watts, *The Way of Zen*, p. 24.
37. D. Suzuki, *Essays* ... Second series, p. 21f.
38. The parallel teaching in the Bible is found in Ezekiel 26, where it is said: '... and I will take away the stony heart out of your flesh and I will give you an heart of flesh, And I will put my spirit within you, and cause you to walk in my statutes, and ye shall keep my judgements, and do them.' (27–28.)
39. R. Wilhelm, *The Secret of the Golden Flower*, p. 46.
40. Frontlets or *phylacteries*.
41. G. Scholem, *Trends in Jewish Mysticism*, p. 136f.

42. Kitzur Sh'lh, 14, 2, in M. H. Harris, *Hebraic Literature*, p. 279.
43. *The Philokalia*, pp. 193, 74, 157, 223.
44. i.e. St Simeon.
45. *The Way of a Pilgrim*, p. 55ff.
46. Similarly, in the *Tibetan Book of the Great Liberation*, a Mahayana text, it is said of a maid-servant of a great dakini (celestial being) that imprinted inside her chest was the sacred mandala image of one hundred deities.

The Rock of Living Waters

For who is God, save the Lord?
And who is a rock, save our God?
2 Samuel, 22, 32

Now let us finish the journey I have described ... As
you have seen it comprises the whole spiritual life
from the very beginning until God absorbs the soul
into Himself and gives it to drink freely of the
fountain of living water which I told you was to be
found at the end of the way.
ST THERESA, The Way of Perfection.

And when Moses prayed for water for his people,
We said: March on to the rock with thy staff. So
there flowed from it twelve springs. Each tribe knew
their drinking place. Eat and drink of the provisions
of Allah, and act not corruptly, making mischief in
the land.
Koran 2, 60

The mystery which lies at the heart of all things is life itself, life seen in a
new light and lived in a new way. It is that more abundant life of which
Tagore says:

Life of my life, I shall ever try to keep my body pure, knowing that
thy living touch is upon all my limbs.[1]

Like the aspect of life in which we daily participate, this hidden life is
entered through a new birth and is seen to grow in waves of
development towards realms where words do not reach. The beginning
and the consummation of this development are linked by a chain of
transformatory experiences, each one of which expresses itself in certain
distinct images and metaphors. It is this fact that explains the almost
endless variety found in the accounts handed down to us by men of
vision, and, what is more, when seen in this light, these texts cease to be
the fanciful utterances of a soul in ecstasy and become, instead,
painstaking attempts to describe, as accurately as words will allow, a

succession of inner happenings. Furthermore, following traditional instructions, in certain circumstances, the chain of experiences can be repeated and verified and the deep human-divine centre within found and lived from.

It appears that there are certain main phases of growth which manifest themselves progressively wherever this development takes place.

The initial phase is marked by a bestowal of certitude, repose and strength often coming, as we have seen, at the height of desperate doubt, unrest and weakness. In this way the discovery of the cave of the heart yields its first fruit. In the midst of flux a point of stillness is found, unmoved and unmoving, and eternally abiding. He who goes through this experience speaks of a place of refuge, of a point of extreme quiescence, of the motionless hub of a moving wheel.

In Tibetan symbolism, at the centre of the wheel of the Teaching stands the sacred syllable OM, representing the first phase in the fourfold ascent of the soul as it is expressed in the holy formula of the *Om Mani Padme Hum*. To the Buddhist the place of refuge is the Buddha, who has shown the way to the point of stillness within, to the diamond of truth,[2] to be discovered in the calm depth at the bottom of the pool of ceaseless becoming. In contemplation, he enters the realm of the first stage of meditative awareness, the first *Jhana*, where all agitations of the mind and body are stilled.

> The ascetic, far from desires; far from any disturbing state of mind, maintaining feeling and thought, in a state of serenity born of detachment and pervaded with fervour and bliss, reaches the first contemplation.[3]

Wherever men pay homage or pray to a superior being, whether regarded as divine or not, words are uttered which reverberate with joy and peace at having found a citadel of strength, where fear and confusion are no more.

As the Buddhist says, 'I take refuge in the Buddha', so the Jew says with Samuel:

> The Lord is my rock, and my fortress and my deliverer; The God of my rock; in him will I trust; he is my shield and the horn of my salvation, my high tower, and my refuge, my saviour.[4]

To the Christian, this rock is the firm ground and the holy root which makes the branches holy; it is, furthermore, as in the Old Testament, spiritual sustenance which unites all believers:

And we are all baptized unto Moses in the cloud and in the sea; And did all eat the same spiritual meat; And did all drink the same spiritual drink: for they drank of that spiritual Rock that followed them: and that Rock was Christ.

1 Corinth. 10, 2–4

Christian mystics of many lands have drunk of that spiritual rock, as did Mechtild of Magdeburg. She says,

I saw with the eyes of my eternity, in bliss and without effort, a Stone. It was like a great mountain[5] and was of different colours; it tasted sweetly of heavenly herbs. I asked the sweet stone who it was. It said *Ego sum Jesus.* Then I went lovingly out of myself and laid my head on Him. I saw that all darkness was shut out from Him and that inwardly He was filled with everlasting light.[6]

When the Muezzin calls the faithful to pay homage to Allah, he cries 'Come to prayer, come to security'. He invites them to seek the Lord, 'the everlasting Refuge', 'the Granter of Security' and the 'Giver of Peace and Rest to the hearts of men'.[7] When they have found that rest, they have found 'the Ka'ba of the heart', 'the stone of sure foundation', which in its earthly form is the goal of the holy pilgrimage. The faithful kiss the black stone and therewith do reverence to, and unite with, that point of repose where the two realms, the divine and human, meet. And if one of them happens to belong to a Dervish order, it is likely that in his belt or girdle he wears a stone, sometimes called *taslim*, and that he repeats the prayer which he utters every time he puts it on: 'O Allah, the rites of the disciples have become my faith; no doubt now exists in my heart; on putting on the *taslim* I have given myself to Thee.'

The symbols and images mentioned so far, the stone, the rock, the refuge, the root, the cave, are all expressive of one particular aspect of the inner centre, stressing its indestructible, everlasting and unchangeable nature. What is experienced is something static, unmoved by life's flux, and ever present. The succeeding phase uses different, even contrasting, metaphors. Here the element of change, of growth and of motion predominates, and the dynamic, instead of the static qualities of the experience take the lead. Characteristic symbols are the seed, the bud, the fountain, the well, spark. The open contrast to what has gone before points to the fact that a new mode of experience has been reached, a mode which is concerned primarily with the emergence of latent powers, the awakening to life of something asleep, and the opening up of possibilities so far closed and inert.

The answer to the question of what the psychological process is which is responsible for this change, has been suggested by C. G. Jung. He shows that any concentration of psychic energy on a point within, such as the concentration in meditation or prayer on the heart centre, necessarily results in a state of inner tension, which, in its turn, produces the feeling of growth or 'swelling'. He points out, further, that in Hindu religious terminology one of the meanings of the word 'Brahman', the Absolute, is psychic energy, 'Brahman' being derived from the term for swelling, that is prayer, conceived as 'the upward surging will of man striving towards the holy, the divine'.[8]

Thus we read in the *Upanishads*, 'By contemplation (*tapasa*), Brahman expands'.[9]

When the Hindu seers speak of the lotus bud, which opens in the heart of man, of the emergence of the *Purusha* as the beginning of liberation or, when Lord Krishna asks Arjuna in the Gita to know him as the eternal seed, the source of all existence, and as that from which everything proceeds, it is this inner dynamic experience which is referred to. Man now sees the Divine as That which is ever creative, as both the self-renewing source of the world and the growing seed in his own being. The within as well as the without now reveal themselves as continuously creative, like a seed which contains all, a spark or a small flame hidden in a secret place which, if fanned, will grow until all is light. The keynote is motion and change and this is perhaps nowhere more clearly expressed than in the following passage, where the emergence of the *Purusha*, the Self, is likened to the flight of an arrow released from the bow, the sacred syllable OM.

Take the great bow of the Upanishads and place an arrow sharp with devotion. Draw the bow with concentration on Him and hit the centre of the mark, the same Everlasting Spirit (*Brahman*).
The bow is the sacred OM, and the arrow is Atman, the Self. Brahman is the mark of the arrow, the aim of the soul. Even as the arrow rests in its mark, let the vigilant self rest in its aim.
Mundaka Upanishad II, 2, 3/4

The emergence of *Purusha*, in Buddhist terms, is the freeing or awakening of wisdom and insight (*bodhi* or *panna*). It is that element which grows in man and transforms him; and, at the same time, it is the cradle of the new, non-individual selfhood leading to supreme enlightenment, *Maya Bodhi*. It is also that subterranean spring of fresh water which figures in the imagery attending the second phase of contemplation, the second *Jhana*:

> As a lake with a subterranean spring; and into this lake there flows no rivulet from East or from West, from North or from South, nor do the clouds pour their rain into it, but only the fresh spring at the bottom wells up and completely pervades it, infuses, fills and saturates it, so that not the smallest part of the lake is left unsaturated with fresh water; just so the ascetic pervades and infuses his body with internal serene calm, born of self-recollection, pervaded with fervour and beatitude.[10]

In the teaching of Mahayana Buddhism, 'the fresh spring at the bottom which wells up' is the emergence of Tathagatahood, the realization of the immanent Buddha-nature in man. As a germ (*garbha*) or element (*datha*) it is present from the beginning in embryonic form and man's endeavours should be directed towards its growth and unfoldment. 'Some call it the Sole Seed', says a Tibetan text.[11]

It reveals itself as another aspect of the sacred syllable OM, for it is enshrined in the word *Mani*, the jewel, of the mantra *Om Mani Padme Hum*. Like the stone of alchemy, this jewel has the power of transformation, for out of it is born the elixir of life.

Later Taoism, with its alchemical tendencies, has seized upon this idea and developed it elaborately. The texts are full of such metaphors as the germinal root, the seed pearl, the embryo or the foetus, and all the stages of growth from conception to maturity are worked out in detail, the goal being complete transmutation and the attainment of saint-hood.

Just as the seed, perishable and destined to die, is born out of the 'place of power', itself immutable and unchanging, so spring water, the symbol of change and fructification, issues out of the rock of salvation, the everlasting refuge. Thus it is said in the Old Testament that when the children of Israel were dying of thirst in the wilderness of Sin, the Lord told Moses, 'Behold I will stand before thee there upon the rock of Horeb; and thou shalt smite the rock, and there shall come water out of it, that the people may drink.'[12,13] Through the presence of the Lord, the rock turns into a standing water, and the flint into a mountain of waters, and man receives nourishment out of the well of salvation whose waters fail not.[14]

In Christian exegesis, the spiritual Rock which became drink to the Children of Israel is Christ. His Church is built upon that Rock and contains the fount of baptismal waters 'produced out of the Rock to quench the thirst of the people'. When the woman of Samaria came to draw water from Jacob's well, Jesus reveals to her the existence of this fountain, for he likens the water he offers her to a well in man, carrying the waters of everlasting life.[15]

The seed which grows in the good earth, the rivers of life that proceed from the throne of God, the gushing springs found in the Garden of Refuge of which the Koran speaks, and the well issuing from the stone or rock, all these point to the same discovery; the discovery of the still centre in the midst of the world's turmoil, revealing itself as a source of heavenly sustenance. When this happens to the seeker, he exclaims in ecstasy, as the Sufi poet and mystic Rumi has done:

Since the fountain-head is abiding, its channel is always bringing forth water. Since neither ceases why should you complain? ...
Do not be afraid that the water will cease to flow: for this water is limitless.[16]

Perhaps the most potent, and certainly the most prevalent, symbol employed in the portrayal of this discovery, is that of the spark. The texts reiterate unceasingly that the seed or well found in the cave of the human heart is, in truth, a seed or well of light, and they maintain that this realization which, so it appears, is often accompanied by an actual experience of luminosity, marks the turning point in a man's life, for it is a sign that a spark of the divine light, always regarded as the highest aspect of supreme reality, has taken birth in his soul. This event, whatever its manner of manifestation, transcends the human sphere, for in it the whole created world partakes. It is cosmic in character and refers to both the human and the divine planes of existence as well as to the inner and outer life of man.

The discovery of the divine spark within can happen gently like the break of dawn, or violently like a sudden flash of thunderous lightning. It has given rise to such seemingly opposing similes as 'a light that shineth in a dark place, until the day dawn, and the day star rises in your heart', or the Lord God as 'a consuming fire'.[17] Both clearly refer to man's first contact with the transcendent light. The first implies slow growth and a steady waxing of intensity. As the Christ child was born in the gloom of the stables, a small star only gradually giving light to the world, so many mystics must have experienced the birth of the inner light. Thus Johannes Tauler, the German 'Friend of God' of the fourteenth century, to whom the words of Isaiah 'For unto us a child is born, unto us a son is given' (9, 6) clearly referred to that beautiful birth which should, and in fact does, take place at any moment in any good and holy soul; and thus, too, Meister Eckhart:

> Therefore, I say that to the extent a person can deny himself and turn away from created things, he will find his unity and blessing in that little spark in the soul, which neither space nor time touches.[18]

When St Paul received the divine light, it happened otherwise. What touched him was a consuming fire. We are told that Saul, on the way to Damascus, was thrown to the ground by the fierceness of the vision of light and he was blinded by its radiance. His companions led him into Damascus, sightless. Thus, too, is related the story of 'Umar's conversion to Islam. He, like Saul, went in anger to stamp out the new religion.

> In short, he was on the way, with naked sword, making for the Prophet's mosque ... Just as 'Umar entered the door of the mosque, he saw as clear as clear that an arrow of light flew from Muhammad, upon whom be peace, and pierced his heart. He uttered a loud cry and fell down insensible. Love and passionate attachment manifested in his soul, and he would that he might dissolve into Muhammad in the extremity of his affection, and become effaced.[19]

Both types of experience occur side by side and they have done so throughout the history of religion. Thus far eastern Buddhism has its gradual as well as its sudden schools of enlightenment, the first could be epitomized by the expression found in Zen texts of a 'maturing enlightenment' brought about by diligently polishing the mirror of the soul until it becomes brilliant and pure; the second would reject this and rather speak of a hidden treasure always brilliant and pure, whose existence is realized in a flash.

Taoism puts great emphasis on the idea of 'maturing enlightenment' and has worked out in detail the various phases of the slow growth of the 'seed pearl' within, but it also knows of the sudden inrush of the light, terrifying and altogether beyond rational explanation. There has come down to us a story of a master and his disciple. It is, set in another context and another world, the story of St Paul on the road to Damascus, as it is likewise the story of innumerable other men who have walked this self-same path.

One night as the disciple walked along the mountain path he felt a sudden lightening circulating within him. There was a roar of thunder in the top of his head, the mountain, the mountain stream, the world and his very self all vanished. This experience lasted for 'about the time it would take for five inches of incense to burn'. After that he felt that he was an entirely different man and that he was purified by his own light. The student was told that even this light must be put aside. His master, indeed, had experienced it frequently over the course of thirty years and had learned to pay no attention to it.[20]

The wise counsel of the master has been repeated through the ages by all great men of wisdom. For, although the first contact with the inner light, be it experienced gradually or suddenly, is indicative of a profound transformation in man, as a physical phenomenon it carries no weight, and is only of significance in so far as it acts as a pointer of the stage reached.

The Chinese disciple felt that he was purified by what he called his own light. In many instances, this is indeed the immediate action of that first contact. It burns away all that resists transformation or stands in its way. It sets alight and consumes in order to create anew. As Plato has seen it in his simile of the cave, man sits in deep shadow, it is the shadow of unregenerate matter, of sin and ignorance. Where this state of darkness has prevailed for a long time, the inrush of light not only causes pain but sears and burns. The light reveals itself under the aspect of fire and flame; 'the flame of the circling sword', as Jewish mystics have called it, here enters the world of man. St Bernard avers that when the soul feels the heat of the burning flame, it is a sign of the nearness of the Lord, and it will cry with the prophet:

> From above has He sent fire into my bones

and again,

> my heart was not within me and while I was
> musing the fire burned forth.[21]

St Catherine of Genoa uses the simile of being plunged in the divine furnace of love, and Richard Rolle, the English mystic, prays

> O Holy Ghost ... Burn my reins and my heart with
> Thy fire that on Thine altar shall endlessly burn,

so that his inmost parts may be ready to receive the light.[22] St John of the Cross describes it thus:

> The fire penetrates the substance of the fuel,
> playing about it, stripping it of its ugliness;
> the fuel is made ready to be all afire itself
> and to be transformed into fire.[23]

Pain and torment accompany this action of the purifying flame, but, as many who have gone through this experience assure us, it is the pain and torment of love.

> O Jesus, Lover, Husband, Tempest, Fire!
> Take me, transform me in thine utmost heat[24]

This ecstatic prayer of Jacobo da Todi sounds like an echo of the words which came to St Catherine of Siena, spoken by her divine lover,

> I, Fire, the Acceptor of sacrifice, ravishing
> away from them their darkness, give the light.[25]

NOTES FOR CHAPTER 11

1. *Gitanjali*, 4.
2. Sanskrit: *Vajra*, Tibetan: *dorje*, meaning the most precious stone, i.e. the diamond.
3. *Majjhima Nikaya*, CXXV.
4. See 2 Samuel 22, 2, 32–33, 47. In Genesis (49, 24) God is called 'the stone of Israel', a metaphor which recurs in the Sabbath prayer where the Lord is addressed as 'the rock of Israel' and where a hymn is sung with this refrain:
   > Rock from whose store we have eaten,
   > Bless him, my faithful companions;
   > Eaten have we and left over,
   > This was the word of the Lord.
5. 'Rock' and 'mountain' are closely related images; indeed, stone, rock and mountain are often interchangeable. In the Koranic verse cited as a motto, for instance, the term translated as 'rock' can also stand for 'mountain' (al-hajar). However, a mountain, as a religious symbol, has so many additional meanings that any attempt to do justice to it would distract from the line of argument pursued here.
6. L. Menzies, *The Revelations of Mechtild of Magdeburg* IV, 3, p. 99.
7. Suras 59, 23; 13, 28.
8. *Psychological Types* (1933 ed.), p. 249.
9. *Mundaka Upanishad* I, 1, 8. *Tapas* has also been translated as 'self-brooding' or 'brooding'.
10. *Digha Nikaya*, II, 82.
11. W. Y. Evans-Wentz, *Tibetan Book of the Great Liberation*, p. 209.
12. Ex. 17, 6; Num. 20, 10.

13. According to an old Jewish legend, a miraculous well accompanied the children of Israel through the desert. It was found in the crag of a rock and they drank from it whenever they rested and were thirsty. This legend is based on the biblical text (Num. 21, 16–18):

  And from thence they went to Beer; that is the well whereof the Lord spake unto Moses, Gather the people together, and I will give them water. Then Israel sang this song, Spring up O well; sing ye unto it: The princes digged the well, the nobles of the people digged it, by the direction of the lawgiver, with their staves ...

  It is this passage to which St Paul refers in 1 Cor. 10, 1–4, quoted above.

14. See Is. 12, 3; 58, 11; Ps. 36, 9; Jer. 2, 13; 17, 13; Sol. 4, 15. Also J. Mitchell, *The City of Revelation*, where the close relationship between 'rock' and 'water' is shown at length.

15. John 4, 14 and 7, 38. See also Revelation, where is mentioned several times 'the living Fountain of Waters' or 'the Fountain of the Water of Life'.

16. M. Smith, *Readings* ... No. 113. The Koran speaks of two Gardens, two Fountains and two Springs, a fact which is said to refer either to this and the next world or the outer and inner life.

17. 2 Peter, 1, 19 and Deut. 4, 24.

18. *Sermons*, Fragment 39, in R. B. Blakney, p. 246.

19. A. J. Arberry, *Discourses of Rumi*, p. 171.

20. C. Y. Chang, *An Introduction to Taoist Yoga*, p. 147. The Review of Religion, March 1956.

21. Cant. XXXI, 4.

22. The Amending of Life, XI. Both quoted in: Sir James Marchant, *The Way to God*, pp. 117 and 199.

23. *The Mystical Doctrine* ... *The Living Flame of Love*, Prologue.

24. Jacopone da Todi, in Sir James Marchant, *The Way to God*, p. 310.

25. Dialogue, Cap. 85, in E. Underhill, *Mysticism*, p. 266. One is here reminded of the saying, traditionally attributed to Christ: Whoever is near unto me is near unto the fire; whoever is far from me, is far from the kingdom. (Origen, *Jerem, Homil.* XX, 3.) (See *Secret Sayings of Jesus*, Fontana Book, p. 170.)

12

The Eye of Wisdom

The eye of the great God,
The eye of the God of glory,
The eye of the King of hosts,
The eye of the King of the living
    Pouring upon us
        At each time and season,
    Pouring upon us
        Gently and generously.
Glory to thee,
    Thou glorious sun.
Glory to thee, thou sun
    Face of the God of life.

                     Gaelic Prayer

The Flame of Will, burning high, rises to his pure
light in the heaven of the mind, wide he extends his
illumination and fronts the Dawn. She comes,
moving upward, laden with all desirable things,
seeking the gods with the oblation, luminous with
clarity.

       SRI AUROBINDO, *Hymns to the Mystic Fire*

To redeem the image, to seek conversion, to match
With a pure heart the kingdom born within the eye
Lies at the quick of being. He shall alone know
The appointed place, who comes out of the east wind
After the frost has stripped him like a tree,
Whose shadowless intent holds out to innocence
The still reflection of simplicity.

      MORWENNA DONNELLY, *The Tragic Image*

From its rootplace in the heart, the spark grows to become a rising
flame or, to use another metaphor, the hidden spring swells into a
mighty river. This inner process, known to all true seekers, is as elusive
of description as it is vital for the 'pilgrim's progress'. That which rises
to take possession of the whole of man,[1] has variously been named holy
love, spiritual energy,[2] vital breath,[3] the serpent power,[4] divine light;
whatever the descriptive terms used, they indicate unmistakably that, at

this point, the focus of attention changes. The frequent allusions to the middle part of the body, notably the heart, are now joined by others all pointing to the region of the head. The insistence with which this shift of emphasis recurs in all the major traditions, makes it impossible to dismiss it as arbitrary or merely fanciful. What is more, a scrutiny of the relevant passages reveals that they contain detailed explanations why, at a certain point, such a shift becomes imperative. Symbolically speaking, the seed gives way to the plant, the flower opens and out of it issues the miracle of new life.

The *Upanishads* contain many passages which refer to this upward motion, and show that through it a connection is established between the heart centre, where the first stirring of the spark occurs, and the centre in the head, the place of full realization. They speak of the supreme bright power residing in the heart which, through mantric intonations, rises like smoke

> to the sky in one column and follows afterwards
> one branch after another.[5]

This column of smoke is the vital channel (*susumma*), carrying the ascending current of energy. Its centre is the heart, its lower part goes down, through the region of the navel (*manipura*), into the rootplace (*muladara*), and its crown fills and overarches the head. In various ways devotees, irrespective of their allegiance, direct their attention, in meditation and contemplation, successively to the different centres, linking the lower with the upper regions of the body. Perhaps the best known text concerning this upward motion is found in the *Chandogya Upanishad*:

> There are a hundred and one arteries of the heart,
> Only one of these passes up to the crown of the head.
> Going up by it, one goes to immortality. (VIII, 6, 6)

All those who have made this inner ascent assure us that it is felt as a stream of increasing volume, as the Sufi poet Jellal-ed-in Rumi has done, of whom it is said that

> a great fire mounted through his body to the top of
> his skull, whence he saw a window open and a thin
> smoke rise to the foot of the celestial throne.[6]

Around the 'subtle path to the head', as Sankara has called the inner channel, there are entwined the two great opposing forces, male and female, active and passive, symbolized by the sun and the moon. Their marriage takes place in the heart; divided yet one they rise, in the same way as a spiral motion embraces the opposites but is in reality one.[7] In the language of Hindu mythology, the union of Indra and his consort Indrani is accomplished in the heart, they ascend as two in embrace and it is said that the two bodily eyes represent the divine lovers;[8] in other words, they represent the two great forces whose interplay sustains all existence.

What is expressed here belongs to the lore expounded by all great religious teachers; they agree that the two eyes symbolize the dyad, the guiding principle of the world and man. On the cosmic plane they are seen as sun and moon, the two luminaries or sources of light or, as Hindu mythology has it, the two eyes of the Universal Man.[9] On the human plane, the two eyes are the organ with which man discriminates, the organs which respond to the endlessly varied shades of light and darkness, furnishing him with a unified picture of the world around him. They are his guiding lights, turned towards the external life.

Even this duality, however, has to be transcended and, on a new level of realization, the two must become one, in the sense that their unitary essence shines forth and overshadows all else. When this is achieved, the dyad gives way to that higher third which is a monad, yet, at the same time, acts as a mediator between the two.[10] This, in religious terminology, is the opening of the third eye. It is an event nearly always referred to by the use of the singular; not the eyes but the eye opens, the eye of knowledge, the eye of wisdom, or, according to the particular tradition in which it occurs, the eye of Shiva, the eye of the universal Atman, the celestial, clarified, superhuman eye of Buddhist teaching, or the eye of eternity of the Christian mystical tradition.

According to Sufi teaching, the moon of the heart rises to become the sun of the eye,[11] or the eye of certainty, and it is on this 'third eye' that the Dervishes concentrate so that the light, through the grace of their teacher, may be imparted to them. As an outward token of this inner process, they light a candle and direct their prayers to the Giver of Light, Allah.

When this eye opens, heart and eye become unified, and he to whom this happens now sees the world with the eye of the heart.[12] With this he penetrates into the region of complete unity and simplicity as Al-Hallaj must have done, for he said,

> I saw my Lord with the Eye of the Heart.
> I said, 'who art Thou?', he answered, 'Thou'.[13]

As the two eyes are the organs of external sight, so the one eye is the organ of inner sight, of *bodhi*, or enlightenment. It is this fact which elucidates the saying of Jesus that the light of the body is the eye, and his assertion,

> if therefore thine eye be single, thy whole
> body shall be full of light.[14]

For the opening of the 'third eye' means new sight and illumination; whereas before man is as though blind and in darkness, now he is given the gift of light.

The miraculous event of the blind receiving sight, so often related in the world's scriptures, must not be understood as referring to one level of meaning alone, neither is it poetic licence. Applied to the spiritual plane, these men really see the world in a new light and in a new way, and as regards the physical, practically all traditions contain stories of men whose bodily sight was restored, the moment the opening of 'the eye' took place. Thus we read of a blind man who accompanied the Russian 'pilgrim' on his travels and was taught by him the Prayer of Jesus. Through it there was kindled in his heart the divine flame which, on certain occasions, blazed up, rose to his head flooding him with light, 'and in the light of this flame he could see'.[15]

From this it becomes clear why that state of enlightenment in which the whole body partakes, has been likened to being filled with eyes, or to having reached 'eyeness'. Thus 'Iraqi, a Sufi poet, could say,

> Glass-like, let all thy body be an eye,
> and thy soul's vision shall be radiant:
> turn back on self and haply thou shalt be
> as in a mirror face to face with Him.[16]

The experience which gives rise to an utterance such as this, is known to many. St Marcarius clearly refers to it in terms of the Christian revelation.

> The soul that is perfectly illuminated by the ineffable beauty of the glory of the light of the face of Christ, and perfectly partakes of the Holy Spirit, and is adjudged worthy to be made the dwelling-place and seat of God, becomes all eyes, all light, all face, all glory and all spirit.[17]

'All eyes, all light, all face', thus can be epitomized Ezekiel's vision of the heavenly throne. The four wheels of the cherubim appeared to him, radiant beyond imagination, and he beheld that each had four faces and 'their whole body, and their backs and their hands and their wings, and the wheels, were full of eyes round about' (Ez. 10, 12). It was also what St John saw, for he spoke of 'four beasts full of eyes before and behind' (4, 6–8). Al-Shadili, a fifteenth century Sufi, calls this state the manifestation of unveiling the eyes or the presence of the transformation of the eyes, and he assures us that when this happens to man he sees nothing else but the beloved's face everywhere, and in ecstasy he cries 'Forenoon Sun of brilliant forehead!'[18]

At this point in the ascending process of illumination, the eye becomes the great symbol of light and the face its surrounding field of radiance. The eye reveals itself, not only as the light of the human organism, but also of the whole of the cosmos. It and the sun in its symbolic meaning, as the supreme light of the world, become synonyms. As such it becomes the celestial eye which sees all, illumines all and contains all.[19] In it can be seen the world and at its innermost point, at its luminous core, resides the divine person, the one who is 'all eye, all face', in all eternity.[20] When man's inner eye is opened he can see that person as the Sufi Kilani did. To him was revealed the pre-existence of Muhammad, in the form of the picture of the prophet in the pupil in the centre of the eye of creation.

What is here referred to is an age-old as well as universal insight. It occurs in many sacred texts, sometimes it determines the symbolic imagery used in religious art, at other times it breaks through in mystic vision, vouchsafed to the few only. In Hindu Scriptures and their commentaries are found long passages dealing with the person in the eye, as this phenomenon is called there. Who is this person in the eye? A clear and unequivocal answer is given in the *Chandogya Upanishad*,

> The person who is seen in the eye, he is the self.
> This is the immortal, the fearless, this is Brahman.[21]

The highest self, then, here appears personified in the eye. The eye, however, as has been shown, is the organ of light and therefore stands for the sun; or, in the language of Hindu mythology, the eye is the child of the sun,[22] just as the eye, when it is freed from death and gains immortality, becomes the sun. It was thus that Prajāpati, the great god, could be called and revered as the self of all, the sun of all, and the eye of all. The person in the eye, then, the self in its divine form, is also the person seen in the sun;[23] these two are not only intimately related but they are in reality one and the same. They rest on each other as the

Upanishads express it, the songs and chants of the one are those of the other, the name of the one is that of the other.[24]

The history of Christianity contains many instances where the divine face and the eye of God, both as the supreme light giving and enlightening channels of grace are placed at the very centre or apex of religious imagery. To the baroque artist, in particular, the eye was the great symbol of that heavenly realm of light he constantly strove to represent on earth. It appears crowning the high altar and it appears in pictorial meditation guides as well as accompanying religious treatises. Nicholaus von der Flue, the Swiss saint, gave the face of Christ, from which rays of light are emitted, the place of honour in the meditation picture he constantly used, and on Jakob Boehme's works, almost as an imprimatur, appears the eye of God surrounded by rays and stars. The latter speaks of the single eye, or the eye of eternity, which he, too, identifies with light and the sun. In it is transcended the duality of the 'right and left eye' of the soul, the former looking forward towards eternity, the latter backward towards time. Unity is reached when, through Christ, the eye of time is taken up into the eye of eternity.

> Never shalt thou arrive at the Unity of Vision or
> Uniformity of Will, but by entering fully into the
> Will of our Saviour Christ, and therein bringing the
> Eye of Time into the Eye of Eternity; and then
> descending by Means of this united through the Light
> of God into the Light of Nature.[25]

When this becomes reality, the person in the eye, the eye of time in the eye of eternity, has taken his abode in the centre of human life; the two eyes of the soul are now governed by the eye of the spirit, as Boehme likes to call it, or again, the heavenly internal eye is seen as having its life in and through the eye, or light, of God. Then visible and invisible manifestations, nature and God, are seen as one.

> My Son, let not the Eye of Nature with the Will of the Wonder
> depart from that Eye which is introverted into the Divine Liberty,
> and into the Eternal Light of the Holy Majesty; but let it draw to
> thee those Wonders by Union with that heavenly internal Eye, which
> are externally wrought out and manifested in visible Nature.[26]

Heart and eye, then, are like two nodal points where the inner light is focused,[27] and in the same way as the heart centre has its bodily location in or near the organ of life, so the eye centre has its bodily location near the organs of sight. Many systems teach that it is to be found on the forehead, at a point half way and slightly above the two eyes. In yoga lore this point (*Ajna chakra*), whose colour is white, is seen as the abode of the 'Divinity whose nature is Light'; in a personalized form it is Shiva, the supreme lord (*Jyotisvarupa-Ishvara*), on whose forehead shines the celestial eye, the eye of Shiva. It is the spot where the deity is visualized in devotional practices, meditations are directed, sacred syllables placed in contemplation, a circle or seed of light is often imagined, and it is here that the Hindu caste mark is worn, that the Taoist master wears the sacred character *dschung*, chiselled in gold, and that the high priest in the synagogue used to carry the plate of pure gold on which were inscribed the words 'Holy to the Lord'.[28] The realization of this centre means freedom from bondage, because it bestows freedom from the pairs of opposites.[29]

There exists an old belief that in the eye there not only resides power which can influence the external world, but that from the eye are emitted rays of light. This belief was held by the Greeks, it still survives in folklore today, and it seems likely that what is referred to is that ancient knowledge of the two eyes as symbols of the creative dyad and the one eye as the symbol of transcendent unity.

Light rays, however, can be creative or destructive, healing or causing ill. For this double aspect of the divine energy, focused in the eye, ancient Egypt had a most potent and telling imagery. There the eye, the healing one, was seen to be interchangeable with the cobra, both were royal insigniae, worn on the forehead of the divine king. Is not this reminiscent of something much nearer home, the good and the evil eye, phenomena believed in and 'used' today as in the remote past?

A grandiose picture of this double function of the light of the eyes, as well as the eye, is drawn in the *Kabbalah*. Out of the first primeval ray, shooting forth from *En-Sof*, the unknowable and ultimate mystery, the first man, Adam Kadmon is created. Streams of light descend from his eyes and it is these which form the raw material, as it were, for the whole of the created world. These mighty rivers of light had to be dammed in, the limitless had to be limited, the formless subjected to form, so as to make possible the creation of the material world. These forms or vessels, however, themselves fashioned out of an admixture of light, could not withstand the onslaught, they burst and broke asunder. The light issuing from the divine eye spelled destruction, it meant, as the great Kabbalist Luria saw it, 'the death of the primeval king'.

On death, however, follows new life and on dissolution, restoration. There broke forth from the forehead of Adam Kadmon[30] rays of light which brought healing and furthered new growth. The period of restitution had dawned (*Tikkun*) and, as Luria teaches, with it the figure of the first man was taking shape in and through the world.[31]

Without the light residing in the divine eye, there could be no life, no created world. The sudden withdrawal of this light, often taking the form of a disappearance of sun and moon from the earth, is an event which constitutes the subject matter of many and various myths. Wherever it is found, there a picture of fright, despair and death is given. In a well-known Indian myth, the main aspects of the light of the eye, its destructive and life-giving nature, its deadly power of devastation, as well as its infinite capacity for restoration and healing, are uniquely presented side by side.

It is said that one day the great God Shiva, in a halo of light, sat in deep meditation on a sacred mountain of Himalaya. Approaching from behind came Uma, his wife, the daughter of Himalaya. Playfully she covered the eyes of her Lord with her hands.

> Instantly life in the universe waned, the sun grew pale, all living things cowered in fear. Then the darkness vanished again, for one blazing eye shone forth on Shiva's brow, a third eye like a second sun. So scorching a flame proceeded from that eye that Himalaya was burnt with all his forests, and the herds of deer and other beasts rushed headlong to Mahadeva's seat to pray for his protection, making the Great God's power to shine with strange brightness ... Then Himalaya's daughter, beholding her father thus destroyed, came forth and stood before the Great God with her hands joined in prayer. Then Mahadeva, seeing Uma's grief, cast benignant looks upon the mountain, and at once Himalaya was restored to his first estate, and became as fair as he had been before the fire. All his trees put forth their flowers, and birds and beasts were gladdened.

Seeing all this happening before her eyes, Uma is puzzled, why did her Lord create a third eye, why did it burn mountain and all vegetation to ashes? The answer of Shiva is that it was for the protection of all creatures, but that its blazing force destroyed even the mountain itself. The manifested world could not endure the divine energy, the 'vessels broke'. But because Uma had stood in prayer before him, the Great God cast healing eyes on the world, restoring it to its erstwhile life and beauty.[32]

NOTES FOR CHAPTER 12

1. Sanskrit: *Mahavayu*.
2. *Ojas*.
3. *Prana*.
4. *Kundalini*.
5. *Maitri Upanishad* VII, 11.
6. *The Whirling Ecstasy*, p. 13.
7. This ascent is depicted in the great symbol of *Raja Yoga*, the King of Yogas, as it is expounded in Patanjali's *Aphorisms*, followed and commented upon by many generations of yogis. It shows the *Kundalini* serpent curling around a staff and reaching up into the centre of a lotus flower which is enhaloed by light.
8. *Satapatha Brahmana* X, 5, 2, 9.
9. In ancient Egypt, sun and moon were seen as the right and left eye of the cosmic falcon.
10. The simile used in Buddhism for this unified vision is as follows:
    As if there were two buildings with
    doors, and a man with good sight,
    standing between them, were to see
    people leaving one house and entering
    the other, going and coming.
    J. Evola, *Doctrine of Awakening*, p. 220.

11. The image of this inner ascent chosen by a modern Sufi movement is the winged heart.
12. Mechtilde of Magdeburg speaks of the Eyes of the Soul and says:
    A light of utmost splendour
    Glows on the eyes of my soul.
    Therein have I seen the inexpressible
    ordering of all things, and
    recognized God's unspeakable Glory.
    L. Menzies, *The Revelations of Mechtild of Magdeburg*, p. 30.
13. Abu Bakr Siraj Ed-Din, *The Book of Certainty*, p. 30.
14. Matt. 6, 22; Luke 11, 34.
15. *The Way of a Pilgrim*, p. 125.
16. 'The Song of the Lovers', in M. Smith, *The Sufi Path of Love*, p. 112.
17. Hom. I, 2, in E. Underhill, *The Mystic Way*, p. 328.
18. E. J. Jurji, *Illumination in Islamic Mysticism*, p. 65.
19. ... the risen sun
    Flooding its orbit with the joy of day—
    That Eye of Heaven, mansion of secret light,
    Whose beams of all that's lovely are the shrine.
    Procreant, puissant, arbiter of Sight,
    Emblem and symbol of the light divine—
    Walter de la Mare, 'The Traveller', p. 32.
20. The Jewish *Kabbalah* knows of two 'Faces'; the 'Great Face', the unknowable source of all whose eye is always open and is without a lid, the other, the 'little face' whose eyes open and close, imparting this rhythm to the universe. The great face is the 'I am' from which nine rays of light proceed, the little face, the creator God.

21. IV, 15, 1 and VIII, 7, 4.
22. In ancient Egypt, the eye is seen as the daughter of the high god. This god had originally one eye, but the texts also speak of a 'little face', i.e. of a man or just a face known as 'He who commands both eyes'. In rites, the symbol of the eye is called *Wedjat*, the hale one (healing one). It is this celestial eye which Horus lost in his fight with Seth and which was brought back by the god Toth, thus restoring the light to mankind.
23. The Eye of Horus, the Egyptian symbol, is sometimes depicted carrying the miniature figure of the sun god in its centre.
24. See *Satapatha Brahmana* VIII, 1, 2, 1–2; also the following Upanishadic text; *Brhad-aranyaka* I, 3, 14; V, 2, 2; *Maitrayana* VI, 6; *Chandogya* I, 7, 5.
25. *The Supersensual Life*, Dialogue II, p. 45f.
26. *ibid.*, p. 47.
27. Buddhism speaks of eye-consciousness, centred in the eye, and of thought-consciousness, centred in the heart. M. Eliade, *Yoga*, p. 195.
28. The Egyptian High God addresses the heavenly eye with the following invocation: Come, then, upon my forehead that you may exalt my beauty. Come, then, in front of me, that I have made you elevated! (R. T. Rundle Clark, *Myth and Symbol in Ancient Egypt*, p. 94.)
29. G. Scholem reports an interesting parallel in this teaching:

    In a powerful speech of the great mystic Abraham ben Eliezer Halevi of Jerusalem (died about 1530) we find a recommendation to those who face martyrdom. He advises them to concentrate in the hour of their last ordeal, on the great Name of God; to imagine its radiant letters between their eyes and to fix all their attention on it. Whoever does this, will not feel the burning flames or the tortures to which he is subjected. G. Scholem, *Trends in Jewish Mysticism*, p. 146.

    In like manner, a Chasidic tale relates of the Baal Schem Tow, the founder of the movement, that once he appeased Sammael, the Lord of Demons who was angry for being called to perform a certain service, by asking his disciples to uncover their foreheads. On them was the sign of the image in which God had created man.
30. According to Islamic belief (both Sunnites and Shiites) the *Nur Muhammadi*, the pre-existent light substance, was incorporated in the act of divine creation in the forehead of Adam, to pass through all generations from prophet to prophet until it finally manifested itself in the seal of all prophets, Muhammad.
31. G. Scholem, *Zur Kabbala*, p. 150ff.
32. Nivedita and A. Coomeraswamy, *Myths of the Hindus and Buddhists*, p. 299ff.

IV

FULFILMENT

13

The Holy Round

He bade us form a circle; we stood with folded
hands, and he was in the middle. And then he said:
Answer me with Amen. Then he began to intone a
hymn of praise and to say: Praise be to Thee, Father.
And we all circled round him and responded to him
with Amen.

ACTS OF ST JOHN

Thou also, if thou wishest, mayest let thyself be led.
Then shalt thou dance in a ring, together with the
angels, around Him who is without beginning or end,
the only true God, and God's Word is part of our
song.

CLEMENT OF ALEXANDRIA

The numinous force or energy which, in its ascending course, informs
the human body, encompasses both the inner and outer life of man. It
expands from a central core, conquering, as we have seen, new
territories and opening new aspects of being. It appears, however, that
at a certain point in this process, expansion ceases and the need is felt to
contain the outgoing forces, to dam them in, and to secure them within
a defined area. In the symbolic language of the sacred texts, this point is
reached when the seed has become a fully grown organism, a plant or a
tree, when the spark has given way to the splendour of the midday sun
and when the child has grown into manhood. Growth, at least for the
time being, is halted, the organism has become self-contained and self-
renewing and so as to protect it from the outside world a 'demarcation
rope',[1] a wall or fence, is thrown around it; in short, the image of the
temenos, the holy enclosure, appears, depicted, more often than not, in
the form of the mandala, a round or square pattern, standing for
integration and wholeness.[2]

This inner process is manifold and so is the symbolic language in
which it finds expression. Its many aspects call for different images and
man, on his pilgrimage, singles them out for special attention according
to his immediate need.

The square or circle thrown round a sacred centre, be that an altar, a shrine or other holy object, can be traced by walking or dancing it, it can be erected materially or it can be represented by word or image. Initially it is mainly the need that is felt to ensure the protection of, and intimate contact with, the numinous centre; the form the *mandala* then takes is that of circular processions, and round dances as well as that of a walled enclosure, a city, a garden, a temple, castle or mansion; at other times, it is the subtle inter-relationship of centre and circumference, the intricate and dynamic pattern linking both, that attracts the attention; where this is the case, the *mandala* takes the shape of an open flower, a lotus, a rose or a wheel.

In what follows, the *mandala* symbolism, as an expression of completion and maturity, will be considered under these various aspects. Circumambulation, the city, the lotus, the rose and the wheel.[3]

The circumambulation around a hallowed spot is perhaps one of the oldest of man's religious activities. Megalithic structures suggest that the rites practised there are likely to have included circular processions and it is probably not too much to say that to this very day, whatever the religion, it includes such ceremonies somewhere in its practices.

The closing of the circle or square is regarded as essential for the rite to be effective, the purpose being the safeguarding and concentration of the influence issuing from the sacred object within a confined area. Furthermore, through the circumambulation, a field of force is created which is fed by the divine potency residing in the centre and there is thus established an intimate relationship between the object of worship and the worshipper. The latter not only becomes an integral part of the sacred space, by himself performing the enclosing rite, but by entering the field of force thus created, he is drawn to the centre, under whose influence he is purified and renewed. The spiral nature of every true circumambulation is thus revealed; it encircles and in doing so closes the magic round; this external movement has its counterpart in the inner domain, where the without is 'excircled' and a re-orientation towards the within takes place. At that point, the 'encircling' motion sets in, it is the spiralling approach to the sacred centre.

In the *Kaushitaki Upanishad* we are given the words spoken during the round ambulation:

> I turn myself with the turn of the Gods.
> I turn myself along with the turn of the Sun (II, 9).

Every worshipper performing this rite, whether he be a Hindu, a Buddhist, a Christian, or a Muslim, could utter these words for they are universal in their application. The 'turn of the Sun' and the 'turn of the gods', these two have been regarded as identical, or at least as symbolically related, since the earliest days of religion. The ritual movement, therefore, follows the direction of the sun's course, for this and not the reverse, the 'withershin motion', is the turn of the gods. It is performed around any sacred object, big or small, including pillars, mounds, prayerwalls or tombs, outside and inside temples and churches, as well as around fields, mountains and even whole cities. In the course of it, prayers are said, *mantras* are recited, the air is purified with holy incense and prayerwheels are turned. All these activities are meant to increase the efficacy of the ritual; they enhance the separation from the world outside the *temenos* and, at the same time, as the prayers and *mantras* indicate, they do what the Buddhists call set in motion the wheel of the Law or, in other words, they send out into the world at large the beneficial forces awakened within the consecrated enclosure.

It is clear that in all these ceremonies the external acts and the inner happenings cannot be separated; and this holds even in those many examples where the partakers of the rite are ignorant of its deeper meaning and only perform it because it is customary to do so. It appears that many and diverse factors combine in making a circular motion around a sacred object, executed in traditional manner, touch something off in the psyche of man which, in all religious cultures, is regarded as akin to an experience of wholeness and integration.

The concentric circles drawn round a numinous centre can be wide or narrow and they can refer mainly to an external movement of the body or an internal motion of the heart or soul of man. The following account is given of one such rite, at one time, perhaps the most famous of all, the circumambulation of the holy city of Lhasa.

> The outer circuit of Lhasa is traversed by what is called the Circular Road. It is an exceedingly sacred road. To walk all round it, is a religious proceeding equivalent to visiting every sacred spot within it. All day long one may see strings of pilgrims wending their pious way, twirling their prayer wheels.[4]

Evidence of similar practices comes from many parts of the world, notably from Hindu, Buddhist and Christian countries.[5] Always, whether performed inside or outside church or temple, their purpose appears to be twofold.

It is to activate the inherent numinosity of the object of worship and, simultaneously, to awaken to life the divinity in man. Thus Ibn Arabi the famous Sufi, not only experienced the great transformatory revelation of his life when he performed the prescribed circumambulations of the *Ka'ba* but he also teaches that the *Ka'ba* 'is animated by those who circle round it'.[6] Thus in his major work *Futuhat*, he says

> Illumined is the Ka'ba by walking round it, while the other houses of men remain in darkness ... And He (who is circling round the Ka'ba) should appear to himself during this rite like the angels circling round the throne of God.[7,8]

As the satellite earth circles the sun, so the faithful circle the holy centre, and therewith create a sphere of influence where higher realms can descend into the lower and the lower can be raised to meet the higher. Intercommunication becomes a reality and the way opens to becoming perfect in God's eyes.

The idea of perfection is also operative in the number of circuits performed. The number seven has in many cultures the connotation of a 'rounding off' and in general of consummation. God created the world in seven days, the seventh heaven is the most exalted, just as the seventh day of the week is a holy day. When the seven is reached, the circle closes and a new beginning on a new level, the 'higher octave', begins.

This transition into a new plane is, in the eyes of religious esotericism, the great mystery of the eighth day,[9] that day when everything is made new and a fresh beginning ensues. In like manner, when the faithful circle the sacred place seven times, they are made new and the secret of the eighth day is revealed to them. The *Ka'ba* is not only encircled seven times by the pilgrims on arrival at Mecca but the pilgrimage (*hajj*)[10] proper is not thought to begin until the eighth day of the month (*dhu'l-Hijja*), after the pilgrims have listened to final instructions on the eve of the seventh day.

Scholars have pointed out the close resemblance of this ceremony with the Festival of the Tabernacle in Jewish worship, when circular processions are performed around the altar, one on the first six days and seven on the seventh day. On that occasion in the synagogues, branches from four different trees, the citron, the palm, the myrtle and the willow, are carried round the altar. The symbolism attending this ceremony is complex but one feature stands out clearly. The number four, too, signifies wholeness, and the four trees, according to traditional interpretations, symbolize the four points of the compass, the four elements, the four principal parts of the human body, and the four types of worshipper. In the procession, therefore, is included, metaphorically, heaven and earth, nature and the outer and inner man, and by partaking in the sacred round the faithful are reminded of their God as the creator of all and of His commandment to seek communion with Him and draw nigh unto Him.

For the Lord has said 'If thou wilt come to My house, then will I come to thy house, but if thou refusest to visit My dwelling, I will neglect to enter yours'.[11]

In Christian worship, the centre around which all processions are performed is the cross on the High Altar. One of the principal days when such processions take place is Palm Sunday. During the blessing of the palm branches, the clergy and laity pray that they may understand 'the mystical significance' of that day. With the words 'let us go forth in peace', the procession forms and the participants are reminded that it was six days before the feast of Passover that the Lord entered the holy city, where on the seventh day, the day of the Last Supper, His ministry came to an end and the mystery of the eighth day of consummation and renewal began.[12]

The 'mystical significance' of the circumambulation has often been experienced by the human soul. The magic round is drawn inwardly, without bodily movement, and man thereby becomes rooted in the divine. In the language of the Bible, the heart is circumcised to the Lord, man becomes His servant having entered the sacred domain. In the Old Testament, this is the great goal put before both the individual and the community.

Thus when Jeremiah exhorts his people to 'Break up your fallow ground, and sow not among thorns. Circumcise yourselves to the Lord, and take away the foreskin of your heart' (IV, 3/4), it is taken to mean that circumcision should be a sign and a seal for the nation, as for every single Jew, to turn away from evil ways and be included in the sacred ground of the Covenant. St Paul, rejecting the purely external act of circumcision, speaks in an identical vein,

He is a Jew, which is one inwardly; and circumcision is that of the Heart, in the spirit, and not in the letter; whose praise is not of men, but of God. (Romans, 2, 29.)

When the inward circumcision happens, then a complete 'revolution', as the East likes to call it (Sanscrit: *Paravritta-sraya*), is taking place in the innermost point of man's being, bringing about the birth of the new man. Here, too, the mystery of the eighth day is invisibly present for the Feast of the Circumcision of Jesus, celebrated on the first of January, the day of renewal of the world through the birth of the second Adam, is on the eighth day after Christmas and is therefore called the octave of our Lord.

And when eight days were accomplished for the circumcising of the child, his name was called JESUS, which was so named of the angel before he was conceived in the womb. (Luke 2, 21.)[13]

What the Old Testament calls the circumcision of the heart, Sufi texts call the *tawaf* of the heart, the circuit round the inner *Ka'ba*. According to some devotees, this is the only true pilgrimage of which the outer is only an external reflection. Like the devout Jew, the Sufi poet Rumi felt in ecstatic joy that his heart had become circumcised by Allah, his beloved; and out of the bliss of that experience he sings:

> He that is my soul's repose,
> Round my heart encircling goes,
> Round my heart and soul of bliss
> He encircling is.[14]

The step from round processions to round dances is a short one and, indeed, we find that ring and whirling dances are performed whenever man feels the desire or inner urge to make visible the invisible happenings taking place in his heart by dancing them out and, therewith, letting the body partake in the experienced transition to new states of being.[15] Such dances are, therefore, mostly the result of, or are intended to lead to, an upsurge of the awakened forces within, evidencing itself in largely spontaneous and unpremeditated movements. When this is the case, then union, often of an ecstatic character, takes place, a union between two worlds or, as it is frequently pictured in this context, between the danced ring and its pivotal point in the centre.

The divine presence, visible or invisible, residing at the centre, the devotee moving in ecstatic joy around it, the intimate relationship of communion which is thus established and which is always communion between opposites, the transforming power of the dance, together with its cosmic reverberations, all these traits are found wherever such rituals are performed which is as much today as in olden times, for ring dances belong to all periods and to the most diverse strata of religious culture. Only one example of an archetypal nature can be cited here. A charming Indian myth tells of the *Rasa Mandala* or the round dance of Krishna and the Gopis.[16] Here all the principal features characteristic of the *mandala* dance are present in essentially the same form and meaning as they appear in other cultures. The Gopis, dancing around the god who, himself, performs the divine dance in the centre of the ring, surrender to him in love and by this very act become united with him, each thinking that she alone is dancing with Krishna.

Then Krishna played and danced with the Gopis. He made his appearance manifold and danced with them in a ring, so that each one thought that Krishna himself was by her side and held her hands; so they whirled round in a circle, the dark Krishna and the fair Braj girls, like a gold and sapphire necklace ... So they spent the time, and even the gods came down from heaven to see the dancing, and wind and water stood still to hearken.[17,18]

In most traditions there is preserved the secret knowledge that the celestial motion is circular and that the heavenly beings follow it both as an expression of their high status and as an act of glorification of the highest.[19] By performing this motion man finds entrance into the celestial spheres, he partakes in 'the general dance', as an old Cornish carol names it and, in the words of Dionysius the Areopagite, he becomes 'united to the beginningless and endless illuminations of the Beautiful and Good.'[20,21]

NOTES FOR CHAPTER 13

1. The demarcation rope or '*shime-nawa*' is one of the central symbols of Shintoism. It is fashioned of strands of twisted rice-straw and stands for the holy enclosure; it is present in every Shinto temple.
2. Useful surveys of the symbolism of the 'sacred round' are given in D. A. Mackenzie: *The Migration of Symbols*; W. Simpson: *The Buddhist Prayer Wheel*; and M. Eliade: *Patterns of Comparative Religion*.
3. For a detailed study of *mandala* symbology as it appears in Hindu and Buddhist Tantrism, see G. Tucci, *Theory and Practice of the Mandala*, London, 1961.
4. J. E. Ellam, *The Religion of Tibet*, p. 99.
5. It is known that in former times, and in some cases to this day, Hindu and Buddhist temples, as well as Christian churches, contained in their structural design provisions for such processions. The Sanskrit term for this rite is *pradakshina*, practised today as in ancient times. At York, Lincoln, Chichester and Fountains Abbey, processional stones can still be seen. Another closely related practice recently revived in some places is that of 'Beating the parish bounds'. In marriage ceremonies, mainly Hindu, Buddhist and Greek Orthodox, the newly wed couple perform circumambulations round the altar or house shrine, only then is the marriage, the becoming one of man and wife, considered complete. In western Christianity the most obvious example is the 'Way of the Cross' in which

priest and worshippers make a circuit of the church, beginning and ending at the altar. This circuit is performed sunwise.

6. The same idea is expressed by St Gregory of Nazianzus, when he speaks of dancing 'the dance of David to the true refreshment of the Ark'. See L. Backman, *Religious Dances*, p. 36.

7. Quoted by F. Meier, in *The Mysteries. Papers from the Eranos Yearbooks*, p. 162.

8. There exists a tradition which relates that after the fall, Adam repenting, prayed to God, and the voice of God was heard: 'O Adam! Out of regard for thy posterity I have caused a house of joy to descend from heaven to earth, around which always make it your duty to perform the tawaf (or circuit), just as the angels in heaven make circular processions around the Great Arch (or Throne).' (See H. A. Rose, *The Darvishes* ... p. 38.)

   The Christian version of this legend is that Adam, on the day of Christ's birthday, 'is resurrected and performs a ring-dance with the angels, raised up to heaven'. (Mentioned by Gregory the Wonder-worker (*c.* 213–270) according to L. Backman, *Religious Dances*, p. 22.)

9. G. H. Mees in *The Key to Genesis*, p. 87, quotes the following from the Epistle of Barnabbas, referring to the words of the Lord spoken on Mount Sinai:
   Finally he saith to them: 'Your new moon and your sabbaths I cannot away with.' Ye see what is His meaning; it is not your present sabbaths which I have made, in the which, when I have set all things at rest, I will make the beginning of the eighth day which is the beginning of another world. Wherefore also we keep the eighth day for rejoicing, in the which also Jesus rose from the dead, and having been manifested, ascended into heaven.
   Mees generally associates the eighth day with the resurrection.

10. In this connection G. E. von Grunebaum points to an illuminating fact, he says: The importance of the circumambulation is reflected in the fact that the original meaning of the root *hajj* is 'to describe a circle'—in other words, the Pilgrimage received its name from this key rite. *Muhammadan Festivals*, p. 30.

11. M. H. Harris, *Hebraic Literature*, p. 391.

12. The early Church took over from the antique world what was known as the 'Mystery of the Ogdoad', the mystery of the number eight. Christ rose on the eighth day, Palm Sunday being the first and Easter Sunday the last (eighth) of the liturgical octave of Easter. This eighth day is, however, also number one, the first day of the new dispensation, the day of Helios, now become the sun of the resurrected Christ. The eighth day is also the day of Baptism when the perfect men are born of whom Clement of Alexandria says:
    They did not remain in the number seven of rest but, through good works, they have assimilated themselves to God and they have now been raised to receive the inheritance of the goodness which belongs to the number eight because they gave themselves to the pure vision of insatiable contemplation.
    (See H. Rahner, *Griechische Mythen in Christlicher Deutung*, p. 111. Also J. Mitchell, *The City of Revelation*, p. 116.)

13. Following Genesis 17, 12.

14. A. J. Arberry, 'The Way in Islam', in *The Aryan Path*, Vol. XXXII, Nos. 7 and 8. July/August 1961.

15. In the writings of Ambrose, Bishop of Milan (340–397) occur the following lines: Let us not be ashamed of a show of reverence which will enrich the cult and deepen the adoration of Christ. For this reason the dance must be in no wise regarded as a mark of reverence for vanity and luxury but as something which

uplifts every living body instead of allowing the limbs to rest motionless upon the ground or the slow feet become numb.
Quoted in L. Backman, *Religious Dances*, p. 25ff.
16. Shepherd girls.
17. Nivedita and A. Coomeraswamy, *Myths and Legends* ... p. 235.
18. Nivedita and A. Coomeraswamy, *Myths and Legends*, p. 235. Other well-known ring-dances are the Rasa-Jattra, or the Dance of the Circle, performed in honour of Vishnu; 'Jesus Round Dance', as mentioned in the Acts of St John, 94–102; The Whirling Dance of the Dervishes; the Tibetan Yogic Dance of the Five Directions, and the Spanish Ribbon Dance, only to mention a few. In Christian documents mention is often made of David's dance before the Ark (2 Sam. 6, 14) as bestowing sanction to such practices. It appears likely that this was in fact a round dance, for the Hebrew term used here denotes a whirling or rotating movement. (See W. O. E. Oesterley, *The Sacred Dance*, p. 10, and C. G. Jung, *Psychology and Religion*, p. 280.)
19. In the early Church it was the customary belief that angels descended during the Kyrie, performing a ring-dance in the 'Angels' Choir'. As an old hymn says: 'Always we are encircled by the angels' ring-dance.' That after the Kyrie the presence of angels is taken for granted, is shown by the reference in High Mass to the archangel Michael and all his elect, standing at the right hand of the altar, as well as by the prayer offered after the elevation of the host.
20. *Divine Names* IV, 8.
21. E. S. Drower reports a ring-dance round the *tevah* (tribane) on the occasion of the festival of *Simhat Torah*, which used to be performed inside the great synagogue of Baghdad. This ritual dance is also mentioned by M. Buber in his *Erzählungen der Chassidim* where it is said:
... the disciples were dancing round in a circle and around the dancing circle twined a ring of blue fire.
(E. S. Drower, *Water into Wine*, p. 39, and M. Buber, *op. cit.*, p. 134.)

14

Symbols of Integration

And I John saw the Holy City, new Jerusalem,
coming from God out of Heaven, prepared as a bride
adorned for her husband. And I heard a great voice
out of Heaven saying, Behold, the tabernacle of God
is with men, and he will dwell with them, and they
shall be his people, and God himself shall be with
them, and be their God.

Revelation.

How wide the leaves,
Extended to their utmost, of this rose,
Whose lowest step embosoms such a space
Of ample radiance! ...
Into the yellow of the rose
Perennial, which, in bright expansiveness,
Lays forth its gradual blooming, redolent,
Of praises to the never-wintering sun,
As one, who fain would speak yet holds his peace,
Beatrice lead me; and, 'Behold', she said,
'This fair assemblage; stoles of snowy white,
How numberless. The city, where we dwell,
Behold how vast.' ...

DANTE, Paradiso.

The cosmic vision of St John the Divine, when he saw the holy city
descend from heaven as a sign of the final redemption of the world, also
applies to man; for when he has made the tabernacle of the living God
his permanent abode, then he himself becomes, what St Paul calls, the
temple of God which is holy. Potentially, man is that city or temple of
divine immanence; for just as the world, purified to reflect God's light,
is seen as the place of divine indwelling, so is the purified man. The
names of this temple are legion. It is called the eleven gated City of
Brahman, the foursquare city of God, the heavenly Jerusalem, the
temple of the living Lord, the ancient house, the elixir field, the castle or
mansion.[1] What Judaism claims for its sacred city, Jerusalem, is equally
claimed by other faiths:

The land of Israel is situated in the centre of the world, and Jerusalem in the centre of the land of Israel, and the Temple in the centre of Jerusalem, and the Holy of Holies in the centre of the Temple, and the foundation-stone on which the world was grounded, is situated in front of the ark.[2]

Here man receives the influx from on high and finds fulfilment of his searchings.

One thing have I desired of the Lord, that will I seek after; that I may dwell in the House of the Lord all the days of my life, to behold the beauty of the Lord, and to enquire in his temple. For in the time of trouble he shall hide me in his pavilion; in the secret of his tabernacle shall he hide me; he shall set me up upon a rock. (Psalm 27, 4/5.)

'To dwell in the house of the Lord for ever' is another way of saying that the kingdom of heaven has been founded on earth. Its seat is man, wholly consecrated to the service of God; for just as every temple or church must be consecrated for the God to become a living presence within it, so man must dedicate and purify himself to become the worthy abode for the divinity.[3]

The *Upanishads* discuss the question of the identification of the body with the City of Brahman at length. They make it clear that the various gates of the City refer to the senses and apertures of the body, and are the points of communication with the world. Yet the real City of Brahman is not this perishable body but the Self, the *Purusha*.

If they should say to him, if, within this City of Brahman, is contained all (that exists), all beings and all desires, then what is left of it when old age overtakes it or when it perishes?
He should say, it (the self within) does not age with old age, it is not killed by the killing (of the body). That (and not the body) is the real City of Brahman.[4]

In such passages, frequent use is made of the Sanscrit term '*setu*' for describing the self as informing the whole of man's being, including the body. Its original meaning is a boundary, a dam, or bank of earth fulfilling two purposes; to act as a borderline between fields and thereby to create an enclosure; and at the same time to serve as a pathway or bridge.[5] Here in a nutshell are the characteristic traits of the City of

Brahman. The field standing for the newly found wholeness which is enclosed and fortified against alien forces; this very fact, however, acts as a bridge by leading to something beyond the boundaries, something emerging out of the City of Brahman, as will become clear later. That the term '*setu*', literally denoting a dam delimiting a field, was chosen to stand for the self, reveals yet another level of meaning. For in the language of religious symbolism, the field is none other than the divine city; like it, it stands for both man and the world. It is that field containing the great treasure of which the Christian parables speak, taking it as a simile of the kingdom of heaven.

> 'Again, the kingdom of heaven is like unto a treasure hid in a field; the which when man hath found, he hideth, and for joy thereof goeth and selleth all that he hath, and buyeth that field.'
>
> Matt. 13, 44

The knowledge of the treasure hidden in the field is common property of all pilgrims of the Way. Theirs is the discovery of the supreme lordship of the 'Knower of the field of all fields', as the *Gita* calls him. By finding him, the One, as a living presence informing all created things, the field becomes ripe with the harvest of life eternal.

Medieval painters have given us pictures telling the same story. The sacred enclosure here is the garden of paradise surrounded by a rose hedge or low wall and peopled by the holy family. Also frequently in the picture is the fountain,[6] or well, and the tree whose trunk is not straight but wound serpentwise. Just as the first paradise, according to Genesis, was a *mandala* structure,[7] so this; it is the second paradise in which the development, begun in the first, has reached consummation. The return has taken place, the Christ child has entered the Garden of Eden and the synthesis of the divine and the human has been accomplished. An altogether new and greater life has dawned, a fact which was well recognized by the Hebrew people, for when later in the Christian story the same image appears, Christ entering Jerusalem, the holy city, they declare the resurrection of life with palm branches crying: hosanna in the highest.

By entering the holy city or the garden, Christ also enters the garden of the soul, an image which is much in evidence in both Christian and non-Christian devotional practices. This garden has to be cleansed and made ready so that the 'Divine Gardener' may enter, plant it anew and thus transform it into a place worthy of the divine king. When this has been achieved, the soul becomes glad with joy and sings,

Lord Jesus hath a garden, full of flowers gay,
Where you and I can gather nosegays all the day ...
O Jesus, all my good and all my bliss! Ah me!
Thy garden make my heart, which ready is for Thee!

Christmas Carol

Allah, too, calls his faithful to prepare for the same event by obedience
and submission to His commands,

O soul that art at rest,
Return to thy Lord, well-pleased, well-pleasing,
So enter among My servants,
And enter My Garden!

Sura, 89, 27–30

In Sufi interpretation, this is the garden of the heart at whose centre
plays a fountain fed from the still higher abode, the garden of the spirit,
where only those are allowed to enter who have attained spiritual
perfection. But all are called and, what is more, those heavenly places
are not only described in detail in the texts, but their earthly reflection is
there for all to see. When a Muslim enters a mosque, he passes through
such a garden;[8] for the forecourt is built as a walled enclosure where
waters flow, reminding him of the need for purification and renewal,[9]
and where often beautiful trees greet him, foreshadowing the trees of
paradise promised to him in the holy book.

When St Augustine wrote his famous treatise, *The City of God*, he
based it on Greek philosophical thought, notably on Plato's *Republic*.
There the picture of two cities is given, one heavenly, the other worldly,
one the idea to be emulated, the other the stark reality to be
transcended. This idea is found in St Paul's writings as well as St
Augustine's. The latter speaks of the house of God and of two cities,
Babylon and Jerusalem, in which two types of love prevail, self-love
and selfless love of God. Those who belong to the House of God, St
Augustine calls the pilgrims who live in this world but whose real home
is the heavenly city,

being by grace predestined, by grace elect, by grace a pilgrim here
below, and by grace a citizen of heaven.[10]

The whole work can be called a long meditation on the heavenly
Jerusalem, showing in detail its many aspects and relationships to the
fallen world of man. In all its complexity, it is a spiritual guide in the
same sense as St Theresa's 'Interior Castle' is, and it is exactly to this

same purpose that seekers of other traditions have used the image of the holy city.

There, too, it appears as a meditational guide, yet not written about so much as painted or drawn with all the minute intricacies pertaining to its symbolism. Notably, Tibetan Buddhism has for centuries resorted to this visual aid. The *lamas* use it freely and often present their pupils with colourful representations of the sacred city printed on silk or other suitable material. Many different versions of these *mandalas* exist; they appear side by side with others, based on the ground plan of the open lotus or wheel. In the case of the city, a beautiful garden is often seen to surround its walls which, at the four cardinal points, are broken by elaborate gateways. The garden itself is enclosed by an encircling line, the whole frequently resting on a mountainous landscape whose peaks touch the sky above.

Within the walls, more concentric circles protect and enshrine the holiest of holies, the goal of the pilgrimage, in some instances, the image of the Buddha, or a sacred word or syllable, in others the diamond sceptre, the *vajra* or *dorje* (see pl. 4). This inner domain is known as the palace which, once again, represents both the hub of the world and the hidden centre in man. Access to it, and to the city as a whole, is only possible through initiation, which, to the worthy, confers the ability to penetrate the successive circles, barring the way to the Buddhist paradise, whatever its meaning in the different schools.[11]

Initiation is followed by many years dedicated to meditation and holy practices until the *mandala* image has been translated into life and the seeker has become one with it; it has, then, served its purpose and can be left behind:

> For the Yogi who hath the perfect Divine Mandala
> Well defined in His own body,
> What need is there of the Mandala
> Outlined on the ground?[12]

It is said that when the Buddha was born, he immediately walked seven steps, and where he touched the ground a lotus sprang up. Later, when the seer Asita saw the child he recognized the future Buddha by certain marks on its body; amongst these were a circle of soft down growing between the eyebrows and wheels marking the soles of the feet.[13]

The seven steps are the stages on the path of integration, whose completion is symbolized by the open lotus, the wheel, and the circle. The lotus flower which has unfolded its petals reveals in the centre the divine seed, the Buddha child, or, in Hindu religion, the child Shiva sitting in the birthplace of the gods, *padma*, the lotus-abode. The new birth takes place in the bud but in time the flower opens, growth is completed, and man finds himself transformed into a lotus.

This appears to be a universal experience, for, just as the Tibetan saint became identified with the *mandala*, so the Egyptian soul at the end of her journey says,

> I am the pure lotus which springeth up from the divine splendour that belongeth to the nostrils of Rā. I have made my way, and I follow on seeking from him who is Horus. I am the pure one who cometh forth out of the Field.

The accompanying vignettes show either a lotus flower in full bloom or the head of a man emerging from a lotus flower which is floating on water.[14]

Do symbols migrate from place to place or are they spontaneously produced, the same or similar images standing for certain basic experiences? This question will never be answered by taking sides unequivocally, for the ramification of influences and the universality of human reactions are such that at every point, singled out for attention, both seem to fuse and an explanation one way or the other does not touch the integral uniqueness of the experience. The open lotus rising out of muddy waters, or the rose born on a stem of thorns, represents such a universal symbol, always telling the story of the man who has accomplished a renewal of his whole being.

In Buddhist meditational practice, man has reached the third *Jhana*, the third of the embodiments or fruits of meditation and the imagery attending it is almost exactly that of *The Egyptian Book of the Dead*. Instead of the lake fed by a subterranean spring used in the second *Jhana*, here the simile is that of a lotus sustained and nourished by the fresh waters of the lake.

> As in a lake with lotus plants some lotus flowers are born in the water, developed in the water, remain below the surface of the water, and draw their nourishment from the depths of the water, and their blooms and their roots are pervaded, infused, filled and saturated with fresh water, so that not the smallest part of any lotus flower is left unsaturated with fresh moisture: just so the ascetic pervades and infuses, fills and saturates his body with purified joy, so that not the smallest part of his body is left unsaturated with purified joy.[15]

Here the lotus primarily indicates a high form of realization reached through deep meditation. It is for this reason that the Buddha, or in the Mahayana Schools of Buddhism, one of the *Bodhisattvas*, is so often depicted in meditation on the open lotus. For in the great mantric formula *Om Mani Padme Hum*, the lotus, *Padme*, represents the third[16] of the successive stages of transformation. Its embodiment, according to Tibetan teaching, is Amithabha Buddha, the Buddha of Boundless Light,[17] who, when he decided to enter the incarnate world for the good of suffering mankind, was heralded by heavenly voices thus:

Hail! Hail! the Lord Amithabha, Protector of Mankind, shall take birth as a Divine Incarnation from a lotus blossom amidst the Jewel Lake.

Tib. Book of Gt. Lib., p. 107

What the lotus is for Indian religion, is the white lily,[18] and the red or golden rose, for the near Eastern religions. Both are seen as emblems of perfection,[19] from whose hidden centre diverse and dynamic patterns radiate out, filling the whole with a life of beauty and harmony.

The Old Testament speaks of the lily as an ornamentation of the temple, the top of pillars, so we are told, being adorned with lily work. The word is *soshan*,[20] deriving from the Egyptian term for lotus, and it seems unlikely that such decorative work was used in the house of God without an awareness of its symbolic meaning.

On medieval paintings, the Madonna as well as the angel of the annunciation carries the lily, the madonna lily as it is called in English, and the same applies to many Christian saints who display it as an emblem of virginity, chastity and saintly perfection. More and more, however, the lily has become the flower of the resurrection, of Easter, the feast of the new birth, as it had been in the later *Kabbalah*.[21] It is this meaning which fired the imagination of many poets, mainly those of the French Renaissance, who make frequent use of the simile of the lily (fleur de lys), often in conjunction with the rose. Such is the case in a mystic poem entitled '*Rosier de Marie*'.

Amour à toi beau lis au milieu des épines,
Fleur qui brille parmi les ruines,
Rose qui sort du tronc desséché d'Israël!
Toi que rêva Jacob mystérieuse échelle,
Par qui la terre voit descendre Dieu en elle
Et l'homme remonter au Ciel.[22]

The image here given of the rose, emerging from the dry trunk of the old dispensation, is symptomatic for the Christian use of this symbol. The picture of the 'full-blown' rose stimulated Christian piety even more deeply and lastingly than did the lily.[23]

The man who enters the Christian *temenos*, a cathedral or church, is greeted by an intricate *mandala* structure crowning the west end, the rose window. From the outside it only shows its structural complexity, the round filled with interlacing lines, meeting at the centre, from which they fan out in all directions. Seen from the inside, from the interior of the sanctuary, it grants a multicoloured vision, diffused with light and throbbing with life. The magic circle has been entered, and this circle reveals itself to be like unto a rose at whose innermost point the Christian mystery is enacted.

When it is said that, according to Indian teaching, the cosmic lotus, thousand-petalled and gold in colour, was the cradle of the creator God Brahman, in Christian imagery, it is God the Father, the Madonna and Child, the Trinity, or Christ alone, who are depicted as occupying the centre of the Mystic Rose or *Mandorla* of Light.[24]

It is likely that in the middle ages the rose window, or the rose in general, reminded the worshippers of their heavenly queen, Mary, the Mother of God, the exemplar of all virtues, and all graces. For, through the litany of the Blessed Virgin, they were familiar with the fact that amongst Mary's adorational names there occur the following: Domus Aurea, House of Gold, Rosa Mystica, Mystical Rose, Regina sacratissima Rosarii, Queen of the most holy Rosary.

The Mother of God is seen as the mystical rose[25] for the same reason as the lotus, in Indian mythology, is originally a symbol of the earth goddess in whose womb the divine child is born. As happened in India, this image of divine incarnation is later made to include the God himself, and eventually the lotus became the symbol of Brahma just as the rose became the symbol of Christ. This rose of roses flowers on a rosebush, or it is seen to spring from a tender root, growing in a rose garden, all similes for Mary, the divine Mother.[26]

> A spotless Rose is blowing,
> Sprung from a tender root,
> Of ancient seers foreshowing
> Of Jesse promised fruit ...
> The Rose which I am singing,
> Whereof Isaiah said,
> Is from its sweet root springing,
> In Mary purest Maid.

The rose, like the lily, is the flower of the resurrection, of the new life entered through the crucifixion, for, according to medieval interpretation, the way of Christ leads through the cross to the rose, *per crucem ad roseam*. The sign of the first is the unadorned cross on which the saviour, crowned with thorns, died; that of the second the floriated cross, often shown with equal arms, whose centre is surrounded by a circle or rose, and whose ends flower forth bearing roses, trefoils or lily-shaped ornaments.[27] It is the cross of the completed sacrifice, the cross of victory[28] and consummation, the sign of the new man. Just as the lotus is seen to rise out of the turbid waters of a pool pure and unstained, so here the rose in all its beauty is born out of a thorn. Its flowering time is Christmas, the nativity of the Lord; for it blooms 'in the cold bleak winter turning our darkness into light', as an old song tells us, and as it can still be seen at Glastonbury, where the sacred thorn, sprung from the staff of Joseph Arimathea, sends forth its blossoms every Christmas-tide.[29] The saying of the Sufi poet, Hafiz, here becomes true: 'without enduring the torment of the thorn one cannot gain the rose'.

The mystic rose is a symbol dear to Islamic Sufism. It occurs in many of its writings, wherever the theme is spiritual love and divine intoxication, and one of the great Dervish orders, the Qadiris, wear it on their caps as a sign of membership.[30] To them it is a constant reminder of the need to delve ever deeper into the mystery of the rose, and thereby to unravel the mystery of God. Was it this a Sufi devotee was engaged in, of whom Sa'di of Shiraz tells in his famous book entitled *The Rose Garden*?

A certain mystic had bowed his head in holy meditation and plunged deep into the sea of divine vision. When he came back to himself, one of his companions said pleasantly, 'What gift dost thou bring to us from the garden where thou hast been?' He answered, 'It was in my mind, when I saw the rose-bush, to fill my skirt with roses and bring them home to you, but their perfume so enravished me that my skirt slipped from my hand.'[31]

The symbol of the rose, and that of the wheel or disc, are closely related. The rose windows are in fact often wheel-shaped with unmistakable spokes radiating out from the hub.[32] Like the rose, the wheel as a sign of spiritual attainment and cosmic unity in diversity, is the common property of practically all the great religious traditions. There is, however, a distinct difference in meaning between the rose and the wheel. Whereas the rose tells the beholder of peace and beauty, the wheel indicates becoming and thus motion within the eternal round. The wheel, therefore, either in the form of the Christian wheel cross or the many-spoked Buddhist wheel of the law, does not so much stand for the person of the saviour or *Avatar*, risen and triumphant, but for the entirety of the message delivered in and to the world.[33] Both are in reality versions of the sunwheel, symbolizing the course of the sun through the four seasons of the year. As such, the wheel combines in itself the heavenly and the earthly spheres, the outer circle standing for eternity, and the enclosed cross or spokes for nature and the world. Thus it revolves, a potent symbol of the Way, reminding man of the eternal law as a means of liberation and salvation from the snares of earthly existence.[34]

When the *Rig Veda*[35] speaks of the immortal wheel which nothing can arrest and on which all beings repose, this is based on the same cosmic vision as is expressed in those Upanishadic passages which tell of the wheel of Brahma, enveloping the whole world, on which the ignorant flutter about like birds. It is man's sacred duty to turn the wheel within himself, by following the prescribed path; those who oppose its movement and do nothing within, are doomed.

He who in this world turns not the wheel that has been set revolving, evil of life, and delighted in the senses, lives in vain.[36]

The turning of the wheel is the path of integration within and of unity without, of the synthesis and transcendence of the opposites whose interplay keep the wheel in motion.

The Buddha's world-liberating act was to set the wheel of the Law (*Dharmachakra*) revolving, an act resulting immediately from his attainment to supreme enlightenment.

And when the royal chariot wheel of the truth had thus been set rolling onwards by the Blessed One, the Gods of the earth gave forth a shout, saying: 'In Benares, at the hermitage of the Migadaya, the supreme wheel of the empire of truth has been set rolling by the Blessed One—that wheel which not by any Samana or Mara, not by any one in the universe, can ever be turned back!'[37]

Thus we read in the Sutta of the foundation of the kingdom of righteousness. When the wheel has turned a complete circle, when a round of existences has been accomplished, the law is fulfilled; man has become like a full circle, whole, and is called a *Chakravarti*,[38] a supreme king, who has turned the wheel of the *Dharma*.

There has come down to us the description of the visions of the *Chakravarti* Maha-Sudassana, the Buddha in one of his former births. The heavenly treasure of the wheel appeared to him with its 'nave, its tire, and all its thousand spokes complete'. After paying homage to the wheel, he says,

> Roll onward, O my lord, the wheel!
> O my Lord go forth and overcome.

This episode from one of his previous lives the Buddha tells to his favourite disciple, Ananda, and he ends with these words:

> Now when the wondrous wheel, Ananda, had gone forth conquering and to conquer o'er the whole earth to its very ocean boundary, it returned back again to the royal city of Kusavati and remained fixed on the open terrace in front of the entrance to the inner apartments of the Great King of Glory, as a glorious adornment to the inner apartment of the Great King of Glory.[39]

Buddhist tradition foretells the return of this great king of glory, who will appear on earth in order to guide mankind; he will be called the king of the golden wheel or the holy king turning the wheel.

Often such visions as these, belonging to eastern religiosity, have a foreign ring to western ears. We are unused to the symbolic language employed and are therefore unresponsive. In this case, however, it is different. For the *Chakravarti's* vision of the wheel moving in the four directions of the globe, together with his appellation 'O my lord, the wheel' makes something reverberate in us which belongs to our own tradition. It is contained in the Bible and it, too, belongs to a vision of the heavenly spheres and of the things to come. The prophet Ezekiel beheld a wondrous sight.[40]

> Now as I beheld the living creatures, behold one wheel upon the earth by the living creatures, with his four faces. The appearance of the wheel and their work was like unto the colour of a beryl: and the four had one likeness: and their appearance and their work was as it were a wheel in the middle of a wheel.

And the prophet saw that wherever the living creatures went there the wheels went and he heard that voices cried unto the wheel within a wheel 'O wheel!'

NOTES FOR CHAPTER 14

1. For a detailed study of the hidden significance of the Cosmic Temple, see J. Mitchell, *The City of Revelation*.
2. Midrash Tillin Terumah, Kedoshim, in M. H. Harris, *Hebraic Literature*, p. 249.
3. We read in St Theresa's 'Way of Perfection', XXVIII, 9: 'Let us realize that we have within us a most splendid palace built entirely of gold and precious stones; ... within this palace dwells the mighty King who has deigned to become your Father, and who is seated on a throne of priceless value—by which I mean your heart.'
4. *Chandogya Upanishad* VIII, 1, 4–5. For parallel passages see *Svetasvatara Upanishad* III, 18, and *Bhagavadgita* V, 13.
5. F. M. Muller, *The Upanishads*, Vol. II, p. 130; also *Brhad-aranyaka Upanishad* IV, 4, 22.
6. 'Maria im Rosenhag', as these pictures are often called, notably in medieval Germany (Rhineland). There is undoubtedly an allusion here to one of the many attributes of the Virgin Mary used widely in the middle ages: *Fons signatur*. (See pp. 145–6 and 179.)
7. It was walled and through it ran the four rivers of life, forming a cross; in its centre stood the tree of life.
8. Every Christian monastery, as well as collegiate churches, have such a walled garden with a well or fountain at its centre. Members of the order use it for walking round it in prayer and meditation.
9. The *Ka'ba* itself contains two 'fountains', the *mizāb ar-rahma*, the waterspout of mercy, and, under a separate roof, the well of zamzam from which Hagar and her son Ishmael drank when they were dying from thirst. Gabriel made it appear miraculously and to this day it is said to have miraculous qualities.
10. *The City of God* XV, 1, 2.
11. There exists a curious parallel to this symbolic use of the 'city' *mandala* as a guide to meditation. In the church of the Holy Trinity at Teinach there is preserved a so-called 'Kabbalistische Lehrtafel' which belonged to the Princess Antonia von Wurttemberg. It is a picture of a temple whose open doors allow the sanctuary to be seen from the outside. In front is a circular garden built round a pond in whose centre, on a rock, stands Christ. Around the cupola are seen groups of the heavenly hosts and the whole picture is filled with symbolic figures telling the story of the Old and New Testament as well as the teaching of a Christianized version of the *Kabbalah*. The whole is encircled by a hedge with a vaulted entrance through which the Princess is seen entering the temple. Every item in the picture is numbered or lettered and the over hundred explanations reach from the crown of the kingdom, the highest manifestation of God, down to the *neophite*, the princess, embarking on the pilgrimage to the Kabbalistic heights. In E. Benz, *Die Christliche Kabbala*, plate.
12. W. Y. Evans-Wentz, *Tibet's Great Yogi Milarepa*, p. 277.
13. In like manner, when Krishna was born, he, the 'Lotus-eyed', revealed his divine nature by carrying certain emblems, including a disc and a lotus flower.
14. *The Egyptian Book of the Dead*, chapter LXXXI A and B. See pl. 3.
15. *Digha Nikaya* II, 82.
16. According to some teachings, there are five *Jhanas*, corresponding to the five *Dhyana* Buddhas, Amitabha being the fourth.

17. Amitabha, in his Bodhisattvic form, is Avalokiteshvara or Padmapani, the saviour of mankind who carries the lotus (*padma*) in his hand (*pani*). For the development of the lotus symbol from the Indian lotus or Earth Goddess to its use by Mahayana Buddhism as the sign of *Prajna Paramita*, the highest embodiment of enlightenment and wisdom, see H. Zimmer, *Myths and Symbols* ..., p. 98ff.

18. The water lily is only another version of the lotus and it is, therefore, not surprising that another version of the above-mentioned Egyptian text is:
    I am the pure Lily coming forth from the Lily of Light ...
    A. Bothwell-Gosse, *The Lily of Light*, p. 48–9.

19. The lily and the rose figure together in the Song of Solomon where it is said 'I am the rose of Sharon, and the Lily of the Valleys', 2, 1. The Golden Rose, *Rosa Aurea*, is blessed by the Pope on the fourth Sunday in Lent. Originally, 'this exquisitely wrought jewel was intended as a reward for perfection in virtue, a symbol of earthly human perfection, a reflection of the heavenly and superhuman attained by many saints'. (A. Bothwell-Gosse, *Immortal Rose*, p. 44.)

20. The Zohar renders it 'rose'. See *Jewish Encyclopedia*, 'lily', 1905 ed.

21. The lily is also an important Masonic symbol. See *Jewish Encyclopedia*, 1905 ed.

22. A. Bothwell-Gosse, *The Lily of Light*, p. 37.

23. According to an Indian legend, Brahma and Vishnu were talking about flowers. Brahma averred that the lotus represented the height of beauty, whereupon Vishnu took a rose and held it up; Brahma agreed to the superiority of the rose. Something similar must have happened in Christianity, although myth and legend are silent about it.

24. Dante speaks of it as 'this rose ... of ample radiance'. See *Paradiso* XXX, quoted above, p. 172.

25. As we sing in the Advent carol:
    > There is no rose of such virtue
    > As is the rose that bare Jesus: Alleluia
    > For in this rose contained was
    > Heaven and earth in little space: Res miranda ...

    The rose is carried by the Patron Saint of South America, called Rose of Lima, who is depicted as holding a rose with the Christchild in it.

26. The rose garden is the 'hortus conclusus' as well as the 'vas spirituale', the shrine of the Spirit, in which the treasures of devotion and love are contained, just as is the case in the 'Rose garden', Gulistan, in Sufi poetry (Sa'di).

27. E. S. Drower in *Water into Wine*, p. 87, speaks of the preference shown by the Nestorian, Jacobite, Orthodox and Armenian Churches for the 'floriated cross', a cross with arms of equal length ending in a trefoil, known in heraldry as the 'cross botonnée'. The floriated cross, which has been connected by some with Aaron's rod that budded, is closely associated with the resurrection; hence it conveys, more than any other cross, the idea of resurgent life. As she points out, it is used in these churches at the ceremony of the feast of the finding of the cross. In this form, it closely resembles the double *dorje* or *vajra*, the Buddhist emblem, often depicted with a lotus in its centre, out of which grows 'the cross', the lotus buds pointing in all four directions.

28. Such 'rose crosses' are fairly frequent in medieval art, especially in Irish art. Usually there is a fifth rose at the centre of the cross, standing for 'Jesus Christ Victor', as the inscription on one such cross signifies. (See A. Rosenberg, *Die Christliche Bildmeditation*, and F. Henry, *Early Christian Irish Art*.)

29. Christian Saints are often shown as crowned with roses, a reminder of the crown of thorns, now bearing flowers through the sacrifice of Christ. St Elisabeth of

Portugal, for instance, is shown, not only with a crown of roses but also as carrying roses in the depth of winter.

30. The description of this rose of the Quadiris is illuminating. It has two outside and two inside rings, as well as three circles, and is made of green cloth. The first circle signifies *sharoat*, or God's law as revealed by His Prophet; the second signifies the *tariqat*, or 'Path' of the Order; the third signifies the *ma'rifat*, or 'knowledge' of God. The three together are a sign that their acquisition has bestowed the hal, or condition, known as the haqiqat, or 'Truth'. (See H. A. Rose, *The Darvishes*, pp. 99–100.)

31. M. Smith, *The Sufi Path of Love*, p. 40.

32. In this form it is sometimes called the rose-wheel; at its centre, God, the Father, or Christ in majesty. It represents the world made perfect, the kingdom of God, or the sacred city.

33. In early Buddhist art, the wheel took the place of the Buddha figure as it appears in later periods. It stood not so much for the Buddha himself, but for his teaching, the *dharma*, as it still does in Buddhist iconography.

34. These two aspects of the wheel are of importance for Indian religions as well as Christianity. The round or wheel of births and deaths is something to be transcended; for man is broken on it, in the same way as in stark reality many a Christian saint was martyred on it, and as Christ was broken on the Cross. Triumph over this aspect of the wheel means the conquest of death and the victory of *dharma*, the wheel of the Law. In Christian symbolism, the cross is now surrounded by a circle, it has been made whole and become the wheel-cross, or the wheel or wreath with candles on it, thus emitting light.

35. V, 1, 164, 2.

36. *Bhagavadgita* III, 16.——

37. *Sacred Books of the East* XI, p. 153ff.

38. The term *Chakravarti* is known to Hinduism, Buddhism, and Jainism. According to the *Vishnu Purana*, the hand of a *Chakravarti* shows the mark of the disc of Vishnu, and likewise, the footprints of the Buddha are said to display the wheel at their centre.

39. *Sacred Books of the East* XI, 251ff.

40. Chapters I and X.

15

The Tree of Victory

I will be as the dew unto Israel: he shall grow as the lily, and cast forth his roots as Lebanon. His branches shall spread, and his beauty shall be as the olive tree, and his smell as Lebanon. They that dwell under his shadow shall return; they shall revive as the corn, and grow as the vine; the scene therefore shall be as the wine of Lebanon.

HOSEA

Seest thou not that God citeth a symbol? 'A good word is as a good tree, its root firm and its branches in heaven, giving its fruit at every season by the leave of its Lord? God citeth symbols for men that they may remember.

KORAN

The Perfect Man is a miniature of Reality; he is the microcosm, in whom are reflected all the perfect attributes of the macrocosm ... The Perfect Man was the cause of the Universe, being the epiphany of God's desire to be known; for only the Perfect Man knows God, loves God, and is loved by God. For Man alone the world was made.

IBN 'ARABI

In the *temenos*, the holy enclosure, there grows a tree which is variously called the cosmic tree, the tree of life, and the tree of knowledge. Its symbolism is intricate,[1] but, whatever its exact connotation in each case, primarily it appears to represent wholeness and fulfilment. It is the tree of the kingdom of heaven grown out of a mustard seed, or, according to *Mahayana* teaching, the tree of life which grows out of the Buddha seed in the human heart and bears the fruit of supreme enlightenment. The seed must die, the soft young shoot must give way to the mighty tree as Ezekiel saw it:

The tender twig that is planted on the high mountains of Israel, that shoots forth into branches and becomes a great cedar and all the birds dwell under it. (17, 23.)

The Buddha attained illumination under this tree which is known as the bodhi tree, the tree of transcendental knowledge, and which, as the myth has it, is none other than the tree of life growing at the centre of the world. Its presence indicates that the Buddha, as other *Avatars* had done before and after him, established afresh the contact with the root of all life and, what is more, that in and through him that organic wholeness was made manifest in which the root and the branches, the one and the many, are unified.

Most religious traditions see in the tree the great symbol of unification of the opposing life forces, of male and female, static and dynamic, permanent and impermanent, or light and darkness. For the tree partakes of the changelessness of the rock on which it stands, as well as of the transiency of the seed out of which it emerges; in it pulsates the rising and falling sap, the female or moon force (*Ida*), as Tantrism sees it, ascending from the root to the crown and the male or sun force (*Pingala*), descending from the highest point down to the earth.

This insight of the living union of the opposites accomplished when organic wholeness, spiritually and physically, has been reached, has found expression in various ways. Often it has given rise to the image of two birds nesting in the tree of life, as we read in the *Upanishads*.

Two birds inseparable friends, cling to the same tree. One of them eats the sweet fruit, the other looks on without eating.[2]

Other passages speak of two selves, both partaking of the fruit of *Karma* and both residing within in the secret abode of the Supreme. They are known as shade and light.[3] Here, according to most commentaries, the opposites referred to are the temporal and the eternal self whose meeting place is the world tree, more specifically the tree of human life. In it the union of the active (*Upaya*) and the passive (*Prajna*) element is accomplished in the same way as two lovers experience union in embrace.[4] The person who does not understand this clings to the tree hopelessly 'grieving, immersed, bewildered by his own impotence'.[5]

Birds belong to trees because they belong to the air. They stand for the spiritual realm, for the higher spheres of life. They have wings, as the soul is said to have wings, and they can take themselves to the heights towards the light of the sun. Often, instead of two birds in the tree or flanking it there are depicted other creatures. Sometimes they are animals of the earth who cannot lift themselves up; they are earthbound and therefore point to the lower realms of nature. At other times, we see strange creatures accompanying the tree, unicorns or lions with wings denoting their link with both spheres, the upper and the lower. Occasionally the birds of the air and the animals of the earth appear together as is the case in a bas-relief in the baptistry of Cividale where two birds with fruits in their beaks appropriately occupy the crown whilst winged creatures in the shape of lions flank the trunk of the tree.[6]

Christianity, alongside other religions, has made ample use of this symbolism. It did so, not only in the form indicated by the last example, but above all, in a way which medieval art used and spread so widely that it is often regarded as typically Christian which, indeed, in a sense, it is. We are referring to pictures of the tree of paradise, encircled spiralwise by the serpent, to the right and left of which stand the first men, Adam and Eve.[7] Here the duality residing in the tree[8] has found a most trenchant expression.

Genesis relates that Adam and Eve plucked the fruit from the tree of knowledge of good and evil, and that from this act of disobedience stems the fall. Genesis, however, also mentions the tree of life as distinct from the tree of knowledge. What is the answer to this riddle? It is impossible here to follow this dispute in detail but, in view of the inherent polarity of the cosmic tree, as it appears in so many traditions, it seems likely, as some scholars have repeatedly pointed out,[9] that at some time a split occurred. For when the intuitive knowledge of the duality in unity of the tree of life is lost, the opposites it enshrines become mutually exclusive; beside the tree of life, there now grows the tree of knowledge of the opposites, of male and female, of good and evil.

At that moment, too, the king-spirit of the tree of life, the serpent, linking in its coils the root with the crown, the earth with the sky, and acting as the protector of enlightened beings,[10] seems to undergo a similar split. The winged serpent which denotes life and light[11] loses its wings, bird and serpent part company. The latter becomes the tempter, the channel of the forces of unregenerate nature.[12] Not until bird and serpent become reconciled can the war between the contraries be resolved. Then, once again, there will be not two but only one tree, the *bodhi* tree of enlightenment, the tree of victory which in Christian interpretation is the cross on which the serpent hangs crucified. 'And as Moses lifted up the serpent in the wilderness, even so must the son of man be lifted up' (John 3, 14). Here the breach has been healed, for at the foot of the cross of Golgotha (Skull Hill) lies a skull or a serpent and at its head appears the bird of the cosmic tree, the dove, the symbol of the holy spirit. Just as Krishna is said to have put an end to the strife between the serpent king Kaliya, residing in the deep, and the sun bird Garuda,[13] so Christ fulfils the ancient prophesy that the spirit of the

Lord shall rest on a branch arising out of the roots of the stem of Jesse. 'The verge of Jesse hath blossomed: A virgin hath brought forth God and man: God hath restored peace, reconciling in himself the highest with the lowest.' (Roman Missal.) (See pl. 5.)

With this the rod of Jesse, which is none other than the tree of life, as it is also the cross, becomes the throne for him who has reconciled the opposites. 'Alleluja, Alleluja, tell the heathen, the Lord is king now, throned on a tree.' This could equally well apply to the tree-shaped lotus which becomes the throne of the All-Enlightened One, the Buddha.[14]

In church or temple, the sacred tree has its place in the innermost sanctuary. This is regarded as its root place as well as the place where the transformation into the tree of enlightenment and victory takes place. (See pl. 6.) There is found the cone or tree of a stupa, there stands the holy candlestick, the *Menorah*,[15] used in Jewish worship, which is often shaped like a tree, there stands the cross on the high altar in a Christian church and there, too, as an ornament, adorning the Holiest of holies, the *mihrab* of a mosque, can be seen the tree of life.

This, however, is not all. For the structure itself of a church or temple taken as a whole, often follows the outlines of the sacred tree. Every church, exoterically as well as esoterically, is none other than the tree of life and as such, in the form of the tree of Golgotha, stands at the centre of the world. The same is claimed for temples of other faiths for they, too, represent the tree.[16] Regarding the Tibetan dagoba, Lama Govinda has the following to say:

> The spire of the *dagoba*, *pagoda* or *chhorten* (as they are called in Tibet) represents this tree of life in its ideal form of the heavenly tree whose branches are the higher worlds which spread one above the other in innumerable planes beyond the summit of Mount Meru, the axis of the universe ... The spiritual rebirth of the world starts in the mind of man and the tree of life grows out of his own heart the centre of his world, and spreads into ever new infinities, into ever higher and purer realms until it has turned into a tree of enlightenment.[17]

The sap of the tree of life is fed from above and therefore descends as it also rises from its root to complete the cycle. Seen under the first aspect the tree derives its life from the heavenly spheres and it is for this reason that it is often said to have its roots in heaven and its branches on earth. This image is found in Indian scriptures where it is called 'that ancient tree, whose roots grow upwards and whose branches grow downwards; that indeed is called the bright, that is called Brahman that

alone is called the immortal. All worlds are contained in it, and no one
goes beyond it. This is that.'[18]

Ruysbroeck, the Flemish mystic of the fourteenth century, calls this
tree the tree of faith which the seeker of God must embrace

And he must climb up into the tree of faith, which grows from above
downwards, for its roots are in the Godhead.[19]

In the same vein, Jewish mystical tradition speaks of the tree of life
which extends from above downwards and Islamic teaching knows it as
'the tree of happiness' whose roots are sunk in the furthest heaven and
whose branches spread over the earth.[20]

Generally speaking, whether seen in its macrocosmic or microcosmic
dimension, and whether visualized as hanging downward or standing
upright, the tree nurtured from above is the symbol of the divine
descent into manifestation. It has to be read from its top downwards, as
it were, for it branches out from the divine unity and, as Jewish
mysticism has expressed it, 'All the divine powers form a succession of
layers and are like a tree'.[21] This is the tree of God, representing the
descending life giving forces. From oneness they ramify and disperse to
give birth to the world in all its diversity. To retrace these stages and
find the way back to unity is man's sacred duty or, as some would say,
the one true purpose of his existence. Its symbol is the tree of life in its
ascending aspect, which often fuses with a closely related symbol, that
of the ascending ladder; both stand for the progressive discovery of the
hidden truths in the outer as well as inner world. As such they signify
the *imitatio dei* and it is therefore altogether in keeping with this
worldwide tradition when a devout Rabbi of the sixteenth century calls
his ethical treatise, dealing with the imitation of God, a 'palm tree'
which he introduces with the words:

It is proper for man to imitate his Creator, resembling Him in both
likeness and image according to the secret of the supernal form.[22]

The secret of the supernal form is enshrined in the sefirothic tree, as
taught in the *Kabbalah*, as also in supernal man, the perfected being in
whom all vital forces have become purified and sanctified and are
directed towards the one goal, the realization of the holy life and the
kingdom of God on earth. In him Adam Kadmon, man as he was
originally created, perfect and whole, has risen again. 'In him' as Martin
Buber has said, 'the lower, earthly man realizes his archetypal image,

the cosmic primordial man who embraces the spheres. He is the reversal of the great flood, in him the world returns to its source.'[23]

In most traditions, the perfect man stands both at the beginning and end of creation, he is the first as well as the new Adam. Individual man stands between both, between the innate image of primordial perfection and the ideal of its renewed realization. The symbols for this ideal are those discussed above, the cross, the lotus, the tree. All these are interchangeable and can stand for the perfected human being, or, on the cosmic level, for universal man. To the *Kabbalists*, for instance, the tree of divine emanations is also man, just as the whole of the created world can be seen under the image of the human form.

According to eastern teaching it is the realization of this essential analogy or, as some would say, identity of the human microcosm and the divine macrocosm which is the precondition for attaining to the highest form of existence, that of the perfect man.[24]

In this context we are not so much concerned with the primordial or the cosmic, as with the prototypal aspect of the perfect man, seen as an ideal for individual man to follow. All traditions report of enlightened beings who have walked this earth and have in this very existence reached the goal of heavenly perfection. Their lives show, however, that the aspects mentioned cannot be clearly separated, for these men have always gathered upon themselves the cosmic numinosity of the first creative emanation of the Godhead, which is the highest as well as the nearest to God and, for that reason, the most consummate image or reflection of Him. As the apex of creation, such a man is seen to embrace, within himself, all potentialities of manifestation, existentially he is the created universe in all its diversity. In religious language he is the first and the last, he is the spirit of God made manifest, he is the light of reality become incarnate. He is also the exemplar, the guide, and the friend of mankind who has appeared so as to alleviate the one great task of all men, the imitation of God.

The manner in which men set about this task varies but essentially they all endeavour to create in themselves what the Taoists call the immortal body, the spirit body or, as the *Kabbalah* puts it, to discover the secret of the heavenly man hidden invisibly inside every one of us. Buddhism calls this immortal body, the *dharma body*, pure and immutable, which manifests itself under various forms. Whatever the subtle differences between these, the goal is always the unfolding in man of the germ of Buddhahood and the complete transformation of the human being. By living the *dharma*, the *dharma-body* takes shape or, as some schools would call it, the body of transformation[25] which is the *dharma-body* in manifestation. When this happens man realizes his essential identity with the Buddha and he will speak similar words to those the Tibetan yogi utters during initiation:

> This uncreate mind of my wretched self is the brilliant lotus-body of the Precious Three in unity.[26]

A closely related idea is found in Jewish mysticism where the Rabbis belonging to the *Chasidic* movement liked to interpret Ezekiel's vision of the throne of God: 'and upon the likeness of the throne was the likeness as the appearance of a man above upon it' (1, 26) as meaning that the human form, here apparently applied to God, in reality refers to the body we ourselves fashion through devoted obedience to the Lord's commandments. 'It is the form which we ourselves mould through our hearts' true service. In this way we create for our creator, who is without image or likeness, for Him alone, blessed be He and blessed be His Name, a human form.'[27]

Many of the perfected men the world has known have borne the marks of their high achievement on their bodies.

The nearness of their realization of the embodiment of truth becomes visible in external signs: their bodies partake of the perfection of their being. The ideal of union with the saviour has impressed itself on the bodily members of many Christian saints. The marks and symbols of the God-Man Christ, his wounds, or his cross appear in the flesh and tell the story of a perfect 'Imitatio'. Fallen man becomes a saintly being and the numinous quality of spirit and soul is, in a measure, shared by the human frame. The body partakes of the transformation into the New Man and in the bliss of this happening men of many traditions and tongues have uttered words like these:

> In the body God is present.
> The body is His temple.
> In the body is the place of pilgrimage
> Of which I am the pilgrim,
> In the body is the incense and candles,
> In the body is the holy offering,
> In the body the oblation ...
>
> He who pervades the universe
> Also dwells in the body:
> Who seeks shall find Him there.
>
> Pīpā[28]

NOTES FOR CHAPTER 15

1. So much so, that it is impossible, even briefly, to indicate all its ramifications; only those aspects will, therefore, be mentioned which have a direct bearing on the particular phase of inner development discussed here. For detailed studies, see R. Cook, *The Tree of Life*, and E. A. S. Butterworth, *The Tree at the Navel of the Earth*.
2. *Mundaka Upanishad* III, 1, 1. Also *Svetasvatara Upanishad* IV, 6.
3. *Katha Upanishad* I, 3, 1.
4. In Hindu mythology this becomes Shiva and his Sakti embracing each other.
5. *Mundaka Upanishad* III, 1, 1.
6. To give even a vague outline of the wide dissemination of this whole imagery is impossible here. It appears everywhere, in the ancient near and middle east, f. i. Chaldea, Assyria, Babylonia, Persia, as well as in Hindu and Buddhist art, and in the Far East, Java, China, Japan. (G. d'Alviella, *The Migration of Symbols*, p. 118ff.)
7. This is an age-old symbol which appears almost parallel with the tree flanked by animals. As Bosch has shown for India, it is conceivable that there was a development from animal representation to the human figure. Earlier reliefs, for instance, depict the serpents' spirits (*nagas*) in their animal form, whereas the later ones show them in human shape by the side of their abode, the tree.
8. In India the pipal and nimba trees are frequently found together and a popular interpretation is that they are man and wife. It is beneath this 'pair' that the stone tablets with double serpents are placed (the nagalkas) for these trees are said to be their home. (H. Zimmer, *Myths and Symbols* ..., p. 72.)
9. It is a recognized fact that the original version of Genesis only knew of one tree and that the mention of a second tree is a later addition. (*Jewish Encyclopedia* IX, 518.)
10. It is said that the Buddha, after attaining illumination, sat for seven days under the *muchilinda tree*, lost in contemplation. During those days wind and rain prevailed and so as to protect the All-Enlightened One from cold and wet the serpent king Muchilinda residing in the tree (*nagaraya*) came forth and coiled seven times round the seated figure of the Buddha, protecting him with his large serpent's hood opened like an umbrella.
11. In the Orphic-Hellenistic tradition it stands for Helios-Dionysus and, more generally, for the God Aeon, 'In the shape of the winged serpent, surrounded by rays and accompanied by the four winds, the Aeon is the celestial solar ether, encompassing the world and penetrating it with its rays'. (See H. Leisegang, 'The Mystery of the Serpent' in *The Mysteries*, Papers from the Eranos Yearbooks, p. 232.)
12. A similar idea is found in certain Kabbalistic teachings where it is said that so long as the two trees remain united—they are regarded as springing from the same root—harmony between the opposites is assured; but when this unity is lost and there are two separate trees, disharmony ensues and evil prevails. (G. Scholem, *Von der Mystischen Gestalt der Gottheit*, Zurich, 1962, p. 59ff.)
13. The myth relates how Krishna as an incarnation of Vishnu, who has both the serpent and the bird (Garuda) as his emblems, not realizing his divinity, is first overpowered by Kaliya and lies inert at the bottom of the serpent pool, into which he had jumped from a tall tree with overhanging branches. Only when his brother Balarama reminds him in powerful words of his divine origin and essence does

Krishna free himself from the deadly embrace of the serpent and trample him underfoot. Then, asked for mercy, he replies:

> You shall not henceforth reside in the waters of the Yamuna, but in the vastness of the ocean. Depart; Moreover, I declare to you that Garuda, the sun-bird of gold, arch enemy of all serpents and my vehicle through the reaches of space, forever shall spare you, whom I have touched. (H. Zimmer, *Myths and Symbols* ..., pp. 85–6.)

Bird and serpent have once more found peace through the unifying touch of the divine, incarnated in man. See pl. 2.

14. See pl. 6.

15. L. Yarden, *The Tree of Light.*

16. The design of a stupa, for instance, is largely based on the four main structural components of a fully grown tree. The root corresponding to the stupa body, the trunk to the main post, the central branches to the pinnacle and the umbrella shaped foliage to the sunshades surmounting the stupa.

 A parallel fourfold division can be traced in the ground plan of the Christian church. First, the *narthex*, the entrance, a chamber sometimes called 'paradise' as the rootplace in or near which the baptismal font is situated, then the nave as the trunk of the tree, the chancel where stem and branches meet, and lastly the apse as the foliaged crown. If here in the cruciform church the tree structure is followed horizontally, in round churches, notably in baptistries, it appears erected vertically, as is the case in the stupa, and reaches from the font, in early times often sunk below floor level, to the domed ceiling frequently decorated to depict the heavenly spheres and topped by a lantern as the pinnacle of the whole structure.

17. Lama A. Govinda, in *Marg.* Vol. IV, 1, p. 9ff; 'Solar and Lunar Symbolism'.

18. *Katha Upanishad* II, 6, 1. See also *Rig Veda* I, 24, 7; and *Bhagavadgita* Chapter 15, where there is a distinction made between the Tree's 'root' which is above, and its 'roots' which grow downwards, symbolizing attachment and desire; these have to be cut so as to achieve liberation.

19. *The Adornment of the Spiritual Marriage*, see C. G. Jung, *Psychology and Religion*, p. 545.

20. For other examples, see M. Eliade, *Patterns of Comparative Religion*, p. 275, and F. D. K. Bosch, *The Golden Germ*, p. 65ff.

21. Book Bahir, in G. Scholem, *Major Trends in Jewish Mysticism*, p. 214.

22. Rabbi Moses Cordovero, *The Palm-Tree of Deborah*, p. 46.

23. M. Buber, *Die Chassidische Botschaft* ... p. 110.

24. In Sufism such a man has been variously called a perfect man (*al-insanu l'Kamil*), a complete man (*al-kamilu'l-tamm*) or a man equipoised between the extremes (*masawi-ut-tarafain*).

25. Buddhism teaches that the immortal body, the dharma-body, pure and immutable, manifests itself under various forms. They are the three (sometimes four, see below) bodies of the all-enlightened one, the *Dharmakaya*, the *Sambhogakaya* and the *Nirmanakaya*, or the absolute body of Buddhahood, the body of bliss and the body of transformation. In a Tantric text it is said of the Buddha Akshobhya:

> He is the dharma-body because he is the embodiment of the Buddhas who are unconditioned; he is the Sambhoga-body because he represents the true nature of constructive consciousness; he is the Self-Existing Body (avabhavika) because this is the single flavour of those three bodies.

Far eastern schools know of two main grades of the body of transformation. Its total manifestation (*Ojin*), taking form in the Tathagatas or Buddhas, and its partial manifestation (*Keshin*) which exists in all those enlightened men in whom the buddha nature has developed sufficiently to transform the whole man.

The founders of some Japanese Buddhist sects like Kobo Daishi or Honen Shonin, as well as others who have reached a high degree of perfection and live a dedicated life of compassion and service, are regarded as Keshin. (See B. L. Suzuki, *Mahayana Buddhism*, p. 44.)

26. D. Snellgrove, *Buddhist Himalaya*, p. 233.
27. Abraham Johashue Herschel von Apta in M. Buber *Erzählungen* ... p. 574.
28. *Sacred Writing of the Sikhs*, p. 237.

16

Transfiguration

Then I saw in my dream that the Shining Men bid them call at the gate; the which, when they did, some looked from above, to wit, Enoch, Moses, and Elijah ...

Now I saw in my dream that these two men went in at the gate: and lo, as they entered, they were transfigured, and they had raiments put on that shone like gold.

JOHN BUNYAN, *The Pilgrim's Progress*

I saw Eternity the other night
Like a great Ring of pure and endless Light,
   All calm as it was bright,
And round beneath it, Time in hours, days, years,
   Driv'n by the spheres
Like a vast shadow mov'd, in which the world
   And all her train were hurl'd: ...

Yet some, who all this while did weep and sing
And sing and weep, soar'd up into the Ring,
   But most would use no wing.
O fools (said I) thus to prefer dark night
   Before true light,
To live in grots, and caves, and hate the day
   Because it shows the way,
The way which from this dead and dark abode
   Leads up to God,
A way, where you might tread the Sun, and be
   More bright than he.
But as I did their madness so discuss
   One whisper'd thus,
This Ring the Bride-groom did for none provide
   But for the Bride.

HENRY VAUGHAN, *The World*

What happens when the pilgrim has completed the circumambulation of the holy shrine, and protective walls enclose the numinous centre, when the images of the four-square city and the tree have appeared and man can be likened to a lotus or a rose in full bloom?

It appears that once more the scenery changes and that perplexing rhythm characteristic of the way asserts itself again. Just as the images of rock and fortress are superseded by their contraries, the perishable seed, the essence of all change, so now. The symbols based on the *mandala* design, standing for a fully grown and delimited organism, give way to something that cannot be defined, that is without boundary or inherent form, something that penetrates all, yet, at the same time, transcends all. To use the colourful imagery of later Taoism, the climb up the sacred mountain now moves close to the summit and the 'hall of jade', the point between the eyes, becomes, in its turn, the germinal vessel out of which rises the golden radiance, bursting open the gate of heaven.

> Then comes the day, happy and great,
> When the diamond tempered and polished,
> Breaks through to dwell in the light.
> The light of the spirits,
> Bright as snow-white linen,
> Here in the Land of the Immortals so pure,
> The Emancipated Child will live and work.[1]

The inner realization which inspired these lines forms part of the spiritual lore of which all great traditions partake. The rising current extends to the crown of the head and what happens there has occasioned the most varied as well as picturesque metaphors. Such images as flames rising from the mountain peak, or a body of light issuing skywards, abound in the portrayal of this, in the literal sense of the word, crowning event.[2]

The Upanishads speak of the door of the sun burst open, of the solar orb which is pierced, of the crossing of all limits and the attainment of the limitless. At the point where the opening takes place, there blossoms the thousand petalled lotus, the *Sahasrāra*, the dwelling-place of Shiva.[3] It covers the crown of the head and hovers, as it were, above the end of the channel which carries the light (*Susumma*) and which it thus transcends.

In this connection, many texts employ the simile of a bird emerging and winging upwards towards the azure of the sky. Thus the fire-bird of Taoist teaching, having first descended into the depth of the soul, now rises like the phoenix, reborn out of the crown of the head. He is that bird which is said to be nesting in the tree of life which now takes to its wings. It flies out of the skylight, as it is said in Tantrism, freed, having become one with the sun, the supreme light.

The winged sundisk, amongst the oldest religious symbols, is expressive of this event. It stands for supreme enlightenment in the sense of a union of life and light. The breach between them is here healed, for darkness has been shed, as the prophet Malachi hears the Lord God of Israel proclaim:

But unto you that fear my name shall the Sun of righteousness arise with healing in his wings. (4, 2.)

The bird of the sun is also the dove of the Holy Spirit rising, surrounded by a halo of light. Like the firebird, it enters into the heart of man at baptism, only to ascend heavenwards when union of the soul with God takes place.

And when the sinner turns to the way of repentance, this light smooths away every trace of sins committed, clothing the former sinner in the garments of incorruption, spun of the Grace of the Holy Spirit.[4]

The soul of man then soars upwards on the wings of the dove.

For the soul turned toward God, fully committed to its desire for incorruptible beauty, is moved by a desire for the transcendent ever anew, and this desire is never filled to satiety. That is why the dove never ceases to move on toward what is before, going on from where it now is, to penetrate that further to which it has not yet come.[5]

Here, too, the dove is visualized as returning to the unseen Light from whence it descended at the Baptism of Jesus when 'the sky opened and the Holy Spirit came down in bodily shape like a dove upon Him' (Luke 3, 21); in the same way, according to Christian iconography, it appears at the Annunciation, flying from on high on rays of light and hovering above the head of the Virgin. It carries on its wings the light divine, and enters into him who is open to receive it. Its touch means victory, and the soul in its new radiance exultantly exclaims

I came from the Isle of Fire, having filled my body with Hikê (vital essence) like 'that bird' who came and filled the world with that which it had not known.[6]

'That which the world had not known is the light which came into the world but which the world knew not, those however who received it became the sons of God'. (John 1, 10–12.)

Pictures of the thousand-petalled lotus, covering the aperture of Brahman at the crown of the head, appear strangely reminiscent of the tonsure of both Tibetan and Roman Catholic monks, and of the skull cap the latter wear over it. They occupy the exact spot of the aperture of Brahman and, furthermore, it is also the place where enlightened beings, a Krishna, a Buddha and the Bodhisattvas bear one of the main marks of their high station, the protuberance, crowning their heads. As the bodily region where the risen light issues forth, the region where the kingly road of divine participation and union culminates, this is the most sacred spot of the human frame. The universal symbol of its awakening, is the nimbus or halo, as well as the golden crown, worn by those exalted beings in whom the divine radiance has risen to transcend the limits of the body. For the boundaries, separating man from the higher realms of light, are here broken through; man now partakes of their glory. This is the reason why, on the cosmic plane, Universal Man, the *Purusha*, as well as Adam Kadmon, are pictured as wearing light crowns, therewith reaching beyond the confines of even the cosmos, and why, for instance, Hindu deities and *Avatars*, like Brahma, Krishna, Vishnu and Shiva, appear with a flaming crown or a halo of light.

Light, crown, and halo are things of many aspects and they have a history of their own which cannot be traced here. It seems likely, however, that one of their main functions is to represent, in a visible form, the highest of those psychic centres, as taught in the East, which, when awakened, is said to give access to 'the breath of *Atman*, the luminous sea in which the separate sparks are all united in one living flame'.[7] It is this living flame which is seen in the *aureoles* of the awakened ones, and which appears in various religious emblems, signs, and sacred objects, always crowning and hallowing them with light. Furthermore, just as a halo is outside the physical body, so is the supreme centre it represents.

'The highest of the inner centres is in the head' says the modern sage Sri Aurobindo, 'just as the deepest is in the heart; but the centre which opens directly to the Self is above the head, altogether outside the physical body, in what is called the subtle body, *sūksma sarīra*'.[8]

When this centre comes into play, man is crowned or, as the *Dervishes* would say, he becomes worthy of wearing the cap (*taj*) which is symbolic of the Light of Muhammad. As a sign of the highest realization, it is white, for it then signifies the white light of God returning unto itself. Such a crown is worn by high religious dignitaries, whatever their particular loyalty. It can take many forms, from the tiara, the triple crown of the pope, the mitre worn by the Jewish high priest, to its Christian equivalent, the bishop's mitre or, again, the pointed cap of the Dalai Lama. Everywhere it symbolizes the fact that the ascent of the inner light has reached the cranial region and that the way is open for the influx of the transcendent light from above.

It is here and only here, at the aperture of Brahman, that the mighty flow of the divine and life-giving waters from the heavens can be received, as it is told in the Indian myth of the birth of the holy Ganga. This river, sacred to this very day, is said to have its source and eternal abode in the centre of the world, the City of Brahman. The ascetic king Bhagiratha undertook to intercede between the god and mankind so that the waters of life should be made to descend upon the parched earth. With arms outstretched, he stood a thousand years, doing the penance of the five fires. Thus he made his bodily, mental and spiritual energies rise to make contact with Brahma, and beg the god for the gift of the waters. The divine reply was that Shiva alone had the power of breaking and sustaining the fall of the mighty torrent by receiving it on his head. This Shiva agreed to do and the point of contact, where the gigantic flow from on high reached the earth region, was the aperture of Brahman, the crown of Shiva's head where his hair formed a high dome. The mighty force thus stayed, the waters divided and flowed down to the mountains and plains. This was an event of light, illumining the sky as though with a hundred suns; it was also an event of redemption for the sacred waters wash away impurities and sin.[9] To this day, the vision of the god receiving the radiant cascades of heavenly waters, and thus becoming the channel of grace and new life, is dear to Sivaite worshippers. As their forebears did, they know that through this divine act they themselves are enabled to receive the heavenly waters of light.

> Thou Fulness consummate, pure Nectar of bliss,
> Mount rising in limitless fire,
> Who camest to stay in my heart always as the
> Vedas and Vedas' desire,
> Didst stream in my soul as a swelling flood,
> bound-bursting with hurtling wave,
> Thine abode hast Thou made in my body today;
> what more of Thy grace can I crave?[10]

From the point of view of the ascent, the light which issues forth at the summit is seen to rise in the form of a flame, broad at the base and tapering to a point, but this same light becomes a flaming drop when viewed under the aspect of the descent. This is, indeed, the imagery used in Tibetan Buddhism. The radiant current having reached the crown of the head, permeating its centre with its glow and heat, illumines and activates the thousand petalled lotus, always depicted with ts petals pointing downwards, from which flaming drops are said to fall, filling the whole body with the fire of enlightenment. The light which finds its way from the centre of the heart to the head, rising in the invisible inner channel now, like a fountain, pours down on all sides, making every part of the body incandescent with light.[11]

The inner transformation in which, in an ascending motion, the bodily centres are awakened to consciousness is thus followed by another, by a descent which 'consists in making these centres into tools of the enlightened consciousness, in which knowledge and feeling, wisdom and love, the brightness of light and the warmth of life become one. The symbol of this integration is the seed-syllable HUM.'[12]

It is the fourth and last in the mantric formula *Om Mani Padme Hum*.

Once this threshold is passed, once the rising flame becomes the falling drop of light, man enters a world diffused with a mysterious radiance.[13] The experience of integration and wholeness, which had expressed itself in such images as the city, the tree, the open flower, now gives rise to visions of light. The City of Brahman, that inner domain, secret and invisible, reveals itself as the seat of divine effulgence which, so we are told, is higher than heaven and greater than the greatest. Jerusalem the holy city now shines with celestial splendour, for the Lord dwelleth in her midst:[14]

> Jerusalem is the light of the world, as it is said, and the Gentiles shall come to Thy light.
>
> Isaiah LX, 3

The lotus and the rose are called golden because of their inner lustre and other *mandala* images such as the garden or the field are portrayed as shining, for they are filled with the divine light.

The same applies to the symbol of the tree. Not only is the tree now seen to harbour the fire spark[15] which, in time, breaks forth as the all penetrating light and ultimately as the sun, but spark, tree and light become one and the world tree shows itself aflame, with light radiating out from the jewelled ornaments with which it is adorned. Images such as this are to be found in traditions as far apart in time and space as the Egyptian, the Japanese, the Hebrew and the Greek. An old incantation from Babylon gives an apt description of the tree of light.

> In Eridu there grows a black kiskanu, it was made in a holy place; its radiance is of shining lapis-lazuli.[16]

Around this tree, people gather to give thanks, and to rejoice, and they set it up in their homes in the form of a lighted tree or a tree-shaped candlestick. The hidden depths of meaning of such festivals are revealed in the words of the eighteenth century Zaddik Rabbi Pinhas. Talking of *Hanukkah*, the Jewish version of this feast of light, he says:

Listen and I will tell you the meaning of the miracle of the light at Hanukkah. The light which was hidden since the days of creation was then revealed. And every year when the lights are lit for Hanukkah, the hidden light is revealed afresh. And it is the light of the Messiah.[17]

The image of the tree, as we have seen, carries in this context the same symbolic meaning as man himself, man made perfect and godlike. Like the lighted *menorah* of Jewish worship, which the early church fathers frequently identified with Christ, so man, having opened himself to the divine influx, is seen to be ablaze with light. He becomes the hero referred to in an old Sumerian text in which the images of tree, light and man are all present.

He, whose body is shining splendour,
Who in the forest of fragrant cedars is cheered with joy,
Standing in the oracle-place Apsu,
Purified with the sparkling lustration.[18]

Here at the beginning of religious history, we are given the archetype 'the Shining One' which in almost endless variations is common to all great spiritual traditions. Krishna, Buddha, Moses, Christ, Muhammad, all these were figures of light, their bodies shone, so their disciples assure us, and they were sources of light, on all levels of meaning. Many of those who followed after them not only saw and believed what they saw or heard but they themselves became channels of light. This is a phenomenon which is reported too frequently and too universally to be ignored or dismissed as phantasy or 'merely' metaphorical. When heart and head, feeling, consciousness and intellect unite, when, in the ritual imagery of the Old Testament, man attains to the state of being when he is given the priestly breast plate and the mitre as signs of his sanctification, then the way is open for the influx of the divine light. Here 'light' stands for a new awareness, embracing and transcending both intellect and feeling, but it also includes the other human functions, sensation, and inner vision or intuition. If this were not so then the transformation we are concerned with here would only be partial and would not affect man as a whole.[19]

All evidence shows that an often overwhelming external appearance, as well as an inner vision of light, accompanies this high level of attainment. Moreover, those who have reached it assure us of two things. One is that such a person appears clad in a shining radiance; he has, as St Paul describes it, put on the 'armour of light' (Rom. 13, 12),[20] and the other is that this radiance, at once, envelops him from without and issues from within.

Such a transformation into light can happen in many ways and on many levels of experience. It can be transmitted or induced by a master, or it can come direct, without human mediation, to those who have completed the spiritual ascent. It may show itself only to a limited number of people or, on rare occasions in the history of mankind, it may take on cosmic dimensions.

At one end of the scale stand initiatory experiences which many a seeker has gone through, at the other such meteoric events as the transfiguration of Christ. To the first, clearly belongs an experience which a western pilgrim has recently had in the East.

Sitting in front of an elderly Indian guru, the latter addressed the young German in a language which he did not understand.

The old man continued speaking still turning towards me. Then he raised his hand ... and touched me gently with the middle finger on my chest, speaking solemnly, almost as though exhorting me; and with a gentle smile on his lips he touched me on the forehead, continuing to speak even more urgently, and looking into my eyes. And then, uttering a sonorous, humming sound, he swiftly touched the crown of my head for a moment.

The humming sound now became a deep rumble. The very columns seemed to tremble, and a throbbing went through my body like an electric current. From the crown of my head it coursed down to my hips. I could no longer see what was around me, and before my eyes a glowing wheel began to turn, whilst a shudder rose up my spine like a serpent wriggling up a tree. The higher it rose the brighter the turning wheel became, purple at first, then yellow and finally radiant white, brighter even than the sun. When I felt the serpent reach the crown of my head I was suffused with a nameless bliss which engulfed everything. It went through every pore in my body, and I had the feeling that I was disintegrating in that radiant white light.[21]

Once again, all the ancient symbols connected with the coming of the light here come to life; they become life, and through its descending flow or, to use tantric imagery, through the dripping down of the nectar stored in the thousand petalled lotus, the whole body is filled with light 'even to the very toes'.[22]

Buddhist monks who advance to the fourth of the *Jhana* meditations tell the same story, of the heart and mind becoming radiant, and of all boundaries crumbling before the power of the light.

> As a man might cloak himself from head to foot in a white mantle, so that not the smallest part of his body was left uncovered by the white mantle: just so the ascetic sits, having his body with a state of extreme equanimity and purity and clarity, so that not the smallest part of his body is left uncovered by the state of extreme equanimity and purity and illumination.
>
> *Digha Nikaya* II, 82

This can be regarded as the classic formula not only for Buddhism but for all the great spiritual systems. What it refers to is a psychophysical phenomenon and it is important that all such utterances should be understood in this twofold way, for illumination experienced in this life applies to both the within and the without of man, manifesting itself on the mental plane as insight and lucidity of perception, on the feeling plane as the glowing flame of love and on the bodily plane as a shining transparency.

When it is said of Buddhist monks who are perfected in virtue, concentration, and wisdom, that they shine like the sun,[23] the same is attested of almost countless other holy men, Hindu, Jewish, Christian and Muslim. It is reported, in our days, that devotees of Ramana Maharshi saw the Saint's body 'shining like the morning sun and round him a halo as of full moons', or he appeared to them as a column of pure light, as indeed the god Siva himself had appeared on the sacred hill of Arunachala.[24] Evelyn Underhill, in her books on Christian mysticism, enumerates many such instances of a 'transfiguring radiance', as she calls it. Thus St Francis, when he prayed at night was, we are told,

> wrapt in a shining cloud as though the wondrous illumination of the body were a witness to the wondrous enlightenment of the mind.[25]

Some of the saints, as did Moses when he returned from Mount Sinai, resplendent with the glory of God shining on his face, have tried to hide this state from the eyes of others.

I was not always able,

says Angela of Foligno,

to conceal my state from my companions, or from the other person with whom I consorted: because at times my countenance was all resplendent and rosy, and my eyes shone like candles.[26]

Mechtild of Magdeburg closes one of her visions, in which the characteristics of the divine Fire was revealed to her, with the ecstatic words

Wouldst thou know my meaning?
Lie down in the Fire
See and taste the Flowing
Godhead through thy being;
Feel the Holy Spirit
Moving and compelling
Thee within the Flowing
Fire and Light of God.[27]

To feel the 'Flowing Light of God' and know the touch of the Holy Spirit, this, too, was the experience of that shining figure of the Eastern Church, St Seraphim. What is perhaps the most endearing and detailed eye-witness account of such a transfiguration is contained in the Revelations of St Seraphim of Sarov. It reverberates through and through with that radiant and almost drunken joy which the gift of the light of God bestows. Walking with a disciple, who later recorded the whole event, the Saint was asked, how one can be certain of being in the spirit of God. The answer given was that, at that very instant, the spirit of God was upon them both and that there was no reason to be afraid of the intensity of the light all around them.

Encouraged by these words, I looked and was seized by holy fear. Imagine in the middle of the sun, dazzling in the brilliance of its noontide rays, the face of the man who is speaking to you. You can see the movements of his lips, the changing expression of his eyes, you can hear his voice, you can feel his hands holding you by the shoulders, but you can see neither his hands nor his body—nothing except the blaze of light which shines around, lighting up with its brilliance the snow covered meadow, and the snowflakes which continue to fall unceasingly.[28]

Ananda, the Buddha's favourite disciple, in wonder beheld a bright lustre going out from the skin of the All-Enlightened one, far outshining the golden garments put upon him, and he is instructed by the master that on only two occasions does the body of a *Tathagata* shine with this transparent brightness; when the *Tathagata* 'is supernally enlightened with incomparable and perfect enlightenment and on the night when he enters Nirvana'.[29]

The story of Christ's transfiguration, as found in the Gospels, is a short one, yet it leaves in its wake an intense brilliance, issuing, so it appears, from the sudden fusion of two worlds, when the divine ray from on high and the holy fire incarnate, and risen from the depth, unite. At that moment, Jesus is heard to talk with Elias and Moses, both men of light who, in their earthly existence, had also been granted the gift of the divine glory.

When this happens, 'the body's house is lighted through the spirit's open door', as a Sufi has said, and man comes and goes in the full light of the 'Sun of the Spirit'. Daniel's vision has become true:

And they that be wise shall shine as the brightness of the firmament: and they that turn to righteousness as the stars for ever and ever (Dan. 12, 3).

Man, having become 'a Shining One', is taken up into the spheres of the eternal splendour, where, so the scriptures of the great faiths assert with an almost monotonous emphasis, sun and moon shine not, the stars are not, no created fire or light exists.[30] Indeed, it is the disappearance of these worldly lights that heralds the break of the new dawn.

When the sun is folded up, and when the stars are dust-coloured ...

says the *Koran*,

and the morning when it brightens, surely it is the Word of a bountiful Messenger, the possessor of strength, established in the presence of the Lord of the Throne.

Then, too, the servants of God need neither celestial nor earthly lights on their way, for the light of God will be upon them.

This is the homecoming and the taking up of light by Light. It is the Ascension when the incarnate light returns to its maker, when the enlightened ones enter the luminous void and the saints the dazzling darkness of God, when the homeless ones, clad in the golden robe, merge into the effulgence of Brahman.

The pilgrims now enter the 'Hall of Light or Illumination',[31] and they speak of the Throne vision where they see the chariot or throne of God, bathed in splendour and attended by shining creatures on clouds of light.

Ezekiel was granted this vision and he fell upon his face before its blinding glory. So did the Rabbis of old who had climbed the ladder of light. We are told that

> Rabbi Eliezer, son of Arach, opened his discourses on the mysteries of the Throne, and no sooner had he begun, than fire came down from heaven and encompassed all the trees of the field which, with one accord, burst into song.[32]

Many a man of vision of the East and West have beheld this ineffable sight; St John the Divine did, so did Dante, who visually was born 'into the ray authentical of sovran light',[33] and it must have been a similar experience which inspired the Sufi writer 'Attār to compose his allegorical poem, 'The Speech of Birds', where the birds see themselves transformed in the unspeakable Glory of the blaze of light issuing from the heavenly Throne. Out of this blaze a voice is heard:

> Come you lost Atoms to your Centre draw,
> And *be* the Eternal Mirror that you saw:
> Rays that have wander'd into Darkness wide
> Return, and back into your Sun subside.[34]

Thus is consummated the Odyssey of the soul; the Way, 'where you might tread the sun, and be more bright than he', ends in an apotheosis of light. It does so today as it has done since the birth of religion; how else can the following lines from Kazantzaki's poem *The Odyssey* be interpreted?

> O Sun, my quick coquetting eye, my red-haired hound, sniff out all quarries that I love, give them swift chase, tell me all that you've seen on earth, all that you've heard, and I shall pass them through my entrails' secret forge till slowly, with profound caresses, play and laughter, stones, water, fire, and earth, shall be transformed to spirit, and the mud-winged and heavy soul, freed of its flesh, shall like a flame serene ascend and fade in sun.[35]

With this the spark's imprisonment in the darkness of matter has ended, its return accomplished, its circular course completed.[36] A new cycle begins, a new spiral turn opens; it opens towards realms where the Biblical command applies 'thou shalt not make unto thee any graven image, or any likeness of anything that is in heaven above, or that is in the earth beneath, or that is in the water under the earth: Thou shalt not bow down thyself to them, nor serve them' (Ex. 20, 4). Here even the highest flight of mystic vision returns silent, as was the case with the Indian seers who uttered the *'neti, neti*, not this not that' or the Buddha who, regarding that world, never broke his silence.

The new turn of the spiral, however, also opens towards another realm, that realm which still struggles in darkness and travail. A new cycle begins, for Christ has come to save all mankind and the Bodhisattvas have vowed not to cease their labours until all sentient beings have been liberated. After the festival of the harvest of light, Pentecost, the shadows gather strength again, those souls not yet freed from the bondage of darkness yearn for the return of the light, so does the earth, all nature, and indeed the whole of creation. And once again the light descends, 'the true light, which lighteth every man that cometh into the world' as in the past, so in the present, and in the future. Thus mankind again awaits Advent and Christmas with hope, hope for the coming of the Messiah, the light-bringer, hope for a new *Avatar* to appear, hope of comprehending the light of Bethlehem and being filled with it and hope for the conquest of the forces of darkness, once more and for ever. In this hope mankind will send prayers and invocation to the heights and contemplate the radiance of the Real. The words or images used will be almost identical all over the world; they will express the yearning 'Lead us from darkness into light', and the minds of all will be fixed on that Light which is called the sun of justice, the effulgence of Brahman, the golden disk, the light of lights, the glory of God, the luminous void, the golden flower, the light of the world.

The answer to this yearning for the light, so the world's religions pay witness, is not a promise of a future gift of light but the realization that to receive the light is the inalienable birthright of man.

The great Prince of Peace and spirits, as He comes forth, casts a cloud about Him; so He comes on upon us; so He encompasseth us; ... Yet still we speak of Him as far above and beyond the starry sky, and of His coming as at a great distance. But, behold! He is already in the midst of us; He breaks forth on our right hand, and on our left, like a flame, round about us, and we perceive Him not. (Peter Sterry.)[37]

In those who do perceive, however, and at this stage it matters little whether they do so under the personal or impersonal aspect of the light, the truth dawns: That light—I am. Then is the spark kindled in the heart, then is the sun born within, and the pilgrimage to the zenith of light, of life, of consciousness, begins.

> O Force-compelled, Fate-driven earth-born race,
> O petty adventurers in an infinite world
> And prisoners of a dwarf humanity,
> How long will you tread the circling tracks of mind
> Around your little self and petty things?
> But not for a changeless littleness were you meant,
> Not for vain repetition were you built;
> Out of the Immortal's substance you were made;
> Your action can be swift revealing steps,
> Your life a changeful mode for growing gods.
> A seer, a strong Creator, is within,
> The immaculate Grandeur broods upon your days,
> Almighty powers are shut in Nature's cells.
> A greater destiny waits you in your front:
> This transient earthly being if he wills
> Can fit his acts to a transcendent scheme.
> He who now stares at the world with ignorant eyes
> Hardly from the Inconscient's night aroused,
> That look at images and not at Truth
> Can fill those orbs with an immortal's sight.
> Yet shall the godhead grow within your hearts,
> You shall awake into the spirit's air
> And feel the breaking walls of mortal mind
> And hear the message which left life's heart dumb
> And look through Nature with sun-gazing lids
> And blow your conch-shells at the Eternal's gate.
> Authors of earth's high change, to you it is given
> To cross the dangerous spaces of the soul
> And touch the mighty Mother stark awake
> And meet the Omnipotent in his house of flesh
> And make of life the million-bodied One.
> The earth you tread is a border screened from heaven,
> The life you lead conceals the light you are.

Sri Aurobindo, *Savitri* IV. 3.

NOTES FOR CHAPTER 16

1. K. L. Reichelt, *Meditation and Piety in the Far East*, p. 119.
2. The Egyptian image for this event, as used, for instance, in the *Book of the Dead*, is a seated figure with the sun disk upon his head. The caption reads: The Chapter of making the transformation into the God who giveth light (in) the darkness. Chapter LXXX.
3. Or, in Buddhist Tantrism, *usnīsa-kamala*, where the ascent of the goddess Candāli reaches the cranial region.
4. In Seraphim. G. P. Fedotov, *A Treasury of Russian Spirituality*, p. 272.
5. St Gregory of Nyssa, quoted in J. Campbell, *The Masks of God*, p. 399.
6. Coffin Text, see R. T. Rundle-Clark, *Myth and Symbol in Ancient Egypt*, p. 247.
7. Sri Krishna Prem, *The Yoga of the Bhagavad Gita*, Commentary ... p. 72f.
8. Sri Aurobindo, *Letters on Yoga*, p. 1165.
9. See *Mahabharata* and *Ramayana*. Also H. Zimmer, *Myths and Symbols in Indian Art* (Bollingen Series VI), p. 112.
10. *Manikkavachakar* (eleventh century), in L. D. Barnett, *The Heart of India*, p. 83f.
11. W. Y. Evans-Wentz, *Tibetan Yoga* ..., p. 172ff; also the same author's *Tibet's Great Yogi Milarepa*, p. 155, and Lama A. Govinda, *Foundations of Tibetan Mysticism*, p. 177.
12. The Sanscrit letters making up the HUM written out in full (the long HUM) are frequently taken as subjects of meditation. They are seen one by one to merge into one another in an ascending order and with this the yogi himself rises up step by step until in his inner realizations the flame-like drop at the apex is reached and he becomes filled with the boundless Void. (See Lama A. Govinda, *Foundations of Tibetan Mysticism*, p. 186ff, and W. Y. Evans-Wentz, *Tibetan Yoga*, p. 335ff.)
13. Jewish mysticism speaks of 'reversing the flow of the divine light (*yihudim*)' without which 'the influx from the highest point in *En Sof* to the lowest terminus in the animal world cannot be brought down'. (R. J. Z. Werblowsky, 'Mystical and Magical Contemplation ...' *History of Religions*, Vol. 1, 1, 1961, p. 33.)
14. For I, saith the Lord, will be unto her (Jerusalem) a wall of fire round about, and will be the glory in the midst of her. (Zechariah, 2, 5.)
    Jerusalem thus became 'a lamp' unto the people, a '*Ner Tamid*', a perpetual light. (See Psalm 132, 17.)
15. According to Hindu lore, Agni, Fire, hides as a spark in the sacred Asvatta tree from which it rises as fire and finally as the sun. This is only one of the many versions of the age-old myth that the sun is born and reborn, ever anew, out of the cosmic tree, as it is also told in the Finnish epos *Kalevala*, where the spark out of which the new sun was to be fashioned was found hidden in the root of an alder tree. (See *Samma Veda*, I, 1, 8, 7; *Rig Veda* I, 65, 1; *Taitri Upanishad* I, 10, 1.)
16. M. Eliade, *Patterns of Comparative Religion*, p. 271.
17. M. Buber, *Tales* ..., p. 124.
18. G. Widengren, *The King and the Tree of Life*, p. 45.
19. Speaking of the experience of light which many Fathers of the Eastern Church have known, V. Lossky says:
    This light (φῶς) or effulgence (ἔλλαμψις) ... is a light which fills at the same time both intellect and senses, revealing itself to the whole man, and not only to one of his faculties. The divine light, being given in mystical experience,

surpasses, at the same time, both senses and intellect. It is immaterial and is not apprehended by the senses; that is why St Symeon, the New Theologian, while affirming its visibility, yet calls it 'invisible fire'. (V. Lossky, *Mystical Theology*, p. 221.)

20. He has 'put on Christ as a garment' (Gal. 3, 27) or, in the language of the Old Testament, he is 'clothed with the garment of Salvation' and has been covered with 'the robe of righteousness' (Isaiah 61, 10). In eastern terms, the body becomes 'the body of illumination and nirvanic realization' (Buddhism); it becomes the diamond body (Tibetan: *Vajrakaya*; Chinese: *Gin Gang Schen*).

21. Hans-Ulrich Rieker, *Beggar among the Dead*, p. 44.

22. W. Y. Evans-Wentz, *Tibet's Great Yogi Milarepa*, p. 34. Another of these picturesque metaphors is 'Milking the Cow of Heaven'.

23. *Ittivutaka* III, 1, 10.

24. A. Osborne, *Ramana Maharshi*, pp. 34, 77 and 90.

25. E. Underhill, *The Mystic Way*, p. 121.

26. E. Underhill, *The Mystic Way*, p. 122.

27. L. Menzies, *The Revelations of Mechtild of Magdeburg*, p. 194.

28. V. Lossky, *Mystical Theology* ... pp. 227–9

29. *Digha Nikaya* XVI.

30. See *Dhammapada* 387; *Upanishads: Mundaka* II, 2, 11; *Svetasvatara* VI, 14; *Katha* II, 2, 15; also Isaiah 60, 19; Revelation 22, 4–5; 1, 16; 21, 23–4; and *Koran*, Sura 81, 1–2, 18–20.

31. The name of the ancient royal sanctuary in Peking (*Ming Tang*).

32. J. Abelson, *The Immanence of God in Rabbinical Literature*, p. 42.

33. Revelation IV; *Paradiso*, 23, 51–2.

34. M. Smith, *The Sufi Path of Love*, No. 176.

35. Nikos Kazantzakis, *The Odyssey, a Modern Sequel*.

36. As the light was with God in the beginning so it will be again at the end. In between lies the graded descent and ascent of the light, its veiling and unveiling, in short its spiral progression. In various forms this teaching is found in most of the great religious traditions. Thus Adam is said to have possessed a body of light before the Fall and so he will again at the end of time. This is made clear in a passage occurring in a Kabbalistic text, where we read that Adam Kadmon (the first created man) wore 'the celestial garment, which is a garment of heavenly light'. But when he was expelled from the Garden of Eden, he became subject to the wants of this world, what was written? 'The Lord God made coats of skin unto Adam and his wife and clothed them: for prior to this they had garments of light, light of that light which was used in the Garden of Eden' (*Sohar* II, 229, 6).

In the same way, the first man created by Ahura Mazda, the God of the Avestan religion, the fair Yima, was a child of light; of him it is said 'Yima stepped forward, in light, southwards, on the way of the sun'.

The Vedic twins Yama and Yami, too, are children of light; their progenitor is Vivasvat, 'the shining forth god'.

37. M. Strong, *Letters of the Scattered Brotherhood*, p. 145.

Bibliography

TEXTS

General

The Bible of the World, edited by R. O. Ballou, London, Kegan Paul, Trench, Trubner & Co., 1940.

'Ethical and Religious Classics of East and West', London, Allen & Unwin, various dates.

Sacred Books of the East, edited by Max Müller, Clarendon Press, Oxford, 1884ff.

Sacred Books of the World, compiled by A. C. Bouquet, London, Penguin Books, 1955.

'Wisdom of the East Series', edited by J. L. Cranmer-Byng, London, John Murray, various dates.

Baha'ism

Baha'u'llah.The Kitab-I-Iqan. The Book of Certitude. Translated by Shoghi Effendi, London, Baha'i Publishing Trust, 1946.

The Glad Tidings of Baha'u'llah. W.o.E., edited by G. Townshend, London, John Murray, 1949.

Buddhism

A Buddhist Bible, edited by D. Goddard, Vermont, Thetford, 1932.

Buddhist Scriptures translation by E. Conze, The Penguin Classics, Harmondsworth, 1959.

Buddhist Texts through the Ages, edited by E. Conze, Oxford, B. Cassirer, 1954.

The Dhammapada, translated by I. Babbit, Oxford University Press, 1936.

Digha-Nikaya, edited by T. W. Rhys Davids and J. E. Carpenter, London, Pali Text Society, 1908ff.

Majjhima-Nikaya, edited by V. Trenckner and Lord Chalmers, London, Pali Text Society, 1888ff.

Manual of Zen Buddhism, edited by D. T. Suzuki, London, Rider & Co., 1950.

Samyutta-Nikaya, edited by L. Feer, London, Pali Text Society, 1884f.

Some Sayings of the Buddha, translated by F. L. Woodward, Oxford University Press, 1945.

See also below: Evans-Wentz, W.Y.

Chinese Religion

The Sacred Books of China, edited by J. Legge, S.B.E. vols., 3, 27 & 28, Oxford, Clarendon Press, 1875, 1885.

I Ching or Book of Changes, the Richard Wilhelm translation rendered into English by Cary F. Baynes, 2 vols. London, Routledge & Kegan Paul, 1951.

Chuang Tzu, H. A. Giles, Shanghai, Kelly & Walsh, 1926.

Confucius:The Analects translated by W. E. Soothill, Oxford University Press, 1947.

Menzius, edited by L. A. Lyall, London, Longmans Green & Co., 1932.

Tao Te Ching, translated by Ch'u Ta-Kao, London, The Buddhist Lodge, 1937.

Tao Te Ching, translated by J. J. L. Duyvendank, W.o.E., London, John Murray, 1954.
See also below: Giles, L.; Waley, A.; Wilhelm, R.

Christianity
The Bible (Authorized Version).
The New English Bible.
The Roman Missal.
The Book of Common Prayer.
The Secret Sayings of Jesus according to the Gospel of St Thomas, R. M. Grant with D. N. Freedman ... English translation by W. R. Schoedel. Fontana Books, Collins, London, 1960.

Egyptian Religion
Egyptian Literature:The Legends of the Gods ..., edited ... by E. A. Wallis Budge, London, Kegan Paul, Trench, Trubner, 1912.
The Book of the Dead, edited by Sir E. A. Wallis Budge, London, Routledge & Kegan Paul, 1951.

Hinduism
The Hymns of the Rig-Veda, translated by R. T. H. Griggith, Benares, 1896.
The Upanishads, translated by F. Max Müller, Oxford University Press, 1926.
The Principal Upanishads, edited ... by S. Radhakrishnan, London, Allen & Unwin, 1953.
Himalayas of the Soul. Translations ... of the Principal Upanishads by J. Mascaro. W.o.E., London, John Murray, 1938.
The Bhagavadgita ... translation ... by S. Radhakrishnan, London, Allen & Unwin, 1948.
The Song of the Lord, Bhagavadgita, translated by E. J. Thomas. W.o.E., London, John Murray, 1931.

Islam
The Holy Qur'ān, Arabic text, translation and commentary by Maulānā Muhammad 'Ali, Lahore, 1951.
The Holy Koran. An Introduction with Selections by A. J. Arberry, London, Allen & Unwin, 1953.
The Sayings of Muhammad, by Allama Sir Abdullah Al-Mamun Al-Suhrawardy. W.o.E., London, John Murray, 1949.

Jainism
Gaina Sutras, edited by H. Jacobi, S.B.E., vols. 22 and 45. Oxford, Clarendon Press, 1884, 1895.

Judaism
The Old Testament (Authorized Version).
Authorised Daily Prayerbook, London, Eyre and Spottiswood, 1954.
Hebraic Literature. Selection from the Talmud, The Midrash, The Kabbalah and the Ana, translated by M. H. Harris, New York, Tudor Publishing Co., 1946.
Die Erzählungen der Chassidim, edited by M. Buber, Zürich, Manesse Verlag, 1949.
Tales of the Hasidim. The early Masters, edited by M. Buber, London, Thames & Hudson, 1956.

Sikhism

The Sacred Writings of the Sikhs, translated by Khushwant Singh, London, Allen & Unwin, 1960.

Zoroastrianism

The Hymns of Zarathustra, translation ... by J. Duchesne-Guillemin, translated from the French by Mrs M. Henning, W.o.E., London, John Murray, 1952.

The Zendavesta, edited by J. Darmsteter, S.B.E., vols. 4, 23, 31, Oxford, Clarendon Press, 1883ff.

The Pahlavi Texts, edited by E. W. West, S.B.E., vols. 5, 18, 47, Oxford, Clarendon Press, 1880ff.

LITERATURE

ABEGG, L. *The Mind of East Asia*, London, Thames and Hudson, 1952.

ABELSON, J. *The Immanence of God in Rabbinical Literature*, London, Bell, 1912.

ABHEDANANDA, SWAMI. See Ramakrishna, Sri.

ALI, A. Y. *The Message of Islam*. W.o.E., London, John Murray, 1949.

ALI, MUHAMMAD. *The Religion of Islam*. The Ahmadiyyah Anjuman Ishā'at Islām, Lahore, 1950.

ALVIELLA, COUNT G. D'. See D'Alviella.

ANSARI OF HERAT. See Singh, S.

Ancient Devotions to the Sacred Heart. See Carthusian Monks.

AQUINAS, THOMAS 'Summa Theologica', *Selected Writings*, London, J. M. Dent, 1946.

ARBERRY, A. J. *Sufism*, London, Allen & Unwin, 1950.

    The Discourses of Rumi, London, John Murray, 1961.

    'The Way in Islam', *The Aryan Path*, vol. 32, No. 7/8, July/August, 1961, pp. 251ff.

AUGUSTINE, SAINT. *An Augustine Synthesis*, by E. Przywara & C. C. Martindale, London, Sheed & Ward, 1945.

AUROBINDO, SRI. Collected Works. Centenary Edition, Pondicherry, 1970.

BACKMAN, E. L. *Religious Dances in the Christian Church and Popular Medicine*, London, Allen & Unwin, 1952.

BANKS, M. M. 'Tangled Thread Mazes'. *Folklore*, vol. XLVI, 1935, pp. 78 & 170.

BARNETT, L. D. *The Heart of India*, W.o.E., London, John Murray, 1924.

    See also Sāntideva.

BARTSCH, H. W. (Editor.) *Kerygma and Myth*, London, S.P.C.K., 1953.

BEIT, H. V. *Symbolik des Märcheus*, Berne, A. Francke, 1952.

BENTZEN, A. *King and Messiah*, London, Lutterworth Press, 1935.

BENZ, E. *Die Christliche Kabbala*, Albae Vigiliae, Zürich, Rhein Verlag, 1958.

BERDYAEV, N. *The Meaning of History*, London, G. Bles, 1936.

BLAKNEY, R. B. See Eckhart.

BOEHME, JACOB. *The Way to Christ*, London, John M. Watkins, 1911.

BORD, J. *Mazes and Labyrinths of the World*, Latimer New Dimensions Ltd., London, 1976.

BOSCH, F. D. K. *The Golden Germ*, S-Gravenhage, Mouton & Co., 1960.

BOTHWELL-GOSSE. A. *The Lily of Light*, London, John M. Watkins, 1935.

    The Rose Immortal, London, John M. Watkins, 1958.

BROOKE, S. C., The Labyrinth Patterns in India. *Folklore*, 64, 1953 pp. 453ff.

BROUGHTON, B. L. *The Vision of Kwannon Sama*, London, Luzac & Co., 1929.
BUBER. M. *Hasidism*, New York, The Philosophical Library, 1948.
  Die Chassidische Botschaft, Heidelberg, Lambert Schneider, 1952.
BUDGE, SIR E. A. WALLIS. *Egyptian Ideas of the Future Life*, London, Kegan Paul, Trench, Trübner, 1900.
BULTMANN, A. See BARTCH, H. W.
BUNYAN, JOHN. *The Pilgrim's Progress*, Oxford University Press, 1921.
BUTTERWORTH, E. A. S. *The Tree at the Navel of the Earth*, Berlin, W. de Gruytar, 1970.
CAMPBELL, J. *The Hero with a Thousand Faces*, London, Allen & Unwin, 1951.
  The Masks of God, vols. I and II, London, Secker & Warburg, 1960, 1962.
CARMICHAEL, A. *The Sun Dances*. Prayers and Blessings from the Gaelic, London, Christian Community Press, 1954.
Carthusian Monks. *Ancient Devotions to the Sacred Heart of Jesus*, London, Burns Oats & Washbourne, 1953.
CHANG CHEN-CHI. *The Practice of Zen*, London, Rider & Co., 1960.
CHANG, C. Y. *An Introduction to Taoist Yoga*. The Review of Religion, March, 1956.
COMENIUS, J. A. See Komensky. J. A.
COOK, R. *The Tree of Life*. London, Thames & Hudson, 1974.
COOMARASWAMY, A. K. See Nivedita, Sister and Coomaraswamy, A. K.
CORDOVERO, RABBI MOSES. *The Palm Tree of Deborah*, translated by L. Jacobs, London, Vallentine, Mitchell, 1960.
D'ALVIELLA, COUNT GOBLET. *The Migration of Symbols*, New York, University Books, 1956.
DANTE ALIGHIERI. *The Vision*: or Hell, Purgatory and Paradise ... translated by the Rev. H. F. Cary, London, F. Warne & Co., 1844.
DE LA MARE, W. J. *The Traveller*, London, Faber & Faber, 1946.
DEEDS, C. N. 'The Labyrinth', *The Labyrinth*, edited by S. H. Hooke, London, S.P.C.K., 1935.
DIONYSIUS THE AREOPAGITE. *On the Divine Names and the Mystical Theology*, by C. E. Rolt, London, S.P.C.K., 1951.
DONNELLY, MORWENNA. 'The Tragic Image', *Renaissance*, The Book of the Guild of St Michael and all Angels, 1945, 1946, Burrow's Press, Cheltenham.
  'Founding the Life Divine', *The Integral Yoga of Sri Aurobindo*, London, Rider & Co., 1955.
DROWER, E. S. *Water into Wine*, London, John Murray, 1956.
ECKHART, MEISTER. *Meister Eckhart*: a Modern Translation by Raymond B. Blakney, London, Harper & Bros., 1941.
ELIADE, MIRCEA. *Patterns of Comparative Religion*, London, Sheed and Ward, 1958.
  The Myth of the Eternal Return, London, Routledge & Kegan Paul, 1955.
  Yoga, Immortality and Freedom, London, Routledge & Kegan Paul, 1958.
  Images and Symbols, London, Harvill Press, 1961.
ELLAM, J. E. *The Religion of Tibet*, W.o.E., London, John Murray, 1927.
ELIOT, T. S. *Four Quartets*, London, Faber & Faber, 1944.
EPSTEIN, I. *Judaism*, London, Epworth Press, 1945.
  Judaism, a Historical Presentation, London, Penguin Books, 1959.
ERANOS YEARBOOKS. *The Mysteries* ... edited by J. Campbell, New York, Pantheon Books, 1955.
  Spirtual Disciplines ... edited by J. Campbell, New York, Pantheon Books, 1960.
EVANS-WENTZ, W. Y. *The Tibetan Book of the Dead*, Oxford University Press, 1957.

The Tibetan Book of the Great Liberation, Oxford University Press, 1954.
Tibet's Great Yogi Milarepa, Oxford University Press, 1958.
EVOLA, J. *The Doctrine of Awakening*, London, Luzac & Co., 1951.
FAUSSET, HUGH I'ANSON. *The Flame and the Light*, London, Abelard Schuman, 1958.
FEDOTOV, G. P. *A Treasury of Russian Spirituality*, London, Sheed & Ward, 1952.
FIELD, D. *The Religion of the Sikhs*. W.o.E., London, John Murray, 1914.
FRAZER, J. G. *The Golden Bough*, London, Macmillan, 1947.
GHAZZALI AL. *The Confessions* ... translated by C. Field, W.o.E., London, John Murray, 1909.
GIBSON, A. *Rockcarvings which link Tintagel with Knossos. Illustrated London News*, London, Jan. 9, 1954.
GILES, L. *Musings of a Chinese Mystic*. Selections from ... Chuang Tzu. W.o.E., London, John Murray, 1906.
   Taoist Teachings from the Book of Lieh Tzŭ, translated by L. Giles. W.o.E., London, John Murray, 1947.
GOODENOUGH, E. R. *Jewish Symbols in the Greco-Roman Period*, New York, Pantheon Books, 8 vols., 1954.
GORDON, E. A. *Symbols of the Way*, Tokyo, Maruzen, 1916.
GOVINDA, LAMA A. *Foundations of Tibetan Mysticism*, London, Rider, 1959.
   Solar and Lunar Symbolism, Marg. Vol. IV, 1. p. 9ff.
GUNTERT, H. 'Labyrinth'. *Sitzungsberichte der Heidelberger Akademie der Wissenschaften*, Phil.-Hist. Klasse, 1932.
GRUNEBAUM, G. E. VON. *Muhammadan Festivals*, New York, H. Schuman, 1947.
HARDWICK, C. *Traditions, Superstitions and Folklore ... their Eastern Origin and Mythical Significance*, Manchester, Simpkin, 1872.
HARRIS, M. H. *Hebraic Literature*, New York, Tudor Publishing Co., 1946.
HEARD, G. *Is God in History?*, London, Faber & Faber, 1951.
HEARN, LAFCADIO. *Kokoro*, London, Gay & Bird, 1905.
HELLO, E. See Ruysbroeck.
HENRY, F. *Early Christian Irish Art*, Dublin, Coln o Lochlain, 1955.
HISAMATSU, S. 'Zen, Present and Future', *The Middle Way*, vol. XXXIII, No. 2, August, 1958.
HOCKE, G. R. *Die Welt als Labyrinth*, Hamburg, Rowohlt, 1957.
HOOKE, S. H. *The Labyrinth*, London, S.P.C.K., 1935.
HUXLEY, A. *On the Margin*, London, Chatto & Windus, 1948.
IBN KHALDUN See ISSAWI.
ISHERWOOD, C. See Patanjali.
ISSAWI, C. *An Arab Philosophy of History*. Selections from the Prolegomena of Ibn Khaldun of Tunis. W.o.E., London, John Murray, 1950.
JABRA, JURJI, E. *Illumination in Islamic Mysticism*, Princetown University Press, 1938.
JACKSON KNIGHT, W. F. See Knight, Jackson, W. F.
JACOBS, L. See Cordovero, Rabbi Moses.
JAINI, J. *Outlines of Jainism*, Cambridge University Press, 1940.
ST JOHN OF THE CROSS. *The Mystical Doctrine* ... An Abridgement made by C. H., London, Sheed & Ward, 1948.
JUNG, C. G. *Psychology and Religion, West and East*, London, Routledge & Kegan Paul, 1958.
   Two Essays in Analytical Psychology, London, Routledge & Kegan Paul, 1953.
   Psychology and Alchemy, London, Routledge & Kegan Paul, 1953.
   The Integration of the Personality, London, Routledge & Kegan Paul, 1952.

Psychological Types, London, Kegan Paul, Trench, Trubner, 1933.

JURJI, E. JABRA. See Jabra Jurji, E.

KADLOUBOVSKY, E. See Philokalia.

KAMAL-UD-DIN, KHWAIA. *Al-Islam*. Woking, The Basheer Muslim Library, 1926.

KAYSER, H. *Vom Klang der Welt*, Zürich, M. Neihans Verlag, 1937.

KAZANTZAKIS, N. *The Odyssey, a Modern Sequel*, London, Secker & Warburg, 1959.

KEMPIS, THOMAS A. See Thomas a Kempis.

KERÉNYI, K. *Labyrinth-Studien*. *Albae Vigiliae*, Zürich, Rhein Verlag, 1950.

KHALDUN, IBN. See Issawi, C.

KHAN, VILAYAT INAYAT. *Stufen einer Meditation nach Zeugnissen der Sufi*, Weilheim, O. W. Barth-Verlag, 1962.

KHAYYÁM, OMAR. *Rubáiyát*, London, Macmillan & Co., 1900.

KINGSLAND, W. *An Anthology of Mysticism and Mystical Philosophy*, London, Methuen & Co., 1935.

KNIGHT, W. F. JACKSON *Cumaean Gates*, Oxford, Blackwell, 1936.

'Maze Symbolism and the Trojan Game', *Antiquity*, vol. VI, 1932.

'Myth and Legend at Troy', *Folklore*, vol. 46, 1935.

KOMENSKY, JOHN AMOS. *The Labyrinth of the World and the Paradise of the Heart*, translated by Count Lutzow, London, Golden Cockerel Press, 1950.

LANDAU, R. *The Philosophy of Ibn-Arabí*, London, Allen & Unwin, 1959.

LAROUSSE. *Encyclopedia of Mythology*, London, Batchworth Press, 1959.

LAYARD, J. 'Maze-dances and the Ritual of the Labyrinth in Malekula', *Folklore*, vol. 47, 1936.

'Labyrinth Rituals in South India', *Folklore*, vol. 48, 1937.

'The Malekulan Journey of the Dead', *Spiritual Disciplines*. Papers from the Eranos Yearbooks, London, Routledge & Kegan Paul, 1960.

LEISEGANG, H. 'The Mystery of the Serpent', *The Mysteries*. Papers from the Eranos Yearbooks, New York, Pantheon Books, 1955.

LONG, G. *The Folklore Calendar*, London, Philip Allan, 1930.

LOSSKY, V. *The Mystical Theology of the Eastern Church*, London, James Clarke, 1957.

MACKENZIE, D. A. *The Migration of Symbols*, London, Kegan Paul, Trench, Trubner, 1926.

MARCHANT, SIR JAMES. *The Way to God*, London, Burns Oates & Washbourne, 1932.

MARTIN, P. W. *Experiment in Depth*, London, Routledge & Kegan Paul, 1955.

MATTHEWS, W. H. *Mazes and Labyrinths*, London, Longmans, 1922, New York, 1970.

MECHTILD OF MAGDEBURG. See Menzies, L.

MEES, G. H. *The Key to the first Chapter of Genesis*, N. Kluwer, Deventer, no date.

MEIER, F. 'The Mystery of the Ka'ba'. *The Mysteries*. Papers from the Eranos Yearbooks, New York, Pantheon Books, 1955.

MENZIES, L. *The Revelations of Mechtild of Magdeburg*, London, Longman, Green, 1953.

MEYER, W. *'Ein Labyrinth mit Versen'*. Sitzungeberichte der Philos.-Hist. Klasse der Königl. Bayrischen Akademie der Wissenschaften, München, 1882, vol. II, 3.

MITCHELL, J. *The City of Revelation*, London, Garnstone Press, 1972.

NEEDHAM, J. *Science and Civilization in China*, vol. 2, History of Scientific Thought, Cambridge University Press, 1956.

NEUMANN, E. *The Origin and History of Consciousness*, London, Routledge & Kegan Paul, 1954.

NICHOLSON, R. A. *Studies in Islamic Mysticism*, Cambridge University Press, 1921.
Rūmī, Poet and Mystic, London, Allen & Unwin, 1950.
NIVEDITA, SISTER AND COOMARASWAMY, A. K. *Myths of the Hindus and Buddhists*, London, Harrap, 1916.
OESTERLEY, W. O. E. *The Sacred Dance*, Cambridge University Press, 1923.
OSBORNE, A. *Ramana Maharshi and the Path of Self-Knowledge*, London, Rider & Co., 1954.
PALLIS, MARCO. *The Way and the Mountain*, London, Owen, 1960.
PALMER, G. E. H. See *Philokalia*.
PATANJALI. *Yoga Aphorisms* ... translated ... by Swami Prabhavananda and C. Isherwood, London, Allen & Unwin, 1953.
PENNICK, N. *Caerdroia, Ancient turf, stone and pavement mazes*, Cambridge, Trumpington, 1974.
PHILOKALIA. *Writings from the Philokalia on The Prayer of the Heart*, translated by E. Kadloubovsky and G. E. H. Palmer, London, Faber & Faber, 1951.
PIKE, ROYSTON. *Encyclopedia of Religion and Religions*, London, Allen & Unwin, 1951.
PILGRIM. *The Way of a Pilgrim*, translated by R. N. French, London, S.P.C.K. 1930.
PLINY. *Natural History*, Loeb's Classical Library, London, 1938.
PLOTINUS. *Select Works*, Thomas Taylor's translation, Bohn's Popular Library, London, A. Bell, 1929.
PRABHAVANANDA. See Patanjali.
PREM, SRI KRISHNA. *The Yoga of the Bhagavad Gita*, London, Watkins, 1938.
PRZYWARA, E. See St Augustine.
PULVER, M. 'The Experience of Light'. *Spiritual Disciplines*. Papers from the Eranos Yearbooks, London, Routledge & Kegan Paul, 1960.
PURCE, J. *The Mystic Spiral*, London, Thames & Hudson, 1974.
RAHNER, H. *Griechische Mythen in Christilicher Deutung*, Zürich, Rhein-Verlag, 1945.
RAMAKRISHNA, SRI. *The Sayings* ... compiled by Swami Abhedananda, New York, Vedanta Society, 1903.
REICHELT, K. L. *Meditation and Piety in the Far East*, London, Lutterworth, 1953.
RIEKER, H. U. *Beggar among the Dead*, London, Rider, 1960.
ROLT, C. E. See Dionysius the Areopagite.
ROSE, H. A. *The Darvishes or Oriental Spiritualism*, by John Brown, edited ... by H. A. Rose, Oxford University Press, 1927.
ROSENBERG, A. *Die Christliche Bildmeditation*, München, Barth Verlag, 1955.
RUMI, JELLALLEDIN. *The Whirling Ecstasy*, Mexico, Ediciones Sol, 1954.
RUNDLE-CLARK, R. T. *Myth and Symbol in Ancient Egypt*, London, Thames & Hudson, 1959.
RUYSBROECK, JOHN. *Flowers of a Mystic Garden*, translated from the French of E. Hello by C.E.S., London, Watkins, 1912.
SAINT AUGUSTINE. See Augustine, St.
SAINT JOHN OF THE CROSS. See John of the Cross, St.
SAINT THERESA OF JESUS. See Teresa of Jesus.
SANTIDEVA. *The Path of Light*, rendered ... into English ... by L. D. Barnett. W.o.E., London, Murray, 1947.
SAUNDERS, K. *Lotuses of the Mahayana*. W.o.E., London, Murray, 1924.
SCHNAPPER, E. B. *One in All*. An Anthology of Religion, W.o.E., London, Murray, 1952.

SCHOLEM, G. G. *Major Trends in Jewish Mysticism*, London, Thames & Hudson, 1955.
　Zur Kabbala und ihrer Symbolik, Zürich, Rhein-Verlag, 1960.
　Von der Mystischen Gestalt der Gottheit, Zürich, Rhein-Verlag, 1962.
SCHUON, F. *L'oeil du Coeur*, Paris, Gallimard, 1950.
SCHWABE, J. *Archetyp und Tierkreis*, Basel, Schwabe, 1951.
　'Symbolon', *Jahrbuch für Symbolforschung*, vol. 1, Basel, Schwabe, 1960.
SIEKMANN, G. R. *The Mystery of Glastonbury Tor*. The Rosicrucian Digest, March 1969.
SIMPSON, W. *The Buddhist Prayer Wheel*, London, Macmillan, 1896.
SINGH, SARDAR SIR JOGENDRA. *The Invocations of Sheikh 'Abdullah Ansari of Herat*, W.o.E., London, Murray, 1939.
SIRAJ ED-DIN, ABU BAKR. *The Book of Certainty*, London, Rider, 1952.
SMITH, M. *Readings from the Mystics of Islam*, London, Luzac, 1950.
　The Sufi Path of Love, London, Luzac, 1954.
SNELLGROVE, D. *Buddhist Himalaya*, Oxford, Cassirer, 1957.
STRONG, M. (Editor). *Letters of the Scattered Brotherhood*, New York, Harper, 1948.
SUZUKI, B. L. *Mahayana Buddhism*, London, The Buddhist Lodge, 1938.
SUZUKI, D. T. *Living by Zen*, London, Rider, 1950.
　Manual of Zen Buddhism, London, Rider, 1950.
　Essays in Zen Buddhism, Second Series. London, Rider, 1950.
TAGORE, A. *Gitanjali*, London, Macmillan, 1913.
TERESA OF JESUS, SAINT. *The Way of Perfection*, London, Burns Oates, 1952.
　The Interior Castle, London, Sands, 1955.
THOMAS A KEMPIS. *The Imitation of Christ*, London, Methuen, 1913.
TUCCI, G. *The Theory and Practice of the Mandala*, London, Rider, 1961.
UNDERHILL, E. *The Mystic Way*, London, Dent, 1913.
　Mysticism, London, Methuen, 1911.
　The Spiral Way, London, Watkins, 1922.
UNIVERSAL PRAYERS. See YATISWARANANDA.
VAUGHAN, HENRY. *The Works of Henry Vaughan*, edited by L. C. Martin, Oxford, Clarendon Press, 1957.
WALEY, A. *The Way and its Power*. A Study of the Tao Te Ching, London, Allen & Unwin, 1956.
WATTS, A. W. *The Way of Zen*, London, Thames & Hudson, 1957.
　Myth and Ritual in Christianity, London, Thames & Hudson, 1959.
WEDEPOHL, E. 'Versuch über Labyrinthe', Der Architekt, VII, 1960.
WERBLOWSKY, R. J. ZWI. 'Mystical and Magical Contemplation. The Kabbalists in Sixteenth Century Safed' *History of Religions*, vol. I, 1, 1961.
WIDENGREN, G. *The King and the Tree of Life*, Universitets Arsekrift No. 14, Uppsala, 1951.
WILHELM, R. *The Secret of the Golden Flower*, London, Kegan Paul, Trench, Trubner, 1945.
　Chinesische Lebensweisheit, Darmstadt, Reichl Verlag, 1922.
YARDEN, L. *The Tree of Light, a Study of the Menorah*, London, East-West Library, 1971.
YATISWARANANDA, SWAMI. *Universal Prayers*, Sri Ramakrishna Math, Mylapore, Madras, 1944.
ZIMMER, H. *Myths and Symbols in Indian Art and Civilisation*, edited by J. Campbell, New York, Pantheon Books, 1953.
　Philosophies of India, edited by J. Campbell, New York, Pantheon Books, 1953.

The King and the Corpse, edited by J. Campbell, New York, Pantheon Books, 1956.
Integrating the Evil, Guild of Pastoral Psychology, Lecture 39, 1943.

INDEX